DEATH TO
THE
INFIDELS

DEATH TO
THE
INFIDELS

RADICAL ISLAM'S WAR
AGAINST THE JEWS

MITCHELL BARD

palgrave
macmillan

First published in 2014 by PALGRAVE MACMILLAN® TRADE
in the United States—a division of St. Martin's Press LLC, 175 Fifth
Avenue, New York, NY 10010.

Where this book is distributed in the UK, Europe and the rest of
the world, this is by Palgrave Macmillan, a division of Macmillan
Publishers Limited, registered in England, company number 785998, of
Houndmills, Basingstoke, Hampshire RG21 6XS.

Palgrave® and Macmillan® are registered trademarks in the United
States, the United Kingdom, Europe and other countries.

ISBN 978-1-137-27907-1

Library of Congress Cataloging-in-Publication Data

Bard, Mitchell Geoffrey, 1959– author.
  Death to the infidels : radical Islam's war against the Jews / Mitchell
G. Bard.
    pages   cm
  ISBN 978-1-137-27907-1 (hardback)
    1. Islam—Relations—Judaism. 2. Judaism—Relations—Islam.
3. Islam—21st century. 4. Islam—20th century. 5. Islamic renewal—
Middle East. 6. Arab-Israeli conflict—Influence. 7. Islam and politics.
I. Title.
BP173.J8B274   2014
297.2'82—dc23

                                                                    2014005894

A catalogue record of the book is available from the British Library.

Design by Letra Libre, Inc.

First edition: September 2014

10 9 8 7 6 5 4 3 2 1

Printed in the United States of America.

CONTENTS

1   Islam and the Jews   1

2   Jews Invade the Heart of Islam   15

3   Arab Unity and Disunity   43

4   From Terrorists to Jihadists   69

5   The Arab Spring's Transformation into the
    Islamic Winter   107

6   Iran and Little Satan   127

7   The Global Jihad   151

8   Jerusalem: Ground Zero of the Conflict   189

9   Shattered Dreams of Peace: From Camp David's
    Success to Obama's Fiasco   209

10 Can the Islamic–Jewish/Israeli Conflict Be
    Resolved?   237

    Notes   263
    Index   276

CHAPTER 1

ISLAM AND THE JEWS

"The Israeli-Palestinian conflict has several dimensions—national, political, territorial, cultural and religious," Israeli journalist Yossi Melman observed. "In the worst case scenarios drawn by Israeli analysts, the most feared and dangerous one is that the religious aspect will take over and dominate the conflict, thus turning it into a religious war, which might draw the billions of Muslims around the globe against Israel."[1]

This is the scenario we now find ourselves in.

Conventional wisdom, as well as the misguided notions of many Muslims, commentators, journalists, and U.S. government Arabists, is that territory, politics, and the Palestinian issue are the root cause of the modern conflict in the Middle East. The easiest way to disprove this belief is to go back to the origins of Islam and trace its development over the centuries with regard to attitudes toward Jews. Though politics later became more important to the dispute between Jews and their neighbors in the Holy Land, the religious dimension has always been the most important factor.

At the outset, a distinction needs to be made between Muslims and Arabs as these terms are not synonymous. Not all Muslims are Arabs and vice versa. Arabs are people who originated in Arabia and now live throughout the Middle East. The overwhelming majority (approximately 90 percent) is Muslim, but others are Christian or members of offshoots of Islam such as Druze and Alawite. Some Arab Christians also have a problem with Jews either because of the assimilation of anti-Semitic Christian teachings, experience with Jews in the holy land or anger toward the Israeli government, while others make a distinction between Jews and Israeli policies. Most Muslims (80 percent) live outside the Middle East in places such as Indonesia, Nigeria, and India or in non-Arab states in the region such as Turkey and Iran.

The word *Islamophobia* was invented to shield Muslims from scrutiny in this era of political correctness. However, no single word can cover the breadth and diversity of the Muslim faith. It is necessary to point out that Muslims have a variety of interpretations of their faith and practices, and not all subscribe to the anti-Semitic or fanatical views that are expressed in the Koran, by their spiritual leaders, or by others claiming to speak for Islam. Islam originated more than 14 centuries ago and has more than 1.5 billion adherents with an assortment of viewpoints and practices. Some of these beliefs are benign, such as those of the Sufis, while others, such as those of jihadis, are dangerous.

Jew hatred among Muslims can be traced to Islam's Holy Scriptures and some of their interpreters—or, some would argue, misinterpreters. Though most Muslims grow up with tolerant religious traditions, a small number of extremists have twisted and misconstrued Islam's Holy Scriptures. Furthermore, radicals often are selective in their interpretation of Islamic sources and pick and choose passages and explanations to fit their needs to motivate, recruit, and brainwash followers.

The good news is that only a fraction of the Muslim world believes the pejorative interpretations. The bad news is that it doesn't require a very high percentage of the world's 1.5 billion Muslims to adopt radical views to pose a threat to Jews, Israel, and the international community.

The interaction between Jews and Muslims is, in historical terms, a relatively recent phenomenon, as Jews trace their history back more than 1,500 years before the birth of Muhammad. Before there were Muslims—or Christians—the Jewish people had a thriving civilization. Jews trace their connection to the Land of Israel to the time of Joshua, more than 3,000 years ago. In fact, for more than 400 years, it was the Jews who had a powerful nation that controlled what the Romans later named Palaestina (the southern portion of what is now called the West Bank) and parts of what is today Egypt, Jordan, Syria, and Lebanon.

Despite the invasion of various empires over the centuries, Jews have lived in their homeland uninterrupted for more than 2,000 years, maintaining a small presence even after most were killed or expelled by the Romans and their successors. Estimates of their population range from a high of 7 million in the first century of the Common Era to approximately 7,000 living under Ottoman domination at the beginning of the nineteenth century. The majority of Jews were deported or provoked to go into exile, what became known as the Diaspora.

Once dispersed, Jews became minorities in the lands in which they lived and adapted their lifestyles, culture, and politics to survive in alien societies.

The story of Jewish-Muslim relations does not begin in the Jews' Holy Land, but in what would later become the Muslims' holiest cities—Mecca and Medina. Jews fleeing persecution from Christians during the centuries after the Roman conquest scattered around the world, and a few tribes settled in the desert wastelands of what is now Saudi Arabia. These Jews, who probably had first been expelled from Palestine by the Romans, settled in Yathrib, which later became known as Medina to commemorate Muhammad's association with the city. Early on, Muhammad respected the Jews and adopted some of their customs (e.g., facing Jerusalem for prayers), but he was angered by the Jews' failure to recognize him as a prophet and their criticism of his distortions of the Old Testament. He subsequently rejected Jewish beliefs and the customs he had adopted (e.g., he changed the direction of prayers to Mecca) and claimed that Abraham was the patriarch of Islam, not Judaism.

"The embittered Muhammad began to cast the Jews in his revelations as a devious and treacherous people, who had persecuted past prophets and falsified the Holy Scriptures," notes historian Ephraim Karsh. "This disengagement was completed on

Muhammad's deathbed in the form of an injunction ordering the expulsion of Jews (and Christians) from the [Arabian] peninsula: 'Two faiths will not live together in the land of the Arabs.'"[2]

Before his death, the tensions between Muhammad and the Jewish tribes escalated, and Muhammad and his followers expelled two of the tribes and murdered all the men from the third, selling the women and children into slavery. Jews in other areas were also besieged but were ultimately allowed to stay on their land in return for an annual tribute of half of their produce.

Muslims believe that God (Allah) spoke to the prophet Muhammad through the angel Gabriel. The revelations to Muhammad were transmitted orally until after the Prophet's death. They were subsequently written down in what became the Koran, a book that followers believe is literally the word of God. The people who were willing to submit to the word and will of God became known as Muslims (i.e., "one who submits").

The enmity of Muslims toward Jews was codified in the Koran, which makes numerous references to Jews that can be interpreted as disparaging. For example: Jews try to introduce corruption (5:64); have always been disobedient (5:78); are cursed and treacherous (5:13); are enemies of Allah, the Prophet, and the angels (2:97–98); "shall have disgrace in this world" and "a grievous chastisement in the hereafter" (5:41); and were "consigned to humiliation and wretchedness" (2:61). Muslims are also instructed "not take the Jews and the Christians for friends" (5:51).

These anti-Jewish views are reinforced in Muslim commentaries. For example, a Hadith (a tradition of the Prophet Muhammad) contains one of the most frequently quoted statements calling for genocide: "On the Day of Judgment, the trees will say, 'Oh Muslim, Oh servant of God, here is a Jew hiding behind me. Come here and kill him.'"

Princeton University professor Bernard Lewis, the doyen of Middle East scholars, explains that one reason for the disproportionate number of critical passages regarding Jews was that Muhammad had more contact with Jews than Christians. He also defeated Jews in battle, creating the image of Jews as weak and unthreatening. Consequently, Muslims worried less about the Jews than the Christians, who were viewed as their rivals in a battle to bring enlightenment to the world.

Islam also has profound theological differences from Judaism that have led to animosity. For example, Muslims believe that the Hebrew Scriptures, though written thousands of years earlier, are falsifications of the Koran. This explains the discrepancy between the two traditions, as in the story of the sacrifice by Abraham of his son. The Torah says Abraham sacrificed Isaac on Mount Moriah in Jerusalem, but Muslims believe Abraham sacrificed Ishmael on Mount Mina near Mecca.

One bizarre and enduring calumny against the Jews is the Islamic belief that ancient Jews were turned into animals for transgressing the word of God. Jews, of course, have been called many disparaging names over the years associated with their looks or wealth, but why the comparison to animals? Islamists find their inspiration in the Koran and the Hadiths. The divine punishment of Jews is mentioned in three Koranic verses: "They are those whom Allah has cast aside and on whom His wrath has fallen and of whom He has made some as apes and swine" (5:60); "You have surely known the end of those from amongst you who transgressed in the matter of the Sabbath, in consequence of which we condemned them: Be ye like apes, despised" (2:65); and "when, instead of amending, they became more persistent in the pursuit of that which they were forbidden, we condemned them: Be ye as apes, despised" (7:166).[3]

Even today, references to Jews (and sometimes "Zionists," used as a synonym) as "the descendants of apes and pigs" are common in mosques and the media in Muslim countries. Here are a handful of examples:

- In a weekly sermon in April 2002, Al-Azhar Sheikh Muhammad Sayyid Tantawi, the highest-ranking cleric in the Sunni Muslim world, called the Jews "the enemies of Allah, descendants of apes and pigs."[4]
- In one of his sermons, Saudi sheikh Abdul Rahman Al-Sudais, imam and preacher at the al-Masjid al-Haram Mosque—the most important mosque in Mecca—beseeched Allah to annihilate the Jews. He also urged the Arabs to give

up peace initiatives with them because they are "the scum of the human race, the rats of the world, the violators of pacts and agreements, the murderers of the prophets, and the offspring of apes and pigs."[5]

- In an August 2001 sermon, Sheikh Ibrahim Madhi, a Palestinian Authority official and imam of the Sheikh Ijlin mosque, Gaza City's main mosque, called on the Palestinian people to forget their internal disagreements and turn all weapons against Jews: "lances must be directed at the Jews, the enemies of Allah, the nation accursed in Allah's book. Allah described [them] as apes and pigs, calf-worshippers, idol-worshippers."[6]

- Referring to Israel's fiftieth anniversary, Hezbollah secretary-general Hassan Nasrallah said the nation was established by "the grandsons of apes and pigs—the Zionist Jews—on the land of Palestine and Jerusalem." He concluded his speech with the slogan "Death to America" and "to the murderers of the prophets, the grandsons of apes and pigs, we say: . . . 'Death to Israel.'"[7]

Christians are also targets of radical Muslims, so it is not surprising that Koranic commentary links transformation into apes and pigs with Christians as well.

Some Muslims do argue these references to apes and pigs should not be taken literally, but as a "metaphor for supposedly believing persons (either Jews or Muslims) who had deliberately and willfully chosen to ignore commandments from God."[8] Nevertheless, these references are primarily directed toward Jews and the impact is dehumanizing. "One could laugh off such rhapsodies of nonsense as the misguided musings of benighted souls," journalist Tibor Krausz notes, "but pervasive Islamic Jew-hatred has real-life consequences. By relentlessly dehumanizing Jews, Islamists seek to legitimize their murder as justified owing to Jews' inherently atavistic and animalist nature. Thus, killing Jews becomes both a religious duty and moral imperative."[9]

The teachings in the Koran should be considered in historical context. For example, some Muslims argue that derogatory references apply only to Jews living at the time of Muhammad, that is, the seventh century. Still, like apologists for terror who try to erase the violent implications of jihad, even as some Muslims use the term to instigate holy war, present-day radical Muslims take Koranic deprecation of Jews literally. "One could reasonably argue," social psychologist Neil Kressel says, "that none of the negative references to Jews require that a contemporary Muslim believer possess hostility to Jews. Moreover, anti-Jewish references in the sacred sources do not explain why hostility to Jews is far more intense today than in many past eras of Islamic history." Kressel adds that "contemporary Christianity possesses at least as strong a religious foundation for Jew-hatred as Islam—in truth, much stronger—yet in the present day much of its potential for bigotry and hatred has been muted."[10]

The disparaging religious teachings have conditioned many Muslims to believe almost any lie about Jews, which helps explain why Hitler's *Mein Kampf* and the *Protocols of the Elders of Zion*, a Russian book fabricating a global Jewish conspiracy to control the world, are bestsellers in the Middle East. These books reinforce the libels of the past. The first popular Arabic edition of the *Protocols* was published in 1951 by Muhammad Khalifa at-Tunisi, who said he translated the book to warn mankind of the danger posed by the Jews. "Even if they were expelled from our countries to any spot of land," he said, "wherever they were, they were enemies of mankind."[11]

The theme of the *Protocols* has been incorporated into a variety of modern forms, including television shows and movies. For example, Egypt produced a 41-part television series, *Knight Without a Horse,* which tells the story of Jews trying to conceal the existence of the *Protocols* out of fear it would reveal their conspiracy to dominate the world. Not to be outdone, Syria produced its own $5 million, 29-part drama, *Al-Shatat,* which depicts Jews engaging in a conspiracy to rule the world and repeats traditional blood libels against Jews.[12]

In addition to the indoctrination of Jew-hatred found in Islamic texts, Muslims are also conditioned by modern media to accept anti-Semitic tropes imported from the Christian world in the early twentieth century. Long before the publication of the *Protocols* and

Hitler's manifesto, Jews were accused of a variety of heinous activities, such as poisoning wells and using the blood of Christians to make matzos for Passover. Though many of these calumnies date back centuries, modern Muslim leaders have repeated them. King Faisal of Saudi Arabia, for example, said that Jews "have a certain day on which they mix the blood of non-Jews into their bread and eat it. It happened that two years ago, while I was in Paris on a visit, the police discovered five murdered children. Their blood had been drained, and it turned out that some Jews had murdered them in order to take their blood and mix it with the bread that they eat on this day."[13] On December 5, 1984, Saudi Arabian UN delegate Marouf al-Dawalibi told the UN Human Rights Commission conference on religious tolerance, "The Talmud says that if a Jew does not drink every year the blood of a non-Jewish man, he will be damned for eternity." More recently, Saudi cleric Salman Al-Odeh said he read about a doctor living with a Jewish family who was asked to bring them human blood. The doctor refused, but discovered that "they were making matzos with human blood."[14]

The Elders of Zion is not the only conspiracy theory circulated in the Muslim world; others include the charge that Jews/Israel/Mossad were responsible for 9/11. For example, Prince Nayef of Saudi Arabia, then interior minister, told a Kuwaiti newspaper that Jews were behind the heinous attacks because they knew they would benefit from subsequent criticism of Islam and Arabs.[15] In 2012, an Egyptian cleric claimed the "elders of Zion" were corrupting Muslims by flooding the Internet with porn and that alcohol and prostitutes would drown Muslim youth in "urges and desires."[16] The Palestinians are masters of the "Big Lie" (the notion that if you tell a lie that's big enough, and you tell it often enough, people will believe you are telling the truth) and have claimed Israelis have done everything from dropping poison candy from planes to kill children in Gaza to injecting Palestinians with HIV.[17]

Anti-Semitic stereotypes are also reinforced in the media in Muslim countries. Jews are often portrayed as Nazis or in Nazi-like cartoons, with hook noses, carrying daggers dripping with the blood of dead children, and with other images meant to dehumanize and humiliate them.[18]

Some Muslim Arabs dismiss accusations of anti-Semitism by arguing that they too are Semites and, therefore, cannot be anti-Semitic. This is pure sophistry. The European Monitoring Centre on Racism and Xenophobia offered a good definition: "Anti-Semitism is a certain perception of Jews, which may be expressed as hatred toward Jews. Rhetorical and physical manifestations of anti-Semitism are directed toward Jewish or non-Jewish individuals and/or their property, toward Jewish community institutions and religious facilities. . . . Such manifestations could also target the state of Israel, conceived as a Jewish collectivity."[19]

Epithets directed at Jews are transmitted by clerics, journalists, Arab officials, and educators, and the teachings filter down to the youngest children. In May 2002, for example, Iqraa, the Saudi-Egyptian satellite television station whose goal is "highlighting the true and tolerant picture of Islam," interviewed a three-and-a-half-year-old Muslim girl about Jews. When the girl was asked whether she liked Jews, she answered, "No." When asked why she didn't like them, she said that Jews were "apes and pigs." "Who said this?" the moderator asked. The girl answered, "Our God." "Where did He say this?" She replied, "In the Koran." When the interview ended, the moderator praised the girl's knowledge and suggested that to be "true Muslims," the next generation of children must receive the same type of education.[20]

Unfortunately, this little girl is not unusual. For example, a slightly older boy appeared on an Egyptian television station in October 2012, reciting, "Oh Islamic nation, oh all Muslims . . . martyrdom on the path of Allah is a religious duty incumbent upon you, oh believers. Pray: 'Oh Allah, destroy Israel'—Amen."[21]

Perhaps the greatest distinction between radicals and other Muslims relates to the concept of jihad, which is often translated as "struggle" or "holy war." Most Muslims interpret jihad benignly, as a struggle within themselves against "evil intentions" and an effort to work toward the moral betterment of society. For centuries, however, the term was used to describe the struggle as one between believers and infidels and the obligation to subjugate or kill nonbelievers. Historian Martin Kramer argues that some scholars selectively interpret the Koran "to turn Islam into a pacifist faith—a kind of oriental Quakerism." Kramer notes that Emile Tyan, author of the article on jihad in the *Encyclopaedia of Islam*, said, "Jihad consists of military action with the object of the expansion of Islam," and efforts to present it as peaceful persuasion or self-defense "disregard entirely the previous doctrine and historical tradition, as well as the texts of the Qur'an and the Sunna."[22] Muhammad said it himself in his farewell address to his followers: "I was ordered to fight all men until they say, 'There is no god but Allah.'"[23] Bernard Lewis adds, however, that limitations were placed on a jihad. "What the classical jurists of Islam never remotely considered," he writes, "is the kind of unprovoked, unannounced mass slaughter of uninvolved civil populations that we saw in New York two weeks ago [September 11, 2001]. For this there is no precedent and no authority in Islam."[24]

The Islamic religion has a more fundamental problem with Jews and the existence of a Jewish state, however. There is a Muslim view that the world is divided into two realms, the House of Islam and the House of War, or the Dar al-Islam and the Dar al-harb. The Dar al-Islam is all those lands in which a Muslim government rules. Non-Muslims may live there on Muslim sufferance. The outside world, which has not yet been subjugated, is called the House of War, and a perpetual state of jihad, of holy war, is imposed by religious law. As Muslim historian Ibn Khaldun explains:

> In the Muslim community, the jihad is a religious duty because of the universalism of the Islamic mission and the obligation [to convert] everybody to Islam either by persuasion or by force. . . . [By contrast] the other religions had no such universal mission and the holy war was [therefore] not a religious duty to them apart from self-defense.[25]

It is then a religious obligation for Muslims to subjugate the infidels and it is unacceptable that non-Muslims should rule over Muslims or that non-Muslims should control Muslim territory. This belief is absolutely fundamental to understanding the intractability of the Israel-Islamic conflict.

Muslims pursuing a holy war against the infidels have consistently made clear their interpretation of jihad. In 1938, for example, long before the creation of Israel, Shiite chief Mujtahid of Iraq asserted that a jihad for Palestine was everyone's duty, and that if the Arabs lost they would suffer "humiliation, death and eternal shame."[26] Today, a Palestinian terrorist organization calls itself Islamic Jihad and does not hide its goal of driving the Jews from Muslims' holy land. Similarly, Hamas says explicitly in its covenant that "Palestine is an Islamic land" and "there is no solution for the Palestine question except through jihad" (Articles 14 and 13).

The territory of Israel is incidental to the broader Islamic goal of achieving dominance over the entire world. "By winning territory and diminishing the size of areas ruled by non-Muslims," Islamic historian Daniel Pipes asserts, "jihad accomplishes two goals: it manifests Islam's claim to replace other faiths, and it brings about the benefit of a just world order."[27]

This reflects the minor role Jews really play on the world stage. Muslims and Christians dominate most of the world and have been engaged in conflict over their respective faiths for more than 13 centuries in a religious war or, if you believe the late Harvard political scientist Samuel Huntington, a "clash of civilizations" that at various times led to open warfare. As Ephraim Karsh notes, however, Muslims, beginning with Muhammad, can set aside questions of faith for pragmatic reasons. If it suits their needs, they cooperate with non-Muslims. That is why Muslim countries today have no qualms about engaging in trade and political cooperation with the "decadent" West and other non-Muslim countries. Moreover, Karsh says, Muhammad's successors "were far less interested in the mass conversion of the conquered populations than in enjoying the fruits of their subjugation. . . . The lands they occupied and ruled became an integral part of the House of Islam whether or not most of their inhabitants became Muslims."[28]

A good example is that, for a time, Muslims and Jews found common cause in fighting the Crusaders. The papal desire to cleanse the region of infidels led to two centuries of bloody crusades (1095–1291), which was the last time Christians were dominant anywhere in the Middle East. "Unlike the early Islamic conquests," Karsh observes, "the crusades were not a drive for world mastery, but a limited endeavor geared toward a specific objective: the liberation of Jerusalem and the Holy Sepulcher from infidel rule."[29] In 1099, the Crusaders captured Jerusalem and slaughtered nearly all the inhabitants—Jews, Muslims, and even Eastern Christians.

Though barred from Jerusalem, Jewish communities remained in other parts of Palestine. The Muslims were defeated because they were in disarray, and it took nearly a century before Saladin built an army strong enough to wage a jihad against the Christians. Adopting the Middle Eastern custom of considering the enemy of my enemy a friend, Jews sided with the Muslims in repelling the Crusaders.

It was not surprising that Jews would seek alliances with the more powerful Muslims given their historic persecution by Christians. Nevertheless, Jews were sometimes treated as severely by Muslims. At best, Jews were tolerated, along with Christians, under a special category created for "People of the Book." Because the two faiths shared a belief in God and Islam viewed Moses and Jesus as prophets, Jews and Christians were treated differently than other subjects of Muslim rule in exchange for their subordination. They were considered *dhimmis* (non-Muslims under Muslim rule), which gave them an element of protection under Muslim rulers but did not change the fact that they were still regarded as infidels who were obligated to recognize the superiority of the true believer—the Muslim.

Moreover, as dhimmis, Jews were required to pay a "tribute" (*jizya*) to the ruler, and were prohibited from building synagogues higher than mosques or homes higher than those of Muslims. Dhimmis could be executed for criticizing the Koran, Islam, or Muhammad, for proselytizing among Muslims, or for touching a Muslim woman. Jews could not drink wine in public, ride horses or camels, pray or mourn in loud voices, give evidence in court against a Muslim, or even stand in the road without showing deference toward Muslims. Dhimmis were excluded from public office and armed service and were forbidden to bear arms. Dhimmis were also sometimes forced to wear distinctive clothing. In the ninth century, for example, Baghdad's Caliph al-Mutawakkil designated a yellow badge for Jews, setting a precedent that would be followed centuries later in Nazi Germany.

While Jews were generally viewed with contempt by their Muslim neighbors, at certain times and places, Jews lived in relative peace and thrived culturally and economically. The myth of the "Golden Age" of Jewry during the period of Muslim rule in Spain (eighth to eleventh century) arose because it was a time when Jewish intellectual, economic, and spiritual life flourished. This did not mean that Jews were treated equally to Muslims; moreover, Jews were still subject to persecution, humiliation, violence, and death. Conditions for Jews in Muslim Spain started to deteriorate in the twelfth century, when the Almovarids gained power.

In most countries Jews fared much worse than in Spain. In 1465, for example, Arab mobs in Fez slaughtered thousands of Jews, leaving only 11 alive, after a Jewish deputy vizier treated a Muslim woman in "an offensive manner." The killings touched off a wave of similar massacres throughout Morocco. Jews also came under attack in the nineteenth century in Marrakesh, where more than 300 Jews were murdered between 1864 and 1880. Hundreds of Jews were killed in Libya in 1785 and massacres occurred in Algiers in 1805, 1815, and 1830. Despite the Koran's prohibition, Jews were forced to convert to Islam or face death in Yemen (1198 and 1678), Morocco (1275, 1465, and 1790–92), and Baghdad (1333 and 1344).[30]

The persecution of Jews in Arab lands reached its nadir in the nineteenth century, when Jews throughout North Africa were forced to live in ghettos and the frequency of anti-Jewish violence increased. Many Jews were executed on charges of apostasy, and ritual murder accusations became commonplace.

After the eleventh century, the Muslims gradually lost their foothold in Spain, but they remained on the march as Turkish Muslims gradually conquered parts of the Balkans, the Mediterranean, and eventually the Levant and North Africa. In 1453, the Turks took over the heart of Christendom, Constantinople, and, centuries later, formally renamed the city Istanbul.

During the Ottoman Empire—which dominated much of Southeast Europe, Western Asia, the Caucasus, North Africa, and the Horn of Africa from roughly 1299 until the end of World War I— Jews fleeing other countries, such as the Sephardic Jews expelled from Spain, were welcomed because they were viewed as a "revenue-producing asset." Jews flourished in places such as Istanbul, Izmir,

Safed, and Salonica. Still, even under the relatively tolerant Ottoman rulers, Jews were oppressed, forced to pay high taxes, and faced ritual murder accusations. H. E. W. Young, British vice-consul in Mosul, wrote in 1909: "The attitude of the Muslims toward the Christians and the Jews is that of a master toward slaves, whom he treats with a certain lordly tolerance so long as they keep their place. Any sign of pretension to equality is promptly repressed."[31]

Today, author Daniel Goldhagen notes, "Anti-Semitism, and its centrality to Islamic civilization, has been ramped up by many orders of magnitude since the 1930s. It is now as ferocious as it has ever been and as central to Islamic civilization as it ever was to Christian civilization."[32]

As a tiny minority, Jews learned to go along to get along with Muslims throughout most of the last 14 centuries. Despite persecution, Jews accepted Muslim rule without challenge for fear of provoking their wrath. Today Jews have a state of their own in the heart of the Muslim world and may be willing to make compromises in the interest of peace with their neighbors; however, as rulers of their own state, the Jews of Israel will not sacrifice their right to self-determination in their homeland and will fight against any Islamic challenges to their sovereignty or survival.

CHAPTER 2

JEWS INVADE THE HEART OF ISLAM

Among Arab Muslims, the age of Muhammad and the Arab conquests that followed, glorious and triumphal moments that took place over the course of the last 1,300 years, remain deeply engraved on the consciousness of the faithful. Muslims consider the emergence of the Prophet and the formulation of the early Islamic community as nothing less than a watershed in the history of mankind.

For many Muslims, especially the radicals, the mission of the faithful is to restore Muslim domination. One thorn in their side—or as they more commonly refer to it, cancer in the Islamic body—is the Jewish presence in the Middle East.

While the Muslims had holy places associated with the Prophet, the three most important being Mecca, Medina, and the al-Aqsa Mosque (not Jerusalem), the Jewish people believed God promised the entire Land of Israel to them. Jews trace their connection to the land to the time more than 3,000 years ago when the Israelites completed the exodus from Egypt and reached the Promised Land. Jews ruled over parts of this land for more than 400 years, longer than the United States has been independent.

After virtually the entire population was expelled by the Romans in the first century, Jews never gave up the belief that the Land of Israel was their homeland and have practiced a number of rituals to remind them of that connection and to encourage them to return. For example, Jews pray each day facing the direction of Jerusalem; a glass is broken during Jewish weddings to remind the newlyweds and witnesses that the Jewish Temple was destroyed; on the holiday of Tisha B'av, Jews commemorate the destruction of the Temple, and participants in the Passover Seder retelling of the Jewish exodus from Egypt sing, "Next Year in Jerusalem."

Muslims, like the Jews, associate the Holy Land with their Holy Scriptures (though Jerusalem is never explicitly mentioned) and also claim the land on the basis of continuous habitation—in their case for 1,300 years. The first Muslims entered the land when they left Arabia and conquered parts of the Byzantine Empire. Muslims often deny the Jewish connection to the area, claim that the Arabs arrived first, that the Jews were interlopers, or that European Jews were descended from a tribe of Turks, the Khazars, who supposedly converted to Judaism in the eighth century and have no relation to the ancient Israelites.

In early debates over the fate of Palestine, Muslims admitted that Arabs first arrived with the Muslim conquest. A large percentage of the people who now call themselves Palestinians actually came from or are descendants of Arabs who left neighboring countries for Palestine during the 1920s and 1930s to take advantage of the improved standard of living created by the Jews. It wasn't until much later that Arabs began to rewrite their history to stake their claim to being the first inhabitants of the land. Thus, the argument is sometimes made that the Palestinians are descendants of the Canaanites (an idea reiterated by Palestinian peace negotiator Saeb Erekat in early 2014)[1] and therefore predate the Jewish connection to the land, a claim that has no historical merit.

Moreover, Muslims never considered the area of Palestine special until after 1967 and Israel's unification of Jerusalem. Nevertheless, today they believe it is Islamic territory, which entitles them to possession. Hypocritically, they dismiss similar claims by the Jews. In fact, the Muslims fighting over the land invented the "limited-liability war," in which they are entitled to hold territory they win in battle, but, if they lose, they have the right to demand the victors give up everything they gained in the fighting. Put simply, Muslims fighting the Israelis believe any conflict should end in their favor, regardless of the cause, the cost, or the outcome—if we win, we win and if we lose, we should also win. This has been the rationale for the Arab political demands regarding Palestine since their defeat in the 1967 War. Often people dismiss the "who came first" argument and claim that what really matters is the party that holds the territory last. After all, if the rightful owners of a territory were the original inhabitants, most existing states would have to return territory to aboriginal peoples.

Prior to the reestablishment of a Jewish state, the Jews were powerless; therefore the Muslim-Jewish conflict was based on religion rather than territory or politics. The emergence of nationalism as a political force in the nineteenth century, however, added a new dimension to the centuries-old clash of beliefs. An Austrian journalist named Theodor Herzl saw the traditional Jewish attempt to go along to get along as futile, as Jews would never be accepted in any society because anti-Semitism is ineradicable. Herzl's conclusion led him to articulate a political form of Zionism, which shifted the Jewish case for returning home from the religious roots of Judaism to the right of Jews as a nation to self-determination in their homeland. Other Jews adopted other Zionist "flavors" that focused on different aspects of building a Jewish homeland, such as physically working the land (Labor Zionism) and restoring Jewish political freedom infused with Judaism (Religious Zionism).

The Political Zionists became more influential in the United States and Great Britain during World War I and increasingly focused on winning international recognition for their objective. Simultaneously, increasing numbers of Jews began to settle in their homeland. Jews had remained in parts of the Land of Israel for roughly 2,000 years, even after most were dispersed around the globe, but their return in large numbers occurred in six distinct periods.

Starting in the 1880s, the move to Palestine was known as the "ingathering of the exiles" or a "returning" to the promised land, thus bearing significant religious and Zionistic significance. The earliest Jews to return to their homeland were Orthodox Jews. Their numbers were small and posed no immediate threat to their Arab and Muslim neighbors. Moreover, the harsh conditions of the land forced many to return to their previous homes. Still Jews kept coming. Pioneers came in greater numbers with the coalescence of Zionism. After years of docility, the Muslim world was not prepared for these assertive Jews.

There was no corresponding Palestinian nationalist sentiment at this point; no movement was "capable of mobilizing many, if not most of the elements of Palestinian society in common cause."[2] In fact, to the extent Arabs or Muslims expressed any nationalist ideas, they were focused on creating "Greater Syria," encompassing Lebanon and Palestine, rather than establishing an independent Palestinian entity. This should not be surprising given the fact that the name "Palestine" has nothing to do with the Palestinians—it is associated with the ancient Philistines who share no common ancestry with the Arabs—and the area was never a state or independent entity in the Muslim Empire.

In 1897, the first Zionist Congress was held in Basel, Switzerland, and declared that the goal of the World Zionist Organization (WZO) founded there would be a "publicly recognized legally secured homeland in Palestine." Subsequently, the movement of Jews became more organized as Jews emigrated together in groups and formed agricultural communes—kibbutzim—and established cities such as Tel Aviv, which was founded in 1909 by middle-class European Jews.

The next waves consisted largely of Jews fleeing from persecution or dreaming of building a life in their homeland. These immigrants were said to be making *aliyah*—literally going up spiritually and physically.

- The First Aliyah (1882–1903) included 20,000–30,000 Jews from Russia, Romania, and Galicia.
- The Second Aliyah (1904–1914) consisted of 35,000–40,000 Jews, many pioneering youth from Russia.
- The Third Aliyah, after World War I (1919–1923), brought another 35,000 youth from Russia, Poland, and Romania.

- The Fourth Aliyah (1924–1931) consisted of 88,000 Jews from Poland.
- The Fifth Aliyah (1932–1938) was stimulated by Nazi persecution and totaled 215,000 Jews.
- During World War II, about 82,000 Jews came to Palestine and another 57,000 reached their homeland after the war.

The Jewish newcomers did not come to steal the land from the inhabitants. They were given financial assistance by wealthy Jews, such as Baron Edmond de Rothschild, and the development arm of the WZO, the Jewish National Fund, which purchased land throughout Palestine. Much of that land was cheap, swampy, and uncultivated. After buying up these areas, Jews sought out Arab landowners who were willing to sell their cultivated land. The sellers soon learned the Jews were prepared to pay exorbitant prices that were hard to turn down. Many Palestinians were understandably upset because the majority of those who lost land—about 80 percent—were debt-ridden peasants, semi-nomads, and Bedouins who often had their homes sold out from under them by wealthy absentee landlords who lived in Cairo, Damascus, and Beirut.

Meanwhile, as World War I dragged on, the British and French were jockeying to protect and expand their interests in the Middle East. François-Georges Picot of France and Sir Mark Sykes of Great Britain signed an agreement in 1916 that divided the expected spoils of the war. Under the agreement, the French were to be given control over Syria and Lebanon and the British were to take responsibility for Iraq and Palestine.

While the British and French were planning on how to carve up the Ottoman Empire, the more immediate issue was winning the war. By 1917, it became clear that defeating Germany and its allies would require U.S. intervention. Some British officials believed that American Jews had extraordinary influence on their government and that promising the Zionists, who were agitating for sovereignty in the Land of Israel, a homeland in Palestine would be an inducement for their supporters in the United States to lobby President Wilson to enter the war. The Zionists' ambition for independence was backed by some British officials as well, some of whom also wished to reward their leader, Chaim Weizmann, for critical discoveries he made as a chemist to help the war effort. Whatever the ultimate reason, the British government expressed support for a Jewish homeland in a letter from Foreign Secretary Lord Arthur Balfour to Lord Rothschild on November 2, 1917, which became known as the Balfour Declaration:

> His Majesty's Government view with favor the establishment in Palestine of a national home for the Jewish people, and will use their best endeavors to facilitate the achievement of this object, it being clearly understood that nothing shall be done which may prejudice the civil and religious rights of existing non-Jewish communities in Palestine or the rights and political status enjoyed by Jews in any other country.

Ironically, Jews were fleeing Palestine in droves just as the British agreed to support a Jewish home there. Their population had grown after the Ottoman government lifted restrictions on immigration in 1913, believing the Turks would benefit from the Jews' wealth and industriousness. Local Arabs immediately began complaining about the surge in the Jewish population, and the Turks reversed their policy a year later. As the war escalated, many Jews fled and others were deported, stimulating even more Jews to leave. By the end of the war, the Jewish population had declined from 85,000 at its outset to 56,000. Meanwhile, no restrictions were placed on Arab immigration; by 1922, that population had grown from 590,000 to 634,000, while the Jewish population had not quite reached its prewar total.

After the war, the British and French proceeded to carry out a modified version of the Sykes-Picot agreement, dividing the Ottoman Empire with the blessing of the participants at the peace conference convened on April 24, 1920, at San Remo, Italy. Artificial postwar demarcation lines became the basis for the borders of the future independent Arab nations of Iraq, Lebanon, Syria, Jordan, and Israel. France and the United Kingdom were awarded "mandates" over land divided on the basis of their imperial interests rather than the welfares of the inhabitants or the logic of the borders. France was assigned the mandate for Syria while Great Britain received mandates for Iraq and Palestine. Consequently, France gained access to vital materials from the region and maintained bases in Syria while Great Britain assumed control of the sea route to India and the Far East through the Suez Canal, ensuring access to supplies of cotton, oil, and other manufactured goods. Ports, bases and, later, airfields built by the British helped strengthen Great Britain's position in the Mediterranean and reinforced its global power.

The mandate for Palestine, formalized by the League of Nations on September 23, 1922, explicitly stated that the Allied powers agreed that Britain would implement the Balfour Declaration and reiterated the intention that foreign control should be temporary. The League said that when the countries could stand on their own, the mandates should end. In essence, Great Britain and France were given the power to decide if and when they would grant their wards independence.

The Arab leaders of the Hashemite dynasty in Arabia, who joined the revolt against the Turks based on British promises of independence, were furious. Faisal ibn Husseini, who led the fight against the Ottomans, became king of Syria after the war, but he was deposed by the French when they were awarded the mandate. The British subsequently offered him the throne of Iraq. Faisal's brother Abdullah also needed a reward, and the British responded by carving a new territory—Transjordan (present-day Jordan)—out of almost 80 percent of historic Palestine on the eastern bank of the Jordan River and installed Abdullah as ruler.

With regard to the Palestine Mandate, it quickly became clear the British had no intention of fulfilling the promise of the Balfour Declaration. They controlled immigration to limit the flow of Jews into the country while simultaneously ignoring a deluge of Arabs who entered Palestine and would later claim to be natives.

Meanwhile, the inhabitants of Palestine had their own rivalries. Contrary to recent historiography, the Arabs in Palestine did not consider themselves Palestinians. In fact, because none of the territories in the Ottoman Empire had formed separate political entities, the people who lived there did not associate with any nationality. They identified themselves according to the towns where they resided and the clans to which they belonged. Thus, for example, a man from Beirut was not Lebanese, he was a Beiruti.

The same was true in Palestine, where two Jerusalem clans vied for influence, the Nashashibis and the el-Husseinis. Like the Hatfields and McCoys of American lore, the two Arab clans had competed for decades and continue to do so. The more business-oriented Nashashibis favored conciliation and, along with their allies, often collaborated with the Jews in hope of reaching an accommodation to live together peacefully. The el-Husseinis, however, were committed Muslims who were militantly anti-British and anti-Zionist and prepared to use intimidation and murder to eliminate and discourage collaborators.

Ultimately, the Husseinis became the dominant political family in Palestine, and Haj Amin el-Husseini emerged as the leading figure in Palestinian politics for nearly three decades. Haj Amin was a radical Muslim and rabid anti-Semite who, in 1919, first began to organize suicide squads, fedayeen, to terrorize Jews in the hope of driving them out of Palestine.

Haj Amin found allies among the British officials, mostly from the British Foreign Office, who had become infatuated with Arab culture and sometimes "went native." (T. E. Lawrence—"Lawrence of Arabia"—is often cited as a prime example.) Even some of those who were not enamored with the exotic peoples of the region believed that Britain's national interest lay with the Arabs because of the size of their population, the economic opportunities they afforded, and, later, their oil reserves and demand for weapons. Some were simply anti-Semitic and used the other arguments as justification for their bigotry. All of these "Arabists" believed Zionist ambitions conflicted with their goal of fostering British-Arab ties.

Originally, Arabists were respected because they spoke Arabic and had an intimate knowledge of the Arab world acquired after years of research and living among the Arabs. Many officials in the U.S. State Department, the OSS (later CIA), and the War (now Defense) Department assimilated the views of the British Foreign Office, however, and the term "Arabist" became associated with diplomats who often could not speak Arabic, spent little or no time in the region and were "politically naïve, elitist and too deferential to exotic cultures."[3]

The heads of the Palestine British Administration consequently worked against Zionism with the aim of sabotaging the Balfour Declaration. The extent to which Great Britain was willing to go to frustrate the Zionists was reflected by the Arabists' complicity in the Palestinian riots.

One British Arabist sympathizer, Colonel Waters Taylor (financial adviser to the Military Administration in Palestine, 1919–1923), met with Haj Amin in Jerusalem on the Wednesday before Easter in 1920 and told el-Husseini that he could show the world that the Arabs of Palestine would not tolerate Jewish domination. He mistakenly persuaded Haj Amin that if sufficient violence occurred in Jerusalem at Easter, Great Britain would forsake support for a Jewish homeland.

Haj Amin took the colonel's advice and organized an Arab mob that attacked Jews and looted their shops. After the violence was quelled, Haj Amin discovered the British authorities did not share Colonel Taylor's view and ordered Haj Amin's arrest. He avoided capture and fled to Jordan. He was subsequently sentenced in absentia to ten years' imprisonment.

Haj Amin still had supporters in the British administration, however, who persuaded Britain's high commissioner for Palestine, Herbert Samuel (paradoxically a Jew), to pardon the man who initiated the violence. Samuel was also convinced to appoint Haj Amin as mufti—the religious leader responsible for interpreting Muslim law in Palestine—after the incumbent mufti of Jerusalem, Kamal el-Husseini, died in 1921.

Haj Amin made his position as mufti the most influential role in Palestine. No Arab could reach an influential position in Palestine without being loyal to the mufti. One way he established control was to create the Supreme Moslem Council, which immediately elected him president. Haj Amin then seized control of all Muslim religious funds in Palestine. The mufti's ascendance introduced the Islamic element into the developing conflict between Jews and Arabs in Palestine.

Haj Amin was not a Palestinian nationalist and did not believe Palestine was a discrete political entity. Rather than independence, he hoped for the reunification of Syria and wrote to Colonial

Secretary Winston Churchill in 1921 demanding that Palestine be reunited with Syria and Transjordan.

The mufti was not the only Muslim voice in Palestine at the time. In fact, some Muslims were pro-Zionist. For example, the mayor of Haifa, Hasan Shukri, who was also the president of the Muslim National Associations, wrote the following to the British government:

> We are certain that without Jewish immigration and financial assistance there will be no future development of our country as may be judged from the fact that the towns inhabited in part by Jews such as Jerusalem, Jaffa, Haifa, and Tiberias are making steady progress while Nablus, Acre, and Nazareth, where no Jews reside, are steadily declining.[4]

This was a minority view, however, and was eclipsed by a more authoritative opinion issued by the first assembly of Muslim religious scholars in 1935, which outlawed land sales to Jews for a variety of reasons. The assembly believed that the sales led to the removal of Muslims from their lands, forced Muslims to accept Jews as rulers, abetted Jews' desire to destroy them, and betrayed and offended Allah. The scholars imposed a variety of sanctions on anyone involved in selling land to Jews, such as isolating them and denying them burial in Muslim graves. Despite the fatwa and other efforts to stigmatize land sales as unpardonable religious and national sins, the sales continued and were often made by prominent Palestinians.[5]

The Arabs who cooperated with the Zionists more broadly did so for personal gain, communal interest, and what they viewed as the national interest, as well as out of pragmatic recognition that Jews could not be dislodged from Palestine, an opposition to violence, and because of personal interactions with Jews, who were friends, neighbors, or employers. Paradoxically, the threats against the mufti's opponents backfired in some cases and stimulated pro-Zionist sympathies because the Muslim "collaborators" and "traitors" were afraid that if a Palestinian state emerged, the mufti would rule it and become an even greater threat to their lives and influence. These Arabs saw the mufti as the real traitor for bringing ruin to the people to further his personal interests rather than those of the Palestinian Arabs.

Haj Amin set a precedent that most Arab countries continue to adhere to today: namely refusing to negotiate directly with the Jews or reach any agreement with them. The mufti's irredentism had a profound impact on the Zionist movement. His uncompromising views forced the Zionists to abandon efforts they were making to reach an agreement with other Palestinian Arabs. These conciliatory Arabs also had to withdraw from discussions with the Jews out of fear of being labeled collaborators, who would be attacked and sometimes killed by the mufti's minions.

In addition to asking Churchill to change the map of the Middle East, the mufti called on the British foreign secretary to restrict Jewish immigration. From 1920–1923, only 8,000 Jews had come to Palestine annually, albeit a significant increase from the 1,806 who came in 1919. Churchill did not impose new limits and immigration steadily increased, reaching a peak of more than 35,000 in 1925. This growth was due primarily to anti-Jewish economic legislation in Poland and Washington's imposition of restrictive quotas.

Under the leadership of the mufti, the Arabs in Palestine discovered that rioting against the Jews was an effective political and military strategy: the British would prevent the Jews from protecting themselves while making little or no effort to interfere with Arab attacks. After each melee, a commission of inquiry would investigate the cause of the riot and conclude that the Arabs were afraid of being displaced as a consequence of Jewish immigration. The disturbances could therefore be stopped by imposing curbs on Jewish immigration.

Staging a riot, subsequently, became the way for the Arabs to halt Jewish immigration. Since the British failed to recognize that the Arabs were upset by the presence of *any* Jews in Palestine, their policy guaranteed an incessant cycle of violence. To appease the Arabs, the British gradually retreated from their obligation under the Balfour Declaration, which convinced many Jews that the British were as much an obstacle to achieving independence as the Arabs.

The British exacerbated the situation by arguing that the influx of Jews threatened the "economic absorptive capacity" of Palestine.

While they feared too many Jews would exceed that capacity, the British ignored the impact of Arab immigrants moving to Palestine without restrictions. This argument was always a bogus one that the British would use to justify limiting Jewish immigration at a time when fewer than 1 million people lived in the same area that now comfortably supports more than 10 million.

It wasn't just the Arabs' fear of being displaced that led to their animus toward the Jews; their hostility toward Jewish immigration also stemmed from their perception of progress as a secular evil meant to undermine traditional Arab and Islamic values. Most *fellaheen* (a peasant or agricultural laborer) actually benefited economically from Jewish settlement; however, they didn't appreciate these improvements because the mufti and other religious leaders preached the immorality of progress and the dangers the progressive Jews posed to Arab culture.

In August 1929, rumors spread of Jews killing Arabs and a Jewish plot to seize control of Muslim holy places on the Temple Mount in Jerusalem. This was the first time during the mandate that religion played a direct role in stoking the conflict in Palestine. It would not be the last, however, as Muslims leaders have found it advantageous to periodically make similar accusations to arouse the local population and the Muslim faithful worldwide.

With a rallying cry to defend the al-Aqsa Mosque, Arab mobs looted Jewish shops and attacked Jewish men, women, and children throughout the country. The most serious attack occurred in the ancient city of Hebron, where Jews believe the Patriarchs Abraham, Isaac, and Jacob and the Matriarchs Sarah, Rebekah, and Leah are buried. Jews lived in Hebron almost continuously throughout the Byzantine, Mameluke, and Ottoman periods. In the early twentieth century, the community in Hebron was small but lived in peace with their Arab neighbors until the night of August 23, 1929, when Arabs went on a rampage against the helpless Jewish community. According to the *Encyclopedia Judaica*:

> The assault was well planned and its aim was well defined: the elimination of the Jewish settlement of Hebron. The rioters did not spare women, children, or the aged; the British gave passive

assent. Sixty-seven were killed, 60 wounded, the community was destroyed, synagogues razed and Torah scrolls burned.

Nearly one-third of the victims were murdered in a single home and then dismembered. Some Arabs did protect Jews, notably Haj Issa el-Kourdieh, who lived in the Jewish Quarter and saved 33 Jews by hiding them in his basement. Other survivors relocated to Jerusalem. After six days of mayhem throughout Palestine, the British finally brought in troops to stop the violence. By the end of the rioting, 135 Jews (including eight Americans) were killed and more than 300 wounded.

The British ignored the mufti's provocations and appointed another commission, led by Sir William Shaw, to investigate the cause of the riots. The Shaw Commission found that the violence occurred due to "racial animosity on the part of the Arabs, consequent upon the disappointment of their political and national aspirations and fear for their economic future." The report claimed that the Arabs feared economic domination by a group who seemed to have, from their perspective, unlimited funding from abroad. The commission reported that the conflict stemmed from different interpretations of British promises to both Arabs and Jews. The commission acknowledged the ambiguity of former British statements and recommended that the government clearly define its intentions for Palestine. It also recommended that the issue of further Jewish immigration be more carefully considered to avoid "a repetition of the excessive immigration of 1925 and 1926."

The rise of Hitler, and the growing persecution of Jews in Nazi Germany in the 1930s, led to a brief reprieve from the British concern with placating the Arabs. The immigration quota was relaxed and the number of Jewish immigrants swelled, reaching a high of more than 66,000 in 1935, nearly double the previous high of 1925. The Arabs objected and the British slashed the quota to less than one-third of the number requested by the Zionist leaders. Consequently Jewish immigration dropped to less than 30,000 the following year and, by 1940, the figure fell below 11,000. The Jewish population still grew from 55,000, just 10 percent of the total population of Palestine before World War I, to almost half a million, more than

30 percent of the country's population, by the start of World War II. No one knows how many thousands of Jews might have survived the Holocaust had the British thrown open the gates to the Jewish homeland.

While the Jews settled as much as possible in areas that were uninhabited or had small Arab populations, Arabs were increasingly drawn to Jewish cities to take advantage of the economic opportunities and improved health services, which dramatically reduced their infant mortality rate and increased their average life expectancy. Palestinian Arabs earned a fraction of Jews' income; nevertheless, the Arabs' per capita income doubled between 1920 and 1937 and exceeded the average incomes of Arabs in Egypt, Syria, Lebanon, and Iraq. This progress simulated even greater immigration from Arab countries—37 percent of the total immigration into pre-state Israel.

With all the focus on Jewish immigration, little attention was paid to the unrestricted Arab influx between the wars that resulted in the non-Jewish population increasing by 380,000. During the 24 years of the mandate (1922–1946), the total population of Palestine increased more than 180 percent, to just under 2 million, while the Arab population alone swelled 118 percent. Arabs would often complain, and still do, that the Jews were not natives of the land they claim, but neither were large numbers of Arabs who moved from neighboring countries before claiming to be Palestinians.

Tensions grew as the Arabs continued to complain of being dispossessed by Jews, even though Jews owned just 9 percent of the land area now known as Israel; 3 percent was held by Arabs who remained in the country while 17 percent belonged to Arabs who left the country. More than 70 percent of the land was owned by the mandatory government.

The impression the mufti and other opponents of Jewish immigration tried to create was that the presence of Jews automatically led to the Arabs' losing their homes and land. In fact, Arabs were selling their land to the Jews. By 1936, for example, more than 90 percent of the land Jews had purchased came from these landowners. The problem for the Palestinians was that nearly 40 percent of the sellers lived in Egypt and Syria and were willing to accept large profits at the expense of any people who might be living on their land. Jews were willing to purchase any available land. Consequently, of the 370,000 acres in Jewish hands, 87,500 acres were swampland and 125,000 acres were lands never before cultivated. These were not areas Arabs were clamoring to hold.

The claim of dispossession was ultimately rejected by yet another British commission, this time led by Lewis French in 1931, which invited Arabs who had lost their land to apply for new territory. The government offered land to any Arabs who were dispossessed, but only 3,200 Arabs applied. Only 600 were found to have legitimate claims and only 100 accepted the British land offer.

The findings of the Lewis Commission did nothing to pacify the Arabs. On the contrary, they became more radicalized by the increase in Jewish immigration and land acquisition and general frustration at the continuation of European rule. In April 1936, a series of attacks on Jewish settlements were led by a friend of the mufti, a Syrian guerrilla named Fawzi el-Kaukji.

As violence continued, the local Arab leaders formed a coalition, the Arab Higher Committee, and made the mufti its leader. The mufti quickly called for a general strike of Arab workers and a boycott of Jewish products, which he hoped would paralyze the country. Violence escalated into terrorist attacks against the Jews and the British in what marked the beginning of the "Arab Revolt."

In May 1936, the British government appointed yet another commission to investigate the cause of the unrest. By the time the commission led by Lord Earl Peel arrived in Palestine in November, 89 Jews had been killed and more than 300 wounded.

Once again, Arab complaints about Jewish land acquisition were found to be baseless, and the commission concluded that any shortage of land was "due less to the amount of land acquired by Jews than to the increase in the Arab population." The commission went further and gave credit to the Jewish presence in Palestine, along with the work of the British administration, for improving the standard of living in the area, which resulted in higher wages and more employment opportunities.

It was nevertheless clear to the commission that the aspirations of the Jews and Arabs were mutually contradictory. In its 1937 report, the commission proposed a seemingly logical solution—divide Palestine into two separate states: one Jewish and one Arab.

The division would not be equal, however, because the Jewish and Arab populations were not divided neatly between two halves of the country. Consequently, the Peel partition plan carved Palestine into a checkerboard of loosely connected areas. The Jewish state was to encompass a minuscule area of Palestine composed of eastern Galilee, the Jezreel Valley, and the coastal plain from Tel Aviv to Acre. The remainder of the country was to be the Arab state.

Most Zionists were dissatisfied that the proposed Jewish state was reduced to a fraction of the historic Land of Israel; nevertheless, they were prepared to accept the Peel plan on the grounds that a small state was better than no state. The Arabs rejected the proposal unequivocally. They could not fathom the idea of 300,000 Arabs consigned to the Jewish state living under "Jewish domination." In fact, they objected to the creation of a Jewish state anywhere on "their" land.

The mufti testified that a Jewish state was unacceptable and that all the Jews who arrived after 1914 should be expelled. Reiterating the "al-Aqsa libel," he speciously argued that if the Jews remained they would try to rebuild their temple and destroy the Muslim shrines on the Temple Mount even though Great Britain was to retain control over Jerusalem. A newspaper controlled by the mufti said "anyone who supports the idea of partition is a traitor," and some Muslim clerics went further and labeled supporters of partition heretics. These labels were essentially licenses for the mufti to kill those who disagreed with him.[6]

The British withdrew the partition plan, but violence escalated to the point where the British finally took action to crush the rebellion. By the time the three-year revolt ended, 415 Jews were dead. The toll on the Arabs was much higher because of clashes with British troops, which left an estimated 5,000 dead, 15,000 wounded, and 5,600 imprisoned. Arabs also killed fewer Jews than their fellow Arabs.

The British also lost patience with the inflammatory rhetoric and violent orchestrations of the Arab Higher Committee and declared the organization illegal. The leaders of the committee either fled or were arrested. The British tried to arrest the mufti, but he escaped to Germany, arriving in Berlin on November 6, 1941. Though pro-Zionist Arabs contemplated a campaign to win public support for reaching an agreement with the Jews, nothing materialized because the mufti's supporters continued to control the political activities of the Palestinian Arabs through continuing violence.

As the possibility of war with Germany grew, the British wanted to secure oil supplies from the Arabs as well as to discourage Middle Eastern leaders from allying with Germany as the Turks had done in World War I. British policy toward the Arabs turned to appeasement. After suppressing their revolt, the British rewarded them with the publication of the 1939 White Paper, which declared the Peel Commission's partition plan unfeasible. The document stated that Palestine would be neither a Jewish state nor an Arab one, but an independent state to be established within ten years. Jewish immigration to Palestine was limited to 75,000 for the first five years, subject to the "economic absorptive capacity" of the country. Worse, and unacceptable for the Zionists, was that future immigration would require Arab consent, effectively putting an end to the possibility of Jews entering the country or becoming a majority. Furthermore, new restrictions were imposed on land acquisition by Jews.

The Zionists considered the White Paper a reversal of the British commitment to a Jewish home in Palestine, which could hardly have come at a worse time. Just six months earlier *Kristallnacht* (the "Night of Broken Glass") had conveyed a strong message to the Jews of Germany and Austria that their future was in danger. More explicit threats to exterminate the Jews by Hitler a few weeks later reinforced the Zionist imperative to open the gates of Palestine to any Jew seeking refuge. The Zionists' leader, David Ben-Gurion, subsequently declared that the Jews would fight with the British against Hitler as though there were no White Paper and fight against the White Paper as though there were no war.

The Zionists viewed the White Paper as a capitulation to Arab violence, which provoked militant Jews to show the British that "Jewish nuisance value was no less dangerous than the Arab variety."[7] Underground Jewish groups, the Irgun and the Stern Gang, subsequently became more violent, targeting British officials and installations in what became an insurgent war to drive the British out of Palestine.

Meanwhile, Haj Amin el-Husseini remained the leader of the Palestinian Arabs from his exile in Berlin, where he became an active supporter of the Nazis. According to historian Robert Wistrich, it was not an accident that the mufti found ideological similarities between National Socialism and Islam, "especially in their authoritarianism, anti-communism and hatred of the Jews."[8]

The mufti hoped Hitler would also have a final solution to the Jewish problem in the Middle East. Hitler said that this was indeed his intention. He said his troops would overrun the Middle East to free the Arabs from the British imperialists. "Germany's objective would then be solely the destruction of the Jewish element residing in the Arab sphere under the protection of British power."[9]

Husseini spent the remainder of the war in Germany, where he did everything he could to sabotage the consideration of any plan to release Jews captured by the Nazis. He also made Arabic radio broadcasts to the Middle East and North Africa, appealing for Muslims to kill Jews and repeating many of the distortions of the Koran to suggest that Jews were out to destroy Islam, that they were hostile to the believers, and that they opposed and tried to kill the Prophet. "Kill the Jews wherever you find them," he said on Berlin Radio in March 1944. "The world will never be at peace until the Jewish race is exterminated." Echoing Nazi propaganda, Husseini told his radio listeners, "The Jews are the germs which have caused all the trouble in the world."[10]

Later, when the full impact of the Holocaust became widely known, radical Muslims would deny it happened, claim Jews exaggerated events, and/or say they deserved it. For example, Sheikh Yusuf al-Qaradawi, a Muslim authority who serves as a moral guide for Hamas and the Muslim Brotherhood, explained why Jews suffered divine retribution:

> Throughout history Allah has imposed on the Jews people who would punish them for their corruption. The last punishment was carried out by Hitler . . . even though they exaggerated this issue. He managed to put them in their place. This was divine

punishment for them. Allah willing, the next time will be at the hands of the believers.[11]

While much has been written about the Jewish lobbying effort to support the creation of a Jewish state, much less attention has been given to the Arab and Muslim campaign to prevent this from happening.[12] Perhaps no one was more outspoken about the Zionist threat than the king of Saudi Arabia, who considered himself the leader of the Muslim world as custodian of the mosques in Mecca and Medina.

A devout Muslim, adhering to the strict Wahhabi brand of Islam, Saud was an unabashed anti-Semite. In 1937, he told a British officer, "Our hatred for the Jews dates from God's condemnation of them for their persecution and rejection of Isa (Jesus) and their subsequent rejection of His chosen Prophet."[13] In the mid-1940s, Saud threatened to execute any Jew who tried to enter the kingdom. He wrote to President Roosevelt in May 1943 in an effort to dissuade him from supporting a Jewish state. "Jews have no right to Palestine," he informed Roosevelt. "God forbid . . . the Allies should, at the end of their struggle, crown their victory by evicting the Arabs from their home."[14] When Roosevelt suggested that the king meet with Zionist representatives in an effort to reach an understanding, Saud told the president's emissary that he was "prepared to talk to anyone, of any religion, except a Jew."[15]

In a face-to-face meeting in February 1945, the king reiterated his opposition to Jewish immigration to Palestine and the creation of a Jewish state. Instead of Palestine, Saud said the Jews should be given the homes of Germans or those in Poland abandoned after their Jewish owners had been murdered. His underlying religious motivation emerged in a subsequent letter to Roosevelt in which he said that Palestine "has been an Arab country since the dawn of history and . . . was never inhabited by Jews for more than a period of time, during which their history in the land was full of murder and cruelty. . . . [There is] religious hostility . . . between the Muslims and the Jews from the beginning of Islam . . . which arose from the treacherous conduct of the Jews towards Islam and the Muslims and their prophet."[16]

Hammering home the point that the conflict is religious, Saud added, "the dispute between the Arab and Jew will be violent and long-lasting and without doubt will lead to more shedding of blood. Even if it is supposed that the Jews will succeed in gaining support for the establishment of a small state by their oppressive and tyrannous means and their money, such a state must perish in a short time. The Arab will isolate such a state from the world and will lay siege to it until it dies by famine. Trade and possible prosperity of the state will be prevented; its end will be the same as that of those crusader states which were forced to relinquish coveted objects in Palestine."[17]

The king undoubtedly believed what he said, but he was also pragmatic enough to realize that his monarchy would depend on the support of the United States. He and his successors continued to complain about the Jews and, later, Israel, but they were not prepared to jeopardize ties with the United States over the Palestine issue.

Another indication that the Arab disposition toward a Jewish state was about religion, and not just politics, was the imposition of the Arab League boycott in 1945. One of the first acts of the League, which was founded that year in Cairo to unify the Arabs, was to declare a boycott that made no distinction between Jews and Zionists: "Jewish products and manufactured goods shall be considered undesirable to the Arab countries." All Arab "institutions, organizations, merchants, commission agents and individuals" were called upon "to refuse to deal in, distribute, or consume Zionist products or manufactured goods." As Israel was still nearly three years from declaring independence, Arab animosity was clearly directed against Jews and not a Jewish state.

Instead of an economic boycott, the mufti's supporters called for a social boycott of Jews to prevent good relations from developing. In addition to opposing the sale of land to Jews, Arabs were told not to rent homes to Jews. "Through the creation of mixed neighborhoods," a mufti-aligned paper wrote, "the Jews seek to prove that coexistence is viable."[18]

The Arabs did what they could to prevent the establishment of a Jewish state, but the Zionists were primarily impeded by the refusal of the British to raise the quota for Jewish immigration above 18,000, even after the war ended and the horrors of the Holocaust were exposed. The Jews' response was to develop a large smuggling effort to bring survivors to their homeland. The British stopped any ships they caught and interned the passengers in camps on Cyprus. After surviving the horrors of concentration camps, 50,000 Jews were confined to new prisons by the British, and 28,000 remained in those camps until the State of Israel welcomed them in 1948.

The Holocaust convinced the Zionists that the safety of Jews around the world depended on the existence of a Jewish state. Jews vowed to never again allow their lives to be at the mercy of others and to ensure they had a haven from danger and a sovereign army that would fight, if necessary, to defend the Jewish people wherever they lived.

The Arabs in Palestine should have been as determined to win independence from the British, but they did not behave that way. Instead, they stayed mostly on the sidelines, watching the Jews fight the British and hoping that Great Britain would stop Jewish immigration and impede the implementation of the Balfour Declaration.

The British public, however, no longer supported their government's involvement in Palestine. They were especially horrified by heinous attacks on British soldiers by the Jewish underground. Seeing no good alternative to end the violence and resolve the conflict between the Jews and Arabs, the British decided to turn the matter over to the United Nations.

The UN created a committee to investigate the cause of the conflict and to try to devise a solution. Like the Peel Commission a decade earlier, the majority of the United Nations Special Committee on Palestine (UNSCOP) recognized that neither side could be forced to accept the demands of the other and, therefore, the logical solution was to divide Palestine into separate Arab and Jewish states. The idea made sense but was difficult to implement because the Jews and Arabs were not neatly divided into two different parts of the country. UNSCOP proposed a checkerboard configuration allotting the areas with the largest concentration of Jews to the Jewish state and those with larger Arab populations to the Arab state. The problem was that Jews lived throughout the country and large numbers of Arabs had settled in Jewish cities, which ensured the Jewish state would have a sizeable Arab population. In addition, the Jewish state was given a swath of territory in the northern part of the country that was barely contiguous with the strip of land along the Mediterranean. The Jewish state ultimately was given more territory because it was also allotted the large, arid Negev desert. The remainder of the country was to form the Arab state.

The UN's proposed borders were based solely on the distribution of the population with no consideration for security. The plan was further complicated by UNSCOP's insistence that Jerusalem remain apart from both states and be administered as an international zone. This arrangement left more than 100,000 Jews in Jerusalem isolated from their state and circumscribed by the Arab state.

As logical as the UN plan may have looked on paper, the reality was that the Muslims could not conceive of sacrificing any Islamic territory or allowing Jews to rule over them. The Zionists were not happy either because their homeland had already been carved up to create Transjordan, and was now being whittled down further to three enclaves, with 60 percent of the territory comprising mostly uninhabited, uncultivable desert. Worse, the Jewish state would not include the holiest city, and ancient capital of the Jewish state, Jerusalem.

Despite their reticence, the Zionists accepted the partition plan, concluding that an internationally recognized state, albeit a small one with indefensible borders, was better than nothing or a return to British control. The Arabs emphatically rejected the partition proposal and left little doubt that they had no intention of compromising. As Arab League secretary Abdel Rahman Hassan Azzam, more commonly known as Azzam Pasha, told Jewish representatives seeking a compromise over partition in September 1947:

> The Arab world is not at all in a compromising mood. The proposed plan may be logical, but the fate of nations is not decided by rational reasoning. . . . You will achieve nothing with talk of compromise or peace. You may perhaps achieve something by force of your arms. We will try to rout you. . . . We succeeded in

expelling the Crusaders, but lost Spain and Persia, and may lose
Palestine. But it is too late for a peaceable solution.

Notice the language used in the threat. It hearkens back to the
glory days of the Islamic Empire when the Muslims expelled the
Crusaders. The conflict was not over land or politics, but the Islamic
desire to return to its glorious past and to retake control over a part
of its heartland.

Azzam Pasha's comment also revealed another key element in the
transformation of the conflict; namely, the Islamic concept of time.
Westerners tend to think of time in terms of hours, days, weeks,
months, and, maybe, years. Muslims' perspective of time extends
over centuries, so setbacks are only seen as temporary and may be reversed. Inter-Muslim feuds, for example, can be carried on for years,
long after the initial cause of the dispute. Muslims have been at odds
with Jews since the time of Muhammad, so it is not surprising to
hear expressions such as this one from Azzam Pasha: "Centuries ago
the Crusaders established themselves in our midst against our will,
and in 200 years we ejected them."[19] From the Muslim perspective,
it may take 200 years to expel the Zionists as well, but Muslims are
confident they will. The reasons for that confidence will be discussed
in chapter 10.

The story of the partition vote at the UN has been often told.[20]
In November 29, 1947, the UN General Assembly voted to recom-
mend the partition of Palestine into a Jewish state and an Arab state
by a vote of 33 to 13, with 10 abstentions. The Jewish state that was
created was allotted roughly 60 percent of the land—6,120 square
miles of the 10,400 in Palestine. More than half of the Jewish state,
however, consisted of the Negev desert. The state was divided into
a coastal section, a northern section, and the Negev. These regions
were connected by narrow corridors. The international zone of Jerusalem was connected to the Jewish state by a narrow road that ran
through the heart of the Arab state. Slightly more than 500,000 Jews
and 350,000 Arabs lived in the Jewish state.

The Jews were still ecstatic, but they knew that they would have
to fight for their independence despite the UN decision. Before the

vote, the Muslims had issued grave warnings if partition was approved. Azzam Pasha, secretary-general of the Arab League, said: "It will be a war of annihilation. It will be a momentous massacre in history that will be talked about like the massacres of the Mongols or the Crusades."[21] Jamal Husseini, the Arab Higher Committee's spokesman, warned that the Arabs would drench "the soil of our beloved country with the last drop of our blood" to prevent the creation of a Jewish state. A few days later, the jurists of Al-Azhar University in Cairo, home of the most influential Islamic scholars, called on the Muslim world to proclaim a jihad against the Jews.

The violence began with rioting and occasional Arab raids and guerilla incursions from beyond Palestine's borders. In a matter of weeks full-scale battles were being fought. Jamal Husseini told the Security Council on April 16, 1948: "The representative of the Jewish Agency told us yesterday that they were not the attackers, that the Arabs had begun the fighting. We did not deny this. We told the whole world that we were going to fight."[22]

Meanwhile, the British impeded the Jews' efforts to defend themselves, imposing an arms embargo against the Jews while continuing to supply the Transjordanian army, which was led by a British officer. The British also continued their human blockade, preventing Jewish immigrants needed in the upcoming fight and future development of the state from entering the country.

On May 14, 1948, Israel declared its independence and called for the Arab population to become citizens in the new state:

> The State of Israel . . . will promote the development of the country for the benefit of all its inhabitants; will be based on the precepts of liberty, justice, and peace . . . will uphold the full social and political equality of all its citizens, without distinction of race, creed, or sex; will guarantee full freedom of conscience, worship, education, and culture . . . we yet call upon the Arab inhabitants of the State of Israel to . . . play their part in the development of the State, with full and equal citizenship.

The following day, the armies of five Arab states invaded. Contrary to revisionist history, Arab leaders were not interested in protecting the Palestinian Arabs or driving the Jews from the land to establish an Arab state. The invaders were really interested in carving Palestine up into pieces that could be annexed to their countries after driving the Jews into the sea.

The Arabs had good reason to believe they would succeed, since their population was several times the size of the Jewish community in Palestine, and, while Israel faced an arms boycott, they had little difficulty acquiring weapons. In addition, they had the benefit of a British general leading Transjordan's legion. Ultimately, however, the five Arab armies mobilized only a fraction of their potential fighters. In fact, the sides were nearly even, with approximately 80,000 Arab soldiers facing 60,000 Jewish fighters.

Very few Palestinians—a few thousand out of a population of 1.3 million—were prepared to fight. "This limited willingness to sacrifice their lives (or personal comfort) for the nation can be seen not only in the low level of mobilization for the decisive war that began in December 1947, but also in their economic activity and involvement in selling land to the Zionists," writes Hillel Cohen, a research fellow at Hebrew University. Those that did fight, Cohen adds, did so primarily to defend their personal belongings rather than the nation as a whole, which is why they restricted their engagements to protect their own village or group of villages.[23] Meanwhile, thousands of Palestinians fled before the war started to avoid being caught in the crossfire. Thousands more left later for the same reason, a handful were driven out by Jewish forces, and most others fled out of fear provoked by their leaders' claims of Jewish massacres and by grandiose predictions about the outcome of the war.

Though a sense of Palestinian nationalism had begun to arise in the 1920s, it had not yet taken root. As UN meditator Folke Bernadotte, a Swede sympathetic to the Arabs, wrote in his diary:

> The Palestinian Arabs have at present no will of their own. Neither have they ever developed any specifically Palestinian nationalism. The demand for a separate Arab state in Palestine

is consequently relatively weak. It would seem as though in existing circumstances most of the Palestinian Arabs would be
quite content to be incorporated in Transjordan.[24]

For Jews and Muslims a critical battle was over the future of
Jerusalem. The Arabs laid siege to the city and placed the 150,000
Jewish inhabitants under constant military pressure. The 2,500
Jews living in the Old City were victims of an Arab blockade that
lasted five months before the Jews were forced to surrender on May
29, 1948.

After nine months of fighting, 6,373 Israelis were killed, nearly
1 percent of the entire Jewish population of 650,000. Arab casualties were estimated at 10,000. As the war dragged on and the
cost escalated, both sides were pressured to agree to a truce. In
December 1948, they did so; however, none of the Arab countries
negotiated a peace agreement with Israel. Instead Egypt, Lebanon,
Jordan, and Syria signed armistice agreements formalizing the
truce; Iraq was the only country that refused to sign an agreement
with Israel.

Though Israel was upset that it failed to gain control of the Old
City of Jerusalem, which was captured by Transjordan, Israeli forces
did expand the territory originally granted to the Jewish state by
the United Nations by about 21 percent. Israel controlled the western half of Jerusalem and most of the surrounding area. Instead of
the partition checkerboard, Israel now had a contiguous territory
stretching from Eilat at the tip of the Negev desert and the Red Sea
in the south up to the border of Lebanon and Syria in the north.

The establishment of Israel marked a monumental turning point
in Muslim history. The outcome of the war was a humiliation and a
disaster. The perception was that a small number of Jews fighting in a
ragtag army had defeated the entire Arab world. This was especially
shameful to Muslims, who could not contemplate that a people who
had been so docile under their rule could now rule over Islamic land
and Muslim Arabs. It was inconceivable that infidels who descended
from apes and pigs had defeated Allah's faithful. "It was bad enough
to be conquered and occupied by the mighty empires of the West, the
British Empire, the French Empire," one Arab writer observed, "but

to suffer this fate at the hands of a few hundred thousand Jews was intolerable."[25]

The Palestinian Arabs refer to the events surrounding the creation of Israel as the *Nakba* (catastrophe). From their perspective it was indeed a disaster as their situation was much worse than it would have been had they accepted partition. No Arab state was created; instead the Arab areas were truncated and annexed by the Palestinians' neighbors. The area now popularly known as the West Bank was occupied by Jordan, as was half of Jerusalem. The Gaza Strip, which had also been part of the Arab state under partition, was occupied by Egypt. Though few of them saw it this way at the time, about 150,000 Palestinians who stayed in the area that became Israel benefited from living in a free democratic society that offered them rights they would have been denied in Arab countries—and that were denied to Palestinian refugees who ended the war in Syria, Jordan, Lebanon, and the Gaza Strip.

For Palestinian Muslim intellectuals, "The very creation of Israel was a travesty. What right did the Jews have to establish a sovereign polity in what had been Muslim land for thirteen centuries and qua Canaanite land in most ancient times. Only the undoing of the Jewish state would result in a proper solution to the ongoing Palestinian problem."[26]

Though many Muslims still had faith that over time they could expel the Zionists, the role of Islam took a temporary backseat in the development of the region as Arab states won their independence from the imperial powers and began to assert more nationalistic goals.

CHAPTER 3

ARAB UNITY AND DISUNITY

Almost from the outset of Islamic history, Muslims were disunited as rival families and factions, Shiites and Sunnis, adopting their own interpretation of Islamic law and competing to be viewed as the rightful successors to the Prophet. Over the course of centuries, one faction would gain dominance for a time; however, rivals inevitably emerged to break up the existing order and instill a new one as dynasties passed from Ummayads to Abbasids to Ottomans.

After nearly 900 years of Muslim empires expanding and contracting, the Turks established the most enduring Islamic reign from 1517 to their defeat in World War I in 1917. Muslim unity was shattered by the rout of the Ottomans. Following the war, the victorious European powers, Britain and France, carved up the former empire into pieces that were designed to fulfill their imperialist ambitions and exploit the region's resources. Instead of Muslim leaders ruling over people across borders, kings were installed by the imperialists and given a population to rule within artificially defined borders.

Many of the leaders of these artificial creations were weak, with no popular constituency, since they had been imposed on the people. The imposition of leaders by foreign powers clashed with the newly formulated notion of self-determination, introduced after the war by Woodrow Wilson, which proposed the principle that a people should be free to determine their own political status. The nationalist idea that territories should be divided into separate units based on ethnicity or some other characteristic of the majority of the population appealed to some of the peoples of the Middle East, but it clashed with the Islamic view that the Muslims constituted a single nation with a common religion, culture, and language; therefore, fundamentalists found it unacceptable for multiple Muslim states to exist. Furthermore, they opposed Zionism because it was unthinkable to embed a Jewish entity in the midst of the Islamic nation.

Any desire for a single Islamic state gave way to the political reality that the region was divided into separate entities, most of which had been created by the imperial powers with little or no regard for the composition of the population. Arab nationalism emerged then as a local reaction to the control exerted over the region's affairs by the colonial powers.

The political situation began to change following World War II as people throughout the region clamored for freedom and an end to foreign rule, which coincided with France and Britain retreating from their colonies as they focused on rebuilding their shattered nations.

Even after the Arab lands won their independence, however, the boundaries of several of them remained those drawn by the imperialists. This was problematic for a number of reasons. For example, some countries, such as Iraq, were given boundaries that included oil fields, which would eventually create greater wealth for Iraqis than for their Syrian neighbors, whose territory had little oil. Besides the distribution of natural resources, the borders also created problematic relations among the people, with Sunni majorities living in places such as Iraq and Syria, while Lebanon had a Christian majority. Iran's population was predominantly Shiite, while neighboring Saudi Arabia was Sunni but with a Shiite minority. These largely artificial divisions were sources of tension then, as they are now.

Despite the differences among the newly independent states, an effort was made to adopt a united front. The first step toward forming a union of Arab states occurred in March 1945 with the formation of the League of Arab States, or Arab League, in Cairo by Egypt, Iraq, Jordan (originally Transjordan), Lebanon, Saudi Arabia, Syria, and Yemen. Other Arab countries became members later as they gained their independence. Even as the League represented a degree of unity, it was actually fractured by inter-Arab rivalries, and while unanimous decisions of the council are supposed to be binding on all members, individual states often ignore them. The League rarely reaches consensus on major issues besides opposition to the creation and existence of a Jewish state and condemnation of Israeli policies.

When Great Britain withdrew from Palestine in 1948, it was the beginning of the end for the imperial powers, as Great Britain and France slowly retreated from the Middle East and the spoils they had seized after World War I were lost forever. Democracy was an alien concept, and the West did little to foster its development in the region. Instead, military men, rather than tribal or religious leaders, began to assert their power and overthrow the leaders imposed on them in countries such as Egypt, Syria, and Iraq.

After a series of coups following World War II, the Syrian government became a dictatorship that allied itself with the Soviet Union against what it viewed as the Zionist menace and the threat of Western imperialism. Despite violent changes in leadership (and another may occur after the current civil war), its anti-Zionist, anti-Western policies have not changed in more than half a century.

Lebanon took an entirely different direction, however, because of its more diverse population of Christians, Muslims, and Druze. The Lebanese established a republic based on the division in the country between the majority Christian Arab population and the minority Muslim and Druze communities. A proportional system was created to allot parliamentary seats to representatives of each faction. The leaders of each group agreed the president would always be a Christian and the prime minister a Muslim. Lebanon also distinguished itself among Arab nations by adopting a more liberal Western-oriented society with greater freedom than its Arab neighbors and a free-market economy. For decades, until the Lebanese civil war in the 1970s, Beirut was considered the Paris of the Middle East.

Lebanese independence has always been fragile because its more powerful neighbor considers Lebanon a part of Syria. The delicate political balance survived until demographic shifts—primarily the emigration of Christians and the growth of the Muslim population—and internecine rivalries aided by Syrian interference caused the system to break down in the 1970s. Syrian forces were "called in" to stop the violence and pacify the country, but they effectively turned Lebanon into a vassal state.

Arabia, meanwhile, never came under imperialist rule. Sharif Hussein, who had been emir of Mecca, was supported by the British because they wanted him to lead a revolt against the Turks during World War I. Hussein subsequently made a series of political errors, including declaring himself King of the Hejaz and, later, Caliph. By overplaying his hand, Hussein provoked the ire of his longtime rival Ibn Saud, who attacked and conquered most of the Arabian Peninsula while the British stood on the sideline. Hussein fled to Cyprus and then to Amman, where his son was king. He died in Amman in 1931 and was buried in Jerusalem.

In addition to his skills as a warrior, Ibn Saud was a shrewd politician. For the next several decades, his principal concern was that Hussein's heirs might seek revenge. In fact, the country that became known as Saudi Arabia almost immediately had border disputes with Hussein's son Abdullah, after Great Britain created Transjordan from territory that included parts of Arabia. To insulate himself, Ibn Saud sought close relations with the British, because they essentially controlled the Hashemite kingdoms in Iraq and Transjordan. After World War II and the collapse of the British Empire, the Saudis turned to the new superpower, the United States, for protection. In fact, the first arms sale made by the United States to Saudi Arabia had nothing to do with Saudi bluster about its opposition to Zionism; it was specifically requested to protect the Sauds from the Hashemites. As other enemies emerged, the Saudis would blackmail the United States to protect them to ensure American access to oil, which slowly became the Saudis' principal bargaining chip. The monarchy Saud established has proven remarkably stable by acting according to one overriding interest: that is, ensuring their royal heads stay on their royal shoulders. The

Saudis will work with the devil, even the Israelis, if it contributes to their survival.

The British supported the Egyptian leadership during the nineteenth century, and, following World War I, Egypt became a protectorate of Great Britain and a site of military facilities for the empire. Even under British dominance, Egypt was the most influential of the Arab states by virtue of its fabled history and advanced culture, the presence of the most prestigious Islamic institution of learning (Al-Azhar University in Cairo), and the region's largest Arab population. As in other Arab countries, however, nationalist feelings were brewing in Egypt, which unlike the artificially created states mapped out by France and Britain, had centuries of history behind it and a homogeneous population. As violent protests against the British presence escalated, Britain unilaterally declared Egyptian independence on February 28, 1922, abolishing the protectorate and establishing an independent Kingdom of Egypt under King Fuad, who had previously held the title of sultan. Fuad's efforts to concentrate power in the monarchy provoked more dissent. The British, however, continued to influence Egyptian affairs, retained control of the Suez Canal Zone, and became the kingdom's de facto protector.

After Fuad died in 1936, his 16-year-old son Farouk inherited the throne. The inexperienced monarch panicked when Italy invaded Ethiopia, and he signed the Anglo-Egyptian Treaty, requiring Britain to withdraw all troops from Egypt, except at the Suez Canal. The danger created by German forces marching through the desert prolonged Britain's stay in Egypt as it became the line in the sand that had to be held to prevent the Axis from potentially overrunning the Middle East. When the Allies halted the German advance in the Battle of Al Alamein (October 23–November 11, 1942), the Nazi threat to the region subsided.

Following the war, British troops were withdrawn to the Suez Canal area in 1947, but nationalist, anti-British feelings intensified. Islamic bigotry and Arab racial animus provoked attacks against European, Christian, and Jewish persons and property. Within five years, most of the small independent businesses, farms, and properties of the white, Christian, and Jewish populations were in ruin, with only the largest businesses managing to survive. The European population fled to the Suez and Alexandria, and the remaining Christian population, mostly Copts, continued to be persecuted but fended for themselves as best they could.

It was not only the British and minorities who were the focus of Egyptian anger. The public was also disenchanted with the leaders throughout the region, especially their own. The failure of the Arab armies to drive the descendants of apes and pigs into the sea humiliated the Arab leaders.

Anger gave way to violence and the situation grew chaotic, which prompted a group of Egyptian military officers to restore order. On July 26, 1952, the "Committee of Free Officers" ordered King Farouk to abdicate. He complied, and Egypt came under the control of a military junta dominated by a charismatic young lieutenant colonel named Gamal Abdel Nasser.

The new regime declared that Islam would be Egypt's official religion, but it had no intention of governing by Islamic principles. Nasser believed in unifying the Arab nations under the banner of pan-Arabism and separated the political sphere from the religious in a way fundamentalists considered blasphemous. When the fundamentalists objected, the military cracked down on them. This left no significant opposition to the officers.

Nasser's ambitions were undermined by emerging nationalist feelings in the region. Despite the artificiality of their imperialist-created borders, the people were developing attachments to their newly independent nations. This was not Western-style secular nationalism, however, because Muslims believe that their faith guides all aspects of life and that religion and politics are intertwined. Arab leaders all gave lip service to Islam's central role in their nations, but many of the men who came to power in these states developed a more idiosyncratic position based on an evolving sense of nationalism. While the countries remained part of the Islamic *umma,* the broader community of Islam established by Muhammad in the seventh century CE, they also had their own separate identities, some based on thousands of years of history living in their lands, even though they may have had other names in the past.

Historically, Muslims were loyal to the umma, not to rulers. This began to change after the French Revolution, when the concept that a government represented the people rather than simply lorded over them became more popular. Arab nationalism was also stirred by a longing for a return to the golden age of Islam, when Muslims dominated the Middle East for more than 1,000 years.

While the Arab states were torn by the conflicting pull of nationalism and pan-Arabism, they did find one unifying principal—hatred of Israel. Muslim fundamentalists believed the Jewish state was a cancer in the Islamic body that must be excised, while the Arab nationalists shared the goal of destroying this "imperialist, colonialist" outpost in the Arab/Islamic heartland.

After 1948, not one Arab country had agreed to sign a peace treaty, and all of them remained vocally hostile. Initially, some still held out hope that Israel could be erased from the map; others looked to isolate it and to maintain constant pressure on its population through a campaign of terror. Arab leaders also stoked public animosity toward Israel by incessant indoctrination through the media and education system.

Pan-Arabism was not a purely political movement interested in uniting the Arab world; it was also infused with anti-Semitism. "Arab and Muslim anti-Semites were very much inspired by Nazi anti-Semitism as well as by German nationalist (and anti-Semitic) authors of the 19th century."[1] Thus, Arab propaganda, especially that emanating from Nasser's Egypt, regularly featured anti-Semitic tropes.

Israel's one hope for peace in the aftermath of the 1948 war hinged on Jordan's King Abdullah, with whom the Zionists had been in contact before and after the war. Though Jordan's Legion had participated in the invasion of Israel and, thanks to British leadership and arms, had fought the most successfully, the Israeli government still believed it could make a deal with Abdullah. Prior to the partition vote, Ben-Gurion had sent Golda Meir to meet with him secretly, and they had reached an understanding that the Jews would not object to Abdullah annexing the area allocated to the Arab state (Abdullah had no interest in creating a Palestinian state; like the other Arab leaders, he hoped to carve out a piece of Palestine for himself). In May, just before the Arab invasion, Meir paid Abdullah a visit in Amman in an effort to dissuade him from joining a campaign against Israel. Abdullah told Meir, however, that he had no choice but to fight with his Arab brethren.

The hope for reaching an agreement with Abdullah after the war ended when an assassin shot him on the steps of the al-Aqsa Mosque in Jerusalem on July 21, 1951. Abdullah's son Talal ruled briefly, but his repeated mental problems led him to be deposed. He was replaced by his grandson Hussein, who ruled the country from 1953 until his death on February 7, 1999. As a young, inexperienced king, Hussein's top priority was to solidify his rule and he was in no position to follow through on his grandfather's initiative with Israel. He did secretly stay in regular contact with Israeli officials throughout his reign, but it would not be until 1995 that he found the courage to sign a peace agreement with Israel.

Meanwhile, Nasser was determined to lead the campaign to restore Arab honor and drive the Jews into the sea. As he rebuilt the Arab war machine, Nasser used terrorists (fedayeen) to wage a war of attrition. "Egypt has decided to dispatch her heroes, the disciples of Pharaoh and the sons of Islam, and they will cleanse the land of Palestine," Nasser said on August 31, 1955. "There will be no peace on Israel's border because we demand vengeance, and vengeance is Israel's death."[2] Notice even the secular-oriented Nasser saw the need to relate his goals to Islam by dispatching both Egyptians and the "sons of Islam" to sustain the campaign against Israel's existence. The terrorist attacks violated the armistice agreement's prohibition on the initiation of hostilities by paramilitary forces; nevertheless, it was Israel that was condemned by the UN Security Council for its counterattacks.

By unleashing Palestinian terrorists, Nasser accomplished multiple objectives. First, he kept pressure on Israel and conveyed the message that Israelis would never have a day of peace. Second, by taking the lead in the rejectionist front against Israel and inflicting pain on the Israeli people, he slowly erased the humiliation of Egypt's failures in the war of 1948 and helped Egyptians regain their pride. Third, as the one country still fighting Israel with more than rhetoric, his standing in the Arab world grew. Meanwhile, Nasser imported arms from the Soviet Bloc to build an arsenal for a direct confrontation with Israel in the future.

Nasser also alienated Arab leaders who resented him taking the credit for fighting the Zionists while leaving others to pay the price. The fedayeen were trained by Egyptian intelligence to engage in hostile action on the border and infiltrate Israel to commit acts of sabotage and murder; however, they frequently operated from bases in Jordan, so the Jordanians bore the brunt of any Israeli retaliation.

Nasser did not believe individual, weak states could regain their honor, defeat the Jews, and permanently expel the imperialists. Nasser stressed the idea that Arab identity transcended the boundaries of individual states and that all the Arab nations should cooperate and, ideally, unite under the banner of pan-Arabism. "While the Arab states paid lip service to notions of unity and formally rejected acceptance of the Jewish state in the aftermath of their defeat, they did not create any effective political mechanism to bind them for collective action against the Zionist interlopers," historians Jacob Lassner and Ilan Troen observed. "To the contrary, they have entered into bitter political rivalries among themselves. The ultimate aim of these anticipated changes was to establish the mutual cooperation necessary to combat external threats and to break the cycle of inter-Arab competition that works to the detriment of the idealized Arab nation."[3]

Nasser's stature grew because of his charisma and defiance of the West. Nasser's ascendance as the dominant figure in the Middle East was especially frightening to the Saudis, who feared he would use his growing influence to subvert their monarchy. In fact, all the conservative kingdoms were worried about Nasser's revolutionary attitude, which was aimed at upsetting the traditional order and replacing the monarchies with progressive regimes willing to follow his lead. The appeal of pan-Arabism was strong among the people who saw themselves as part of a larger Arab community, but leaders of Arab states, besides the monarchies, were concerned that this populism could turn against them. Moreover, they recognized that Nasser did not view pan-Arabism as a partnership; he expected all the Arabs to unite *behind him*.

The United States was concerned with the growing power of Nasser, but the Arabists in the State Department remained convinced the root of all problems in the region was the creation of Israel. Eisenhower's secretary of state, John Foster Dulles, believed that Truman had "gone overboard in favor of Israel," and gave a speech expressing the need for the United States to "allay the deep resentment against it that has resulted from the creation of Israel."[4] The administration's principal concern was that the Soviets would spread their influence to the Middle East by taking advantage of the resentment Dulles spoke about. This led the Eisenhower administration to focus on bolstering the fiercely anti-communist conservative Arab regimes (who, ironically, would later turn to the communists for arms when they could not get what they wanted from the United States).

U.S.-Egyptian relations deteriorated after the United States failed to finance the Aswan Dam and Nasser recognized China and flirted with the Soviet Union. Meanwhile, hostility between Egypt, Great Britain, France, and Israel intensified. The escalation continued with the Egyptian blockade of the Straits of Tiran, Israel's only supply route with Asia, and Nasser's nationalization of the Suez Canal on July 26, 1956. Ominously, less than two weeks later, on October 25, Egypt signed a tripartite agreement with Syria and Jordan that placed Nasser in command of all three armies. This was the first big step toward achieving Nasser's pan-Arab vision.

Nasser's actions were a serious provocation to the Europeans. The Suez Canal had been built in 1869 and was privately owned by a French company. Although an agreement was later reached on compensation for the shareholders and the right of France and Great Britain to use the canal, both nations were furious with Nasser's action and considered it a threat to their interests. They were already angered by Nasser's interference in their former colonies and effort to build a pan-Arab front against the West. The United States also condemned Nasser, but cautioned its allies against any military reaction.

Ignoring Eisenhower's warning, the British and French colluded with Israel to invade Egypt with the intention of capturing the canal and defeating the Egyptian army so soundly that Nasser would be unable to stay in power. While Britain and France were primarily concerned with their economic interest in the canal, and the broader threat Nasser posed to their regional allies, the Israelis were motivated by the need to stop Egyptian terror attacks, which had been unceasing since the end of the 1948 War, to open the Straits of Tiran, and to demonstrate that Israel's military might was sufficient to crush the Egyptian army and its allies. Rather than continue to fight a war of attrition with the terrorists and wait for Nasser and his allies to build their forces up sufficiently to wage a new war, Israel's prime minister, David Ben-Gurion, decided to launch a preemptive strike.

Eisenhower was personally offended because the attack took place a week before the presidential election, his allies didn't consult him, and he feared the war could expand into a wider conflict that might draw in the Soviets. Eisenhower said he was committed to aiding whomever was the victim of aggression and also believed that if force were permitted to settle a political dispute like Suez, then the future of the United Nations was in danger.

Ben-Gurion expected his European allies to give him cover against the opposition of the United States, but he was mistaken. After being condemned for their involvement in the war, Britain and France quickly left the battlefield to the Israelis and ultimately lost their longstanding influence in Egypt. Though Israel succeeded in conquering the Sinai Desert and threatening Nasser's regime, the gains were quickly erased due to pressure from the United States, the Soviet Union, and the Non-Aligned Movement in the United Nations. Eisenhower told Ben-Gurion, "Despite the present, temporary interests that Israel has in common with France and Britain, you ought not to forget that the strength of Israel and her future are bound up with the United States."[5] The president backed up his words with threats to discontinue all U.S. assistance, impose UN sanctions, and expel Israel from the United Nations. Eisenhower forced Israel to withdraw its forces without first reaching an agreement with Egypt, thereby sowing the seeds for the next war.

Despite setbacks during the war, Nasser emerged with even greater prestige in the region as a result of the humiliation of France, Britain, and Israel, and the backing he received from the United States and the international community. This improved his chances to implement his vision of a unified Arab world under his leadership.

It took some time, but Eisenhower recognized the implication of his shortsighted policy as Nasser worked to subvert American interests in the region. He was especially concerned with the increasingly

cozy relationship Egypt was developing with the Soviets, who succeeded in infiltrating the region, just as he had feared. By 1957,
Eisenhower concluded that America's interests would be served by
the overthrow of Nasser.

Eisenhower initially hoped King Saud could become the leader
of the Arabs, but quickly realized this was a mistake. Rather than
oppose Nasser, the first thing the king did was send his brother to
meet with him. Saud also withdrew his support for the Eisenhower
Doctrine, which said countries could request American economic
or military assistance if they were threatened by armed aggression
from another state. When Nasser began to accuse him of being an
American stooge, Saud feared his people, backed by Nasser, might
rise up against him, and Saud lacked confidence in America's ability
to keep him on the throne.[6] Nasser succeeded in temporarily driving
a wedge between the United States and Saudi Arabia, but Nasser did
not abandon his effort to undermine the monarchy, and within a few
years the two countries were fighting a proxy war in Yemen.

In 1958, Nasser finally convinced Syria to form the United Arab
Republic (UAR). Syrian political parties were dissolved and the army
placed under Egyptian control. Nasser was not content with this
single alliance; he foresaw the entire Arab world coming under his
leadership. Toward that end, the UAR did what it could to foment
rebellions in "conservative" states. Nasser's anti-Western, pan-Arab
propaganda helped roil the public and destabilize the regimes in
Lebanon and Jordan, which provoked Eisenhower to dispatch U.S.
troops to shore up the governments of both countries.

The Syrians did not remain content under Nasser's domination.
They were angered by Nasser's socialization of what had been a
largely free-market economy (and one that allowed Syrians a higher
standard of living than the Egyptians). Syrian military officials
chafed under the leadership of Egyptian officers, who were given
more responsibility, better arms, and other advantages. In 1961, a
group of Syrian army officers staged a coup and declared Syria's independence from the UAR.

Though Nasser remained immensely popular with the Arab public, he feared he was losing ground and decided to embark on a new

quest to gain prestige and primacy in the region. This time the focus was Yemen, where the ruler died in 1961 and was replaced by
a group of pro-Nasser army officers who seized power. The ruler's
son, however, had fled, and he launched a revolt against the military
with the support of Jordan and Saudi Arabia, both of which feared
the spread of the revolutionary forces unleashed in Yemen. Nasser
decided he could win a quick and easy victory to restore his image
by sending troops to back the military junta.

Overall the Yemen adventure turned into a debacle, Egypt's
Vietnam, as at least 70,000 Egyptian troops became mired in the
war from 1962–67 before Nasser abandoned the campaign.

Nasser's setbacks led him to seek an issue on which there was an
Arab consensus—the eradication of Israel. He was neither the first
nor the last Muslim leader to discover that railing against Israel was
an effective tactic to distract the public from domestic issues, to gain
favor, and to mobilize the masses. Paradoxically, the 1956 military
setback strengthened Nasser's case for pan-Arabism. Arab unity, he
said, "is our way to the restoration of Palestine and restoration of the
rights of the people of Palestine." Even as the Palestinians were kept
in squalid refugee camps in Egyptian-occupied Gaza and other Arab
states, their cause was a means to an end—rallying the Arab world
under Nasser's leadership to erase the humiliation of 1948 and drive
the Jews into the sea. He left no doubt of his intentions when he declared, "Our path to Palestine will be covered with blood."[7]

To cement his leadership, Nasser convened the first all-Arab
summit in Cairo in 1964 to discuss the "Israel threat." The participants decided to establish a new cadre of fedayeen to harass Israel while they prepared for a broader confrontation. The Palestine
Liberation Organization (PLO) subsequently was formed, with its
objectives spelled out in a National Covenant that reflected Nasser's
pan-Arabism. For example, Article 3 states: "The Palestinian Arab
people has the legitimate right to its homeland and is an inseparable
part of the Arab Nation. It shares the sufferings and aspirations of
the Arab Nation and its struggle for freedom, sovereignty, progress
and unity." The document repeatedly calls for the liberation of Palestine, that is, the destruction of Israel; states that Israel and Zionism

are "illegal"; and makes clear that it is the entire Arab nation's duty to help the Palestinians achieve their objectives:

> The liberation of Palestine from an Arab view point, is a national duty. Its responsibilities fall upon the entire Arab Nation, Governments and peoples, the Palestinian people being in the foreground. For this purpose the Arab Nation must mobilize its military spiritual and material potentialities, specifically, it must give to the Palestinian Arab people all possible support and backing and place at its disposal all opportunities and means to enable them to perform their roles in liberating their homeland (Article 14).

It is striking that the document does not call for the creation of a Palestinian state; in fact, it tacitly recognizes the occupation of the West Bank by Jordan and the Gaza Strip by Egypt.

The most immediate impact of the establishment of the PLO was to provide the Arab nations with a paramilitary force to terrorize Israel. The PLO activities were reinforced by an increasingly belligerent Syrian government that tried to divert the Jordan River to stop Israel's construction of a National Water Carrier to supply the country with water from the Jordan River. Syrian artillery also used the strategic high ground of the Golan Heights to attack the construction engineers and bombard the Israeli farms in the valley below.

As the Syrian military bombardment and terrorist attacks intensified, Nasser's rhetoric became increasingly bellicose. In 1965, he announced, "We shall not enter Palestine with its soil covered in sand; we shall enter it with its soil saturated in blood." Later he said the goal of the Arabs was "the eradication of Israel."

The threats against Israel were a rallying point for pan-Arabism and even the Saudis chimed in that "either Zionism and Israel [must] renounce their project of creating a state in the bosom of the Arab nation, or the Arabs must have the necessary will and power to retake their fatherland by force."[8]

Egyptian troops began moving into the Sinai and massing near the Israeli border on Israel's Independence Day. Three days later,

May 18, 1967, Syrian troops were prepared for battle along the Golan Heights.

When Israel withdrew from the Sinai following the 1956 War, a UN Emergency Force (UNEF) was stationed there as a deterrent to another conflagration. Nasser, however, ordered the peacekeepers to withdraw on May 16 without the approval of the General Assembly. Following the UNEF withdrawal, Cairo Radio's Voice of the Arabs proclaimed in a broadcast on May 18, 1967:

> As of today, there no longer exists an international emergency force to protect Israel. We shall exercise patience no more. We shall not complain any more to the UN about Israel. The sole method we shall apply against Israel is total war, which will result in the extermination of Zionist existence.

An enthusiastic echo was heard May 20 from Syrian defense minister Hafez Assad:

> Our forces are now entirely ready not only to repulse the aggression, but to initiate the act of liberation itself, and to explode the Zionist presence in the Arab homeland. The Syrian army, with its finger on the trigger, is united. I, as a military man, believe that the time has come to enter into a battle of annihilation.

Repeating the provocation of 1956, Nasser ordered the closure of the Straits of Tiran to all Israeli shipping and all ships bound for Eilat. The blockade was illegal and President Johnson hoped to bust it, but he had difficulty finding countries to help. Nevertheless, he warned the Israelis not to take any precipitous action because the United States would not help them if they started a war.

Nasser made no secret of his desire to fight. "Our basic objective will be the destruction of Israel," he said on May 27. As far as he was concerned the war of 1948 had never ended.

Although pan-Arabism had failed to this point, the Arab states rallied around Nasser and joined in the campaign to restore their honor and crush the Jewish state. Approximately 465,000 troops, more than 2,800 tanks, and 800 aircraft were poised on Israel's borders for an attack.

After King Hussein of Jordan signed a defense pact with Egypt on May 30, Nasser announced:

> The armies of Egypt, Jordan, Syria, and Lebanon are poised on the borders of Israel to face the challenge, while standing behind us are the armies of Iraq, Algeria, Kuwait, Sudan, and the whole Arab nation. This act will astound the world. Today they will know that the Arabs are arranged for battle, the critical hour has arrived. We have reached the stage of serious action and not declarations.

As a small country that heavily relies on reserves, Israel could not afford to wait for months for diplomacy to defuse the situation. The economy would grind to a halt and public anxiety would increase. Israel's leaders also were unwilling to stand by while its sea lane was interdicted or risk waiting for an invasion that would put the country on the defensive. Consequently, the government decided to take preemptive action. On June 5, the order was given to attack Egypt.

Israel was immediately fighting on fronts in the north and south against Egyptian and Syrian forces. They hoped to avoid the need to spread their forces to a third front, so Prime Minister Levi Eshkol sent a message on June 5 to King Hussein saying Israel would not attack Jordan unless he initiated hostilities. Hussein was reluctant to join the fighting, but his defense pact with Egypt left him no choice. Furthermore, the Egyptians convinced Hussein that a group of planes Jordan picked up on radar were Egyptians attacking Israel. Perhaps sensing the possibility of victory, Hussein ordered his forces to start shelling West Jerusalem. Only later did Hussein learn that the planes that were spotted were Israel's, returning from destroying the Egyptian air force on the ground.

Israeli forces made short work of the Jordanian Legion and were given the order after just three days of fighting to recapture the Old City in Jerusalem. The city was quickly secured by Israeli paratroopers, unifying Jerusalem for the first time in nearly two decades.

When the Soviets began to threaten intervention, Israel took the Americans' advice to accept a cease-fire, which went into effect on June 10.

The pan-Arab forces under Nasser were routed in just six days, with Israeli forces in position to march on Cairo, Damascus, and Amman. Israeli political leaders had no desire to fight in the Arab capitals and were satisfied with unifying Jerusalem and capturing the Sinai, Golan Heights, Gaza Strip, and West Bank, which tripled the size of the area Israel controlled from 8,000 to 26,000 square miles.

The victory came at a high cost. Israel lost twice as many men—776 dead and 2,586 wounded—in proportion to its total population as the United States lost in eight years of fighting in Vietnam. The death toll on the Arab side was 15,000 Egyptians, 2,500 Syrians, and 800 Jordanians.

It is difficult to minimize the psychological impact of the debacle. The fact that the Jews, inferiors who did not follow the words of Allah, could thrash the warriors of God was incomprehensible. The shock and embarrassment were overwhelming, penetrating the psyche of Arab leaders and public alike.

> The magnitude of the defeat was far too large to be shrugged off with the customary blame placed on external powers and their regional lackeys, and a painful process of reckoning ensued, not only among intellectuals and political dissidents, but also among some of the leaders responsible for the 1967 debacle. . . . Jordan's King Hussein . . . had no desire to take on Israel, and the impetuous decision to join Nasser's bandwagon in the fateful summer of 1967 stemmed from his reluctance to miss out on what seemed at the time an imminent pan-Arab triumph over Israel. When defeat came, the king quickly blamed it on pan-Arab ideals and rhetoric, which in his opinion bore little relation to reality and "enabled the Arabs to goad each other on to their destruction."[9]

The Israelis, however, had expected the military victory to convince the Arab states that they could not be driven out of Palestine, and it was now in their interest to negotiate a peace settlement. Israel even expressed its willingness to give up most of the territory it had won in exchange for a guarantee of peace. The Arab leaders provided their answer at a meeting held in Khartoum in August 1967: "*no* peace with Israel, *no* negotiations with Israel, *no* recognition of Israel."

In the aftermath of the debacle, the Arabs tried to reverse their military defeat in the political arena and to establish a new doctrine of the limited liability war in which they could attack Israel with the expectation that they would either drive the Jews into the sea or convince the international community to force Israel to give up any territorial gains.

This was the Arab basis for supporting UN Security Council Resolution 242, which unanimously passed on November 22, 1967. The resolution was intended to provide guidelines for a peace settlement, essentially calling on Israel to withdraw from territory it captured in exchange for peace with secure and defensible borders. The resolution very deliberately called on Israel to withdraw from unspecified territory, but the Arab states chose to interpret it differently, claiming that Israel was required to evacuate all the territory; that is, to give up all the land Israelis fought and died for defending themselves. The Arab view, which persists to this day, is that Israel is responsible for making all of the concessions while the Arab states have no obligations.

Nowhere does 242 call for the establishment of a Palestinian state; in fact, the Palestinians are not mentioned at all. Ironically, while Arab nationalism grew in newborn states, among Palestinians it largely dissipated as they were dispersed to Lebanon, Syria, Gaza, Jordan, and Iraq and for 19 years focused on rolling back the clock to pre-Zionist times. Palestinians also believed 1948 was a fluke—the Arabs had not fully mobilized—and could still drive the Jews from the land. Thus, they made no effort at state-building and no demands that Jordan create a Palestinian state in the area the Hashemites subsequently called their own, or that Egypt give them sovereignty in the occupied Gaza Strip. While the Egyptians' only use for the Palestinians was as tools of violence against Israel,

Jordan integrated them into society. Tens of thousands of Palestinians subsumed whatever national identity they felt to become loyal to a Hashemite monarchy transplanted from its Arabian home to a state artificially created by an imperialist government carved out of historic Palestine. Even when the Palestinian population became a majority (estimated as high as 70 percent) in Jordan, no effort was made to turn the country into the Palestinian state.

The 1967 War was, nevertheless, an important catalyst for the evolution of a new, more robust Palestinian nationalism that had previously lain dormant for 19 years. The Palestinians became disenchanted with pan-Arabism as a result of its failure to unify the Arab world and destroy Israel. Up until the humiliating defeat in 1967, Palestinians still held out hope that the Arab world would hand them Palestine on a platter. The failures in 1948, 1956, 1967, and, later, 1973, convinced the Palestinians they would have to win their independence on their own.

Paradoxically, the largely secular Muslim leadership of the Palestinians was motivated by their Islamic roots. "More than anything else," Lassner and Troen observed, "the very presence of a Jewish authority on sacred Muslim soil served to stimulate national consciousness and develop a greater sense of unity in the territories and the Palestinian Diaspora. An evolving sense of common cause has allowed Palestinians to increasingly mobilize their human resources toward a single objective: putting an end to the humiliating occupation and establishing a state that represents all Palestinians." Lacking the will to resume fighting, the Arab states turned the PLO loose to "engage the Zionist enemy in the occupied territories and Israel proper."[10]

The 1967 War also introduced the Israelis to another problem that they had underestimated, that is, the indoctrination of Palestinian children with misinformation. Palestinian children were exposed to materials that omitted the Jewish connection to the land, were given maps that did not show a country called Israel, only Palestine, and were supplied with content that was blatantly anti-Semitic. These books were produced in Syria, Jordan, and Egypt, but were funded and disseminated by the United Nations Relief and Works Agency, the only international welfare organization created to administer one specific refugee population. This issue of incitement in textbooks, art, and media has been an ongoing problem since Israel captured the territories because the propaganda has produced generations of young Palestinians who believe that Israel has no right to exist, that Jews are infidels with a litany of negative characteristics, and that martyrdom in the course of killing Jews is a ticket to Paradise. Israelis asked then as now how peace could be achieved with the Palestinians if they fed their children a steady diet of hatred.

Nasser's death on September 28, 1970, hastened the decline of pan-Arabism, but one last gasp came three years later when Anwar Sadat, Nasser's successor, once again led the Arabs into battle. For Sadat, the goal was not really the destruction of Israel, which he did not believe was likely given Israel's military strength and its support from the United States. What Sadat felt he and the other Arabs needed most was to erase and avenge the humiliation of their 1967 defeat.

Initially, Sadat offered Israel peace on his terms: namely, total capitulation. Israel would have to return all the territories captured in 1967, including Jerusalem, and, even then, he did not assure Israel the conflict would be over. Moreover, he repeatedly threatened to renew the war with Israel. After 1967, Israelis had grown overconfident and did not take the threats seriously.

Sadat was very serious, however, and sent a letter to King Faisal of Saudi Arabia on April 17, 1973, informing him of his intention to attack Israel. "Sadat acknowledged unashamedly in this letter that he did not expect to win a war against Israel, but he explained that only by restoring Arab honor and displaying Arab courage on the battlefield could he hope to capture the attention of Washington and persuade Henry Kissinger to support a peace process."[11]

Egypt and Syria planned to launch a simultaneous surprise attack on the holiest day of the Jewish calendar, Yom Kippur, October 6, 1973. Israel's leaders were not surprised, but Prime Minister Golda Meir had not been given sufficient warning to prepare the nation for war. Meir knew that a preemptive strike would improve

Israel's chances for victory and reduce the likely number of casualties, but Israeli forces were not in position to launch an attack and Meir was afraid of the U.S. reaction if Israel struck first. She knew American support was vital and, despite Arab provocations, believed U.S.-Israel relations would be put at risk if Israel started the war. Consequently, she rejected her chief of staff's recommendation to mobilize the Israel Defense Forces (IDF) hours before the attack. When Israel did begin to mobilize, the United States was informed in the hope that the Arabs could be restrained, but, as Meir had anticipated, she was warned by Secretary of State Henry Kissinger not to shoot first.

As Israelis were praying in synagogues around the country, Egypt and Syria mobilized their armies on Israel's northern and southern borders. Approximately 180 Israeli tanks faced 1,400 Syrian tanks on the Golan Heights, while fewer than 500 Israeli defenders with only three tanks were attacked by 600,000 Egyptian soldiers backed by 2,000 tanks and 550 aircraft along the Suez Canal.

In the last gasp of pan-Arabism, at least nine Arab states, including four non–Middle Eastern nations (Libya, Sudan, Algeria, and Morocco), contributed to the war effort. America's supposed ally, Saudi Arabia, and other Gulf States imposed an oil embargo on the United States and other Western nations considered supporters of Israel. The one country that did not fight was Jordan, which did not want to repeat the mistake of 1967 by challenging the superior Israeli forces. King Hussein sent a token force to Syria so he could say his country did participate, but his troops did not attack Israel from the east, allowing Israel to fight on two fronts instead of three.

After initially facing catastrophe, the IDF mobilized its full strength and, with the assistance of a U.S. airlift (which might not have been granted if Israel had struck first), drove the Egyptians and Syrians back. Once again, Israel was in position to attack the Arab capitals. Egypt's Third Army, one of two army units that attacked Israel, was surrounded by Israeli forces in the Sinai that were prepared to wipe out the Egyptian soldiers. At that point Egypt was prepared to accept a cease-fire. Under U.S. pressure, Israel agreed to stop its advance, and, in January 1974, Kissinger negotiated a partial Israeli withdrawal from the Sinai that also freed the Third Army.

Negotiations with Hafez Assad were more difficult, but Kissinger succeeded in reaching a separation of forces agreement in May, which established a UN-policed buffer zone, a reduction in troop deployment, and the return of the Israeli-captured town of Kuneitra to Syria.

In between the two agreements with the principal belligerents, Saudi Arabia and the other members of the Organization of the Petroleum Exporting Countries (OPEC) agreed to end the oil embargo.

As in the case of 1948, one notable aspect of the 1973 War is that it was fought with little concern for the Palestinians. Egypt went to war with the hope, but little prospect, of defeating Israel. The primary objective was to restore Arab honor. Any references to helping the Palestinians were mere lip service, so, not surprisingly, the war and the embargo ended without any concessions regarding Palestinian demands.

The two erstwhile allies, Egypt and Syria, also adopted very different postwar approaches. The United States provided Syria financial assistance for the first time in 30 years, hoping to establish a relationship with Assad and prompt him to agree to a peace settlement with Israel. Assad, as he would for the length of his presidency, charmed American Arabists in the State Department—as well as Jimmy Carter—with professions of his interest in peace. His actions, however, belied those words, as he later made Damascus the headquarters for many terrorist groups, built up a proxy army (Hezbollah) in Lebanon with the help of the Iranians, and did everything he could to sabotage American peace efforts. He became one of the leaders of the Rejectionist Front, the Arab states that remained committed to destroying Israel.

The 1973 War was costly for both sides. By the end of the fighting, 2,688 Israeli, 7,700 Egyptian, and 3,500 Syrian soldiers had been killed.

Israel is such a small country (a population of only 3.3 million in 1973) that the public is hypersensitive to casualties. The number of dead and wounded was devastating as nearly every citizen knew someone who had been killed or injured. Compare this with the

United States, which has been fighting two wars for more than a decade and has lost nearly 7,000. Yet relatively few Americans have a personal connection to the casualties. A political backlash followed the war as the Israeli public demanded answers for why the government was not better prepared, why it did not have better intelligence about Arab intentions, and why the IDF did not take the kind of preemptive action that had been so successful in 1967.

More fundamentally, the war traumatized the entire country. Israelis had emerged from the 1967 War thumping their chests, convinced their forces were superior to those of the Arabs and that they had proved, once and for all, no combination of Arab armies could defeat them; the Arabs would have to reconcile themselves to Israel's permanent place in the Middle East. The 1973 War shredded this confidence and reinforced the long-held fear, prompted by centuries of Jewish history and the Holocaust, that no matter what Jews do, Jew-haters will seek to destroy them, that no matter how strong the Jewish people become, annihilation is still a possibility. Though it may sound extreme, this psychological component of the conflict in the Middle East cannot be underestimated. Given this Israeli concern, it is not surprising that since 1973, Israelis have adopted a fortress mentality. They do not trust the Arabs or Muslims and are willing to make peace only on their terms, which, first and foremost, must guarantee, to the extent possible, their own security.

The psychological impact on the Egyptians was no less earthshaking, but in a polar opposite direction. Paradoxically, although Egypt lost the war on the battlefield, with Israeli troops prepared to march on Cairo and the Third Army saved by the United States from annihilation, Egyptians considered the "Ramadan War" a great victory. (Arabs refer to the 1973 War by the holy month during which it occurred; Jews refer to it as the "Yom Kippur War.") They surprised the arrogant Israelis and nearly defeated them. If not for U.S. support, many believed, they would have driven the Jews into the sea. This was not Sadat's true objective; he was more interested in erasing the humiliation of 1967. As Egyptian chief of staff Sa'ad Shazli said on October 8, 1973, "The war has retrieved Arab honor." This psychological shift was critical to Sadat's strategic decision to change alliances from the Soviet Union to the United States and make peace with Israel. Once he had made this commitment, he was willing to sacrifice the interests of the wider Arab world and, specifically, those of the Palestinians to advance Egypt's own parochial interests. This was the final nail in the coffin of pan-Arabism.

As in 1967, Israel's victory did not convince the Arab states that peace was a better alternative to war. In a show of Arab solidarity after the war, Saudi Arabia, Kuwait, and the United Arab Emirates pledged billions of dollars in economic and military aid to the frontline parties in the conflict with Israel—Syria, Jordan, Egypt, and the PLO. The Arab states, however, had no desire to create any new alliance or to contemplate another round of fighting with Israel. Instead, they focused their opposition to Israel on arming terrorist proxies, engaging in rhetorical bombast, seeking condemnation of Israel at international forums, and, in recent years, working to isolate and delegitimize the Jewish state.

The 1973 War was a watershed because it ended the Arab fantasy of destroying Israel, in part because the United States had clearly chosen a side for the first time and made it clear it would not allow Israel to be defeated. Despite the common perception that the region is in a constant state of turmoil, with the Arab-Israeli conflict as the principal source of instability, it has been more than 40 years since Israeli and Arab armies met on the battlefield. Though formally maintaining a state of belligerency, Iraq, Saudi Arabia, Libya, and Syria have avoided attacking Israel. It is true that Syria has used Hezbollah and Palestinian terrorists as proxies to attack Israel, but Syria has not launched an attack from Syrian soil since 1973. Israel did fight a war with the PLO in Lebanon during which Syrian forces were very briefly engaged, but the Lebanese army stood on the sidelines in 1982 and 2006, and Israel's military campaigns were confined to confrontations with the Palestinian terrorist groups and Hezbollah.

Lassner and Troen conclude that the "once compelling dream of pan-Arabism has been eviscerated. . . . Although there is little if any talk of a single Arab government—most discussion envisages a loose framework in which independent Arab states work cooperatively to solve common problems—individual Arabs, even the leaders of Arab states till pay lip service to unity. The concept of an Arab nation has lost none of its appeal. Despite the continued absence of a unified Arab state or confederation of states, and despite the lingering resentment against false calls for political union, virtually all Arabs believe in the reality of an inclusive Arab nation, or if you wish, Arab people."[12]

CHAPTER 4

FROM TERRORISTS
TO JIHADISTS

Violence directed at the Jews in Palestine has been going on from the days of the Israelites, so it was no surprise that the first new Jewish settlers became targets when they arrived in the late nineteenth century. Generally, attacks on Jews were a reaction to their mere presence in Palestine, though disputes also broke out over water and property rights. Initially, the Jews hired Arabs as guards, but new immigrants were concerned about relying on non-Jews and in 1907 formed a secret society, Bar Giora (named after Simeon Bar Giora, the Jewish military leader in the war against Rome in the first century), to guard the settlements and develop new ones. Two years later, Bar Giora merged with a new organization—Hashomer (Guild of Watchman)—to form a self-defense organization that was established by newcomers from Russia who had experienced pogroms there and wanted to ensure they had their own guards to protect themselves.

In the first decades of the twentieth century, Arab leaders in Palestine were determined to prevent the growth of the Jewish community and, following the Balfour Declaration, to obstruct the establishment of a Jewish state. Fears of dispossession and the imposition of colonial interlopers by imperialist powers provoked resistance on economic and political grounds.

Hostility to Jews was also fueled by the Arabs' unfamiliarity with Jews or Judaism beyond the teachings of the Koran and the pejorative interpretations of many clerics. Attacks on Jews were motivated by religious fervor stoked by the Mufti of Jerusalem, who wanted to cleanse Islamic land of the Jews. He also incited Muslims against Jews by circulating rumors that the Jews were going to destroy the al-Aqsa Mosque (the "al-Aqsa is in danger" libel). Muslims became more agitated following Israel's establishment when Western Jerusalem fell under the authority of the Jews, even though Jews were banned from the Old City and could no longer be accused of threatening the holy mosque.

Nasser's pursuit of pan-Arabism dominated regional Arab politics of the 1950s and 1960s and wasn't put to rest until Nasser's death, with Israel's victory in 1973 adding the final nail to the coffin. Nevertheless, like the mufti before him, Nasser appreciated the role of terrorism in threatening Israeli lives. The fedayeen were not motivated by Islamic fervor, but were the most effective weapons in Egypt's arsenal while it recovered from the shock of losing the war in 1948. During the six years preceding the 1956 War, 364 Israelis were wounded and 101 killed. Until he nationalized the Suez Canal and blockaded the Straits of Tiran, the terror attacks allowed Nasser to maintain a steady level of violence against the Jews that remained just below the threshold that would provoke a resumption of war. As the one country continuing to fight the Zionists, moreover, Egypt established itself as the vanguard against Israel.

Terrorism did not threaten Israel's survival, but the ongoing attacks placed a great psychological and economic burden on the country. Israel maintained a relatively small standing army, relying primarily on reserves in the event of war, which meant that Israel had a small force that could fight in an emergency, that threats provoking the mobilization of reserves could virtually paralyze the country, and that an enemy's initial thrust would have to be withstood long enough to complete the mobilization.

The 1956 War temporarily ended the activities of the fedayeen, though periodic terrorist attacks continued throughout the decade. For the most part Israel's immediate neighbors placed curbs on Palestinian political and military activities out of fear any organized

militia might be turned against their leaders. In 1959, a group of former students from Cairo, including Yasser Arafat, who had moved to
the Gulf to get jobs, came together in Kuwait to unify disparate Palestinian groups under an organization they called Fatah. The group
made the liberation of Palestine its highest priority and clashed with
Nasser's pan-Arab vision by arguing that Arab unity could only be
achieved *after* the Palestinians liberated Palestine.

The Arab League's decision to create the PLO in 1964 signaled a
recommitment to the use of terror against the Jews by not only Egypt
but the entire Arab world, which demonstrated that the war with
Israel was ongoing. When the Arab League established the PLO,
Ahmed Shukeiri, a one-time Saudi delegate to the United Nations,
was tasked with waging a terror campaign, and he established the
Palestine Liberation Army of the PLO to do so. The PLA was not
meant to seriously threaten Israel; rather, like Nasser's fedayeen, the
"army's" goal was to sustain an ongoing low-intensity conflict with
Israel that was controlled by the Arab states. Arafat's Fatah did not
want to be under Nasser's thumb and maintained its independence,
carrying out its own guerrilla operations until after the 1967 War,
when the PLO was viewed as having been part of the catastrophe.
This led to Shukeiri being replaced by Arafat as chairman of the
PLO and Fatah becoming the dominant faction.

The PLO was fashioned as a nationalist organization rather than
a religious one. The members of the Arab League, especially Egypt,
were not interested in creating an organization that believed in taking its directions from the Koran rather than Nasser. The Egyptian
leader had long experience with radical Muslims who challenged his
authority in the form of the Muslim Brotherhood.

The Brotherhood was organized in the late 1920s by Hassan
al-Banna as an anti-Western, pro-Islamic movement. Over time, it
served as the inspiration and sometimes funder of radical Muslim
organizations around the world. The Brotherhood adopted the ideology of Sayyid Qutb, who believed the Muslim world was no longer
faithful to the Prophet's vision. He blamed the ruling governments
(one reason he was executed by Nasser) and called for a return to
the Islam of Muhammad. "The sovereignty of God," he said, must
replace the rule of man."[1] The organization's motto is: God is our

goal. The Prophet is our leader. The Koran is our constitution. Jihad is our way. Death in the service of God is the loftiest of our wishes. God is great. God is great.

The Brotherhood sent some fighters to join the war against Israel in 1948–49 and maintained that no Jewish state could exist on Muslim soil and it was a religious duty to drive out the unbelievers. Israel was a minor issue for the group, however, which sought a restoration of the Islamic empire starting with the removal of the government in Cairo, which ruled largely by fiat rather than Sharia law. In response to the Brotherhood's subversive activities, the organization was banned by the government in 1948 and al-Banna was killed by government agents in 1949. After a period of disarray, the Brotherhood regrouped and focused on building a nationwide network of public services that the state often failed to provide, which helped the Brothers win a following, especially among the Egyptian underclass. Nasser and Sadat both viewed the Brotherhood as a threat to their rule and tried to suppress it by jailing many of its members and responding ruthlessly to any opposition. It would not be until the Islamic Winter of 2010 that the Brotherhood would temporarily get out from under the government's thumb and use the first democratic election in Egypt to seize power. Before the Brotherhood could consolidate its gains and impose its fundamentalist vision on the country, the military ousted the elected officials and once again banned the organization.

Islamists such as the Brotherhood have existed for some time, but they were kept in check by authoritarian leaders who recognized them as a threat. Ironically, over time those same dictators would kill off the non-Islamist opposition, clearing the way for the Islamists to gain power.

The PLO would eventually also challenge Arab leaders, but it started out with their backing. Nevertheless, like the divisions that doomed pan-Arabism, the PLO has its own schisms, which emerged after it became the umbrella in the late 1960s for a variety of groups that shared the goal of liberating Palestine but had different ideas about how to accomplish this objective and what they would do afterward. Factions include the Popular Front for the Liberation of Palestine (PFLP), Popular Democratic Front for the Liberation of Palestine

(PDFLP), Popular Front for the Liberation of Palestine-General Command (PFLP-GC), and Fatah.

The PFLP was founded in 1967 by George Habash, a Christian originally from Lod, a city located today near Ben-Gurion Airport. It became the second largest faction of the PLO and one of the most ideological, with a Marxist-Leninist orientation. Like Nasser, Habash supported the overthrow of conservative Arab regimes in addition to the liberation of Palestine. The PFLP has been responsible for numerous international attacks, including hijackings that killed at least 20 Americans. More recently, the group has been involved in mortar and rocket attacks from Gaza, and, in 2001, it assassinated Israel's tourism minister, Rehavam Ze'evi. The PFLP insists on the creation of a Palestinian state that would replace Israel but in which Jews may be citizens.

The Popular Democratic Front for the Liberation of Palestine is another Marxist-Leninist group that split from the PFLP in 1969. Led by Naif Hawatmeh, the PDFLP was most active in terrorist operations in the 1970s. The group has become more pragmatic in recent years and its positions now align with Fatah.

The PFLP-GC is another offshoot of the PFLP created in 1968 because its leader, Ahmed Jibril, a former captain in the Syrian army, thought the Habash group was more interested in politics than armed resistance. The group is backed by Syria and Iran and was especially active in the 1970s and 1980s. More recently, it has attempted to attack Israel with hot air balloons and motorized hang gliders. The group was based in Damascus and has fought beside Bashar Assad's forces in the Syrian civil war. The terrorists also have bases in Lebanon from which they have fired rockets into Israel.

Besides using violence to achieve their goal, the groups have little in common. Some are more ideological than others, but none were inspired by Islam. In fact, the PFLP are godless Marxist/Leninists whose founder was a Christian. Nevertheless, the Islamic influence was not entirely missing: for example, the name of the largest faction, Fatah, comes from the first letters of the Arabic phrase *Harakat al-Tahrir al-Watani al Filastini*, which means the Movement for the (National) Liberation of Palestine. Because the letters *H*, *T*, and *F* have a connotation of sudden death in Arabic, they were reversed and rendered *Fath*, which means "conquest by means of jihad (holy war)" in Arabic.

The PLO's "constitution" was a set of principles laid out in the Palestine National Charter, or Palestinian Covenant, which was initially drafted by Shukeiri in 1964. Article 22, for example, states that "Zionism is a political movement organically related to world imperialism and hostile to all movements of liberation and progress in the world. It is a racist and fascist movement in its formation; aggressive, expansionist, and colonialist in its aims; and fascist and Nazi in its methods. Israel is the tool of the Zionist movement." Article 19 declares: "The partitioning of Palestine in 1947 and the establishment of Israel are fundamentally null and void." The covenant euphemistically calls for the destruction of Israel and has been an ongoing source of Israeli concerns regarding the trustworthiness of Palestinians to end the conflict even if a peace agreement is signed (a fear that proved justified following the Oslo agreement).

The PLO's belligerent rhetoric was matched by deeds. Terrorist attacks by the PLO and Fatah intensified in the years preceding the 1967 War. In 1965, for example, 35 raids were conducted against Israel. In 1966, the number increased to 41. In just the first four months of 1967, 37 attacks were launched.

While the PLO and its supporters regard themselves as freedom fighters, their targets are rarely government or military installations or personnel but invariably innocent civilians. Israel's enemies rationalize any attacks as legitimate because of real and imagined sins committed by Jews since the beginning of the twentieth century. One rationale often given for killing civilians is that since most Israelis serve in the military they are all legitimate targets whether or not they are in uniform. Nowhere else in the world, however, is the murder of civilians considered a legitimate form of resistance.

Prior to 1967, the following terrorist attacks were conducted against Israel:

- January 1, 1965—Israel: Palestinian terrorists attempt to bomb the National Water Carrier—the first attack carried out by the PLO's Fatah faction.

- July 5, 1965—Mitzpe Massua, Israel: A Fatah cell plants explosives near Beit Guvrin, and on the railroad tracks to Jerusalem near Kfar Battir.
- May 16, 1966—Northern Galilee region, Israel: Two Israelis are killed when their jeep hits a terrorist landmine. Tracks lead into Syria.
- July 13, 1966—Almagor, Israel: Two soldiers and one civilian are killed when their truck strikes a terrorist landmine.

Unlike the 1950s, Nasser kept his hands clean in the 1960s by giving orders from Cairo for attacks originating from outside Egypt. King Hussein was particularly concerned because he recognized that Jordan would bear the brunt of any Israeli responses to PLO missions conducted from his country and feared the combination of his inability to control the terrorists and Israeli retaliation could weaken his authority. He also understood that his rule, along with other conservative regimes in the region, was a target of Nasser's "progressive" pan-Arabist ambitions. Consequently, Hussein feared the PLO might try to depose him with Nasser's help. In response, Hussein closed the PLO's offices in Jerusalem, arrested many of the group's members, and withdrew recognition of the organization by the beginning of 1967.

Nasser and his friends in the region unleashed a torrent of criticism on Hussein for betraying the Arab cause. This heightened Hussein's fear for his throne and led him to the disastrous decision to ignore Israeli warnings and attack Jerusalem in June 1967.

When Israel captured the West Bank and Gaza Strip in 1967, the PLO believed it would have bases for attacks that were now closer to Israel's population centers. Though controlled by Israel, the expectation was that they could mobilize the Arab population for armed resistance. The PLO also believed that Arab citizens of Israel, who had grown accustomed to life in a democratic state, albeit with elements of discrimination, would become a fifth column that would rise up against the Jews and undermine the state from within. Arafat quickly learned the Israeli Arabs were not interested in joining his campaign to liberate Palestine.

The PLO did succeed in establishing a base of operations in Jordan, much to the chagrin of the king. Jordan already hosted Palestinian refugee camps, and the majority of Jordan's citizens were Palestinians. The PLO became more brazen in its defiance of the king and built an army from refugees who seethed at their confinement in camps. Seeing the threat to his regime growing, King Hussein decided to sign an agreement in July 1970 with Arafat to head off any rebellion, but it quickly became moot when Palestinians hijacked TWA and KLM airliners and landed them at the airport in Amman.

Even though the passengers were rescued, tensions between Palestinian radicals and Hussein intensified. The king's troops fought battles with the PLO's "army," and the Syrians escalated the crisis by sending tanks across the border on September 19 to support the Palestinians. Now Hussein was not the only one concerned; the United States was worried that its ally would be defeated by the Soviet-backed Syrians. The Israelis also feared that Hussein would lose power to more radical, anti-Israel leaders from Syria or the PLO.

Hussein asked the United States to intervene; however, President Nixon was not interested in another military engagement during the war in Vietnam. He suggested that Israel could help him. The Israelis were prepared to defend the king, but, in the end, Hussein's troops drove the invaders out, making it unnecessary for Israel to intercede.

After Hussein's forces repulsed the Syrians, they directed their fire at the PLO, killing and wounding thousands of Palestinians and forcing the leadership along with thousands of refugees into Syria and Lebanon. The Palestinians refer to this period as "Black September."

Arafat and his minions soon managed to create another mini state, this time in Lebanon, where the weak government was unable and unwilling to exert its authority over the Palestinians. Southern Lebanon became a new base of operations for terrorist attacks against Israel, but the PLO was not content with attacking local Israelis; Arafat decided to expand the battlefield to target Jews and Israelis around the world.

The global campaign against Israel and the Jews by the PLO was largely an outgrowth of the realization that the Arab states were unlikely to liberate Palestine, and, therefore, the Palestinians would have to do it themselves. Naively, the PLO may have thought it could bomb the Jews out of their homeland, but that was never realistic. Instead, they wanted to instill fear in Jews around the world and to attract publicity for their cause through their terrorist campaign. This strategy began a few months after the 1967 War and resulted in the murder of more than 200 Israelis between 1968 and 1972. Among the more heinous attacks were:

- July 22, 1968—Rome, Italy: The PFLP carries out first hijacking, diverting an El Al flight to Algiers. Thirty-two Jewish passengers are held hostage for five weeks.
- September 4, 1968—Tel Aviv, Israel: One killed and 71 wounded by three bombs that explode in city center.
- November 22, 1968—Jerusalem, Israel: Twelve killed and 52 injured by a car bomb in the Mahaneh Yehuda market.
- December 26, 1968—Athens, Greece: PFLP gunmen kill an Israeli mechanic at Athens airport.
- February 18, 1969—Zurich, Switzerland: A pilot and three passengers are killed by terrorists that attack an El Al Boeing 707 on the airport runway.
- February 21, 1969—Jerusalem, Israel: Two killed and 20 injured by a bomb that detonates in a crowded supermarket.
- October 22, 1969—Haifa, Israel: Four killed and 20 wounded by terrorist bombs in five apartments.
- February 10, 1970—Zurich, Switzerland: One killed and 11 wounded by three Arab terrorists who unsuccessfully attempt to hijack an El Al flight at Zurich airport.
- May 22, 1970—Avivim, Israel: Terrorists attack school bus, killing 12 (9 of whom are children), and wounding 24.
- September 6, 1970—Dawson Field, Jordan: Three airliners holding more than 400 passengers are hijacked and taken to the Jordanian airport by the PFLP. The hostages are released in exchange for terrorists held in Germany, Switzerland, and England.
- May 8, 1972—Lod Airport, Israel: One passenger and five Israeli soldiers killed during a rescue operation by

Israeli commandos on a hijacked Belgian airliner; the
four Palestinian Black September terrorists are killed. The
hostages are freed.

- May 30, 1972—Lod Airport, Israel: Twenty-six killed and 78
  wounded after PFLP and Japanese Red Army terrorists open
  fire in the passenger terminal.
- September 19, 1972—London, England: A Black September
  letter bomb kills Ami Shehori, an attaché at the Israeli
  embassy in London.

The attack that attracted the most attention occurred September
5, 1972, during the Summer Olympics in Munich, West Germany,
when members of the PLO calling themselves Black September infiltrated the Olympic village where the Israeli team was staying. Two
members of the Israeli Olympic team were murdered while fighting
the terrorists to help their comrades escape; nine other Israeli ath-
letes were taken hostage and ultimately killed by the terrorists after
an unsuccessful rescue attempt by West German authorities. Bassam
Abu Sharif, a member of the PFLP at the time, said the motive for
the operation was to attract publicity for the Palestinian cause and
to win the release of Palestinian prisoners.

The years of terror did not change the status of the Palestinians
on the ground. It did significantly raise the profile of their cause, as
Abu Sharif and his fellow terrorists hoped, but the crimes also tarred
the Palestinians with the image of being barbarians. The hijackings,
in particular, forced every country to increase their security to prevent terrorism. The resolve of Israelis was strengthened, and they
became more determined to prove they could not be intimidated.
Moreover, they wanted to impose a high cost on any group that
attacked Jews anywhere and began to track down the perpetrators
of these acts and kill them. The Mossad's Operation Wrath of God
targeted the men who carried out the Munich massacre. According
to George Jonas in *Vengeance: The True Story of an Israeli Counter-
Terrorist Team*, 8 of the 11 men targeted for death were killed. Of
the remaining three, one died of natural causes and the other two
were assassinated, but it is not known for sure if they were killed by

Israeli agents. Terrorism did not end, but those contemplating violence got the message that they could not attack Jews with impunity.

The Palestinians had renewed hope that the Arab states would finally drive the Jews into the sea in 1973, but this was not Sadat's intention. He had no interest in liberating Palestine for the Palestinians; his goal was to restore Egyptian honor. Sadat got what he wanted, but that left the Palestinians in the same position as they were before the war. It now became clear that the Palestinians could not depend on the Arab states to deliver Palestine to them.

Arafat subsequently decided it was necessary to alter the PLO approach and pursue a dual strategy of continuing the "armed struggle" while simultaneously waging a diplomatic war against Israel. One of the first steps in the diplomatic strategy was to seek universal recognition from the Arab leaders that the PLO would control its own destiny. Up to that point, Jordan's King Hussein had hoped to regain the territory he lost in 1967 and considered himself the spokesman for the Palestinians. Israel, too, saw Jordan as a potential partner for peace and, in most scenarios, envisioned some type of confederation between the West Bank and Jordan that would relieve Israel of the responsibility for the Palestinians living there. More hardline Israelis took the position (and some still do) that Jordan was Palestine—historically, geographically, and demographically—and therefore the Palestinians already had a state and did not need another one. They believed Israel should annex "Greater Israel," that is, all the territory captured in 1967.

The PLO began to assume responsibility for the fate of all Palestinians in October 1974, when the Arab states decided at a conference in Rabat to recognize the PLO as the sole, legitimate representative of the Palestinian people. This gave the organization an immediate political authenticity that was further bolstered by the international recognition Arafat received when he was invited to address the United Nations General Assembly on November 13.

The sight of the terror mastermind Arafat standing in front of the international organization created to promote peace was galling for Israelis. More significantly, Israel recognized that it would now be fighting the PLO on both the military and political fronts.

King Hussein had no choice but to join the Arab consensus, which he knew ended his hope of regaining the West Bank and Jerusalem. He would still have influence over discussions about the future of the disputed territories, but Rabat eliminated his role as a negotiator for the Palestinians.

While the PLO had newfound status on the world stage, the earth shifted underneath the Palestinians with Sadat's decision to make peace with Israel.

The Palestinians and their supporters were furious with Sadat, whom they believed sold them out to achieve his own objectives, which was true in the end. Nevertheless, the Palestinians squandered an opportunity to take the first step toward independence when they turned down Israel's autonomy proposal. At the time, a relatively small number of Jewish settlers lived in the disputed territories, but Arafat and his successor's rejection of autonomy and subsequent peace offers are largely to blame for the explosion in the settler population from 10,000 in 1979 to more than 320,000 in 2013. They would never admit it, but the Palestinians were responsible for the growth in settlements because of their recalcitrance, and, should an agreement be signed in the future, it will inevitably leave the Palestinians with a much smaller state than would have been possible years earlier.

The PLO's refusal to accept the autonomy proposal reinforced the image of the Palestinians as rejectionists. Though their goals did not change, Arafat eventually recognized that calling for the destruction of Israel was not a wise political tactic. He and other PLO spokesmen learned to speak in more moderate terms when they addressed English-speaking audiences. Meanwhile, their rhetoric remained extreme whenever they spoke to their constituents. Prior to the Internet age, it was rare for people outside Israel or ministries of foreign affairs to have access to translations of Arabic, so the media and Western public was easily misled by Arafat's doublespeak. Israel publicized the difference between what he said in Arabic and English, but a certain level of mistrust of Israeli motives, combined with poor public relations, typically left the Palestinian view in the minds of many listeners, particularly in Europe. This ability to get away with propaganda in English began to change in the late 1990s as translations became more available on the Internet and groups such as the Middle East Media Research Institute (MEMRI) and Palestine Media Watch (PMW) began to circulate the extremist remarks by Arab officials, clerics, and journalists that appeared in Arabic.

One goal of the PLO diplomatic offensive was to persuade the international community that it was interested only in gaining sovereignty over the disputed territories—the West Bank and Gaza Strip. However, Palestinian documents, rhetoric (in Arabic), and policy called for the liberation of the disputed territories first, followed by the reconquest of the rest of Palestine. This became known as the strategy of stages, and many Israelis and analysts believe this remains the ultimate policy of the PLO, which symbolically is reflected to this day by the PLO and Palestinian Authority insignia, as well as official maps, which show Palestine without Israel.

Amid the excitement over the end of the longstanding conflict between Israel and Egypt, a new, ominous threat emerged from another part of the Middle East. In 1979, the Iranian revolution swept the pro-Israel, pro-American shah from power and replaced him with the theocratic rule of Ayatollah Khomeini. The example of the Iranian people uprooting their government was inspiring for many Arabs; for many Muslims it was a clarion call to begin the reestablishment of the caliphate and to demand stricter adherence to Islamic law and tradition.

One of the first places the impact of the Iranian revolution was felt was Egypt, where the fundamentalists of the Muslim Brotherhood were rejuvenated. The Egyptian public was already angry with Sadat. Many resented the fact that he had unilaterally decided to sign the peace treaty, were enraged by the abandonment of the Palestinians and the campaign to destroy Israel, and upset that Egypt had become a pariah in the region. Muslim fundamentalists shared the general public's feelings, but were especially outraged by the recognition of Israel's right to a state in the Islamic heartland.

Sadat tried to address his internal problems and negotiated loans to improve the lives of the people, but he also outlawed protests, which only created greater anger among his critics. In an effort to mollify the religious extremists, he announced that the Sharia would be the basis of all new Egyptian law. It was too late, however, as the religious extremists believed he was a traitor. On October 6, 1981, Sadat was reviewing Egyptian troops during a parade celebrating, ironically, the Egyptian "victory" in the 1973 War. Suddenly a group of soldiers dismounted from a truck and approached the reviewing stand. The leader of the assassination squad, Lieutenant Khalid Islambouli, threw grenades at Sadat while other men in the truck sprayed the area with gunfire. In just two minutes, Sadat was mortally wounded along with 11 others sitting near him; another 28 were wounded, including Vice President Hosni Mubarak and 4 U.S. officers. One of the attackers was killed, and three others were injured and arrested by security forces.

Later, it was learned the murderers were Muslim radicals associated with an offshoot of the Muslim Brotherhood. Islambouli and the other assassins were tried, found guilty, sentenced to death, and executed by firing squad in April 1982. Years later, the mother of Islambouli expressed pride in her son. She said he was influenced by the Iranian revolution and hoped the fervor would spread throughout the region. "I am very proud that my son killed Anwar Al-Sadat," Mrs. Qadriya told Iran's state-run Fars news agency. "[The government] called him a terrorist, a criminal, and a murderer, but they didn't say that was he was defending Islam. They didn't say anything about the oppressed people in Palestine, about Camp David, or how Sadat sold out the country to the Jews and violated the honor of the Islamic nation." Mrs. Qadriya, who is also the grandmother-in-law of Osama Bin Laden's son, said she was proud to see that Iran had named a street in Tehran for her son.[2]

Sadat's assassination was another milestone in the transformation of the conflict from politics to religion. The extremists sent a powerful message to other Arab leaders of the possible consequences for committing the heresy of recognizing the Jewish state.

After signing the treaty with Egypt, Israelis were initially optimistic that other nations would follow Sadat's example, but the backlash against Sadat, and his murder, quickly killed that hope. In fact, instead of a wider peace, Israel soon found itself in another war.

After Jordan drove the PLO out of the country in Black September, the terrorists regrouped in Lebanon. Before long they repeated the pattern they had followed in Jordan by essentially creating a Palestinian state within Lebanon that the Lebanese government and army could not control. Using southern Lebanon as a base, the Palestinians made repeated incursions into Israel. In 1978, the Israel Defense Forces (IDF) responded by sending troops in to force the PLO further from their border. After doing so, the Israelis left and were replaced by UN troops who quickly proved unable and unwilling to take action to prevent the PLO's return to areas near the border or the group's smuggling of weapons.

The PLO terror campaign was not limited to the Middle East. After the 1973 War, while Arafat was pretending to be a diplomat, the PLO was carrying out attacks worldwide. More than 200 Israelis were killed between 1974 and 1982. These were some of the more odious cases:

- May 15, 1974—Maalot, Israel: Twenty-seven killed, 21 of whom were children, and 78 wounded by PFLP terrorists who attack a school and take 115 people hostage.
- March 5, 1975—Tel Aviv, Israel: Terrorists take over the Savoy hotel; four people are killed.
- July 4, 1975—Jerusalem, Israel: Fourteen killed and 80 injured in Zion Square bombing attack, in which the bomb is hidden in a refrigerator.
- June 27, 1976—Entebbe, Uganda: An Air France airliner is hijacked by a joint German/PFLP terrorist group, which diverts the flight to Entebbe airport and holds 98 Jews and Israelis hostage. On July 4, Israeli commandos fly to Uganda to rescue the hostages. All the terrorists are killed, as well as three passengers and operation leader Lieutenant Colonel Yonatan Netanyahu.
- August 11, 1976—Istanbul, Turkey: Four killed and 20 wounded by PFLP and Japanese Red Army terrorists in an attack at Istanbul airport.
- March 11, 1978—Glilot Junction, Israel: Thirty-six killed and more than 100 injured in a bus hijacking by a female-led Palestinian terrorist gang.

- April 7, 1980—Kibbutz Misgav-Am, Israel: Terrorists attack the children's house on the kibbutz, leaving three dead, one of whom is a child.
- June 3, 1982—London, England: Abu Nidal organization attempts to kill the Israeli ambassador to London, Shlomo Argov, severely wounding him.

PLO attacks and Israeli counterstrikes increased in frequency and thousands of Israelis were forced to flee their homes or to spend large amounts of time in bomb shelters. The attack on Ambassador Argov in London was the last straw for Israeli prime minister Menachem Begin, who decided the situation had become intolerable. On June 6, 1982, the first of 80,000 troops crossed the Lebanese border in Operation Peace for Galilee with the objective of eliminating the terrorists' ability to threaten Israeli citizens living in the north.

The Israeli operation was so successful in pushing the PLO away from the border that Defense Minister Ariel Sharon decided to expand it with the goal of driving the PLO out of Lebanon altogether. After besieging Beirut, a deal was negotiated for Israeli forces to withdraw and Arafat to leave the country. In August 1982, Arafat and his closest associates were evacuated from Beirut to Tunisia. The IDF left Beirut, but not Lebanon. In the meantime a multinational peacekeeping force that included U.S. troops replaced the Israelis in Beirut.

One of the unintended consequences of the Israeli defeat of the PLO was the elimination of one of the most powerful forces in Lebanon, which strengthened the position of Shiite Muslims. Unknowingly, Israel had sowed the seeds for a new terror threat, the next step in the Islamization of the conflict.

Revolutionary Iran saw an opening created by the weakening Lebanese state and the growing anger toward the Israelis who remained in Lebanon, as well as the Western peacekeepers from the United States and Europe who replaced the departing Israeli forces in Beirut. Shiite clergymen educated in Iran and inspired by Khomeini mobilized their co-religionists in 1982, and the recruits began to receive weapons and training from Iranian revolutionary guards to create a guerrilla force. They aimed to first drive the Westerners and Israel from Lebanon, then seize control of the government, establish an Islamic republic in Lebanon, and, finally, join the jihad to destroy Israel and restore the caliphate. The organization took the name Hezbollah (or "Party of God"), which comes from a Koranic verse promising victory for those who join the Party of God.

After years of failing to radicalize the region, Iran finally succeeded in creating an ally, albeit a non-state organization, that would work to achieve Iran's pan-Islamic vision. Paradoxically, Iran was aided in this effort by Syria, whose leader, Bashar Assad, was not a Muslim fundamentalist and, worse, came from the Alawite sect of Islam that Sunnis consider heretical. In fact, the same year Hezbollah was founded, Assad killed as many as 20,000 in the town of Hama to eliminate the threat posed to his regime by the Syrian branch of the Muslim Brotherhood. For Assad, the alliance with Iran had nothing to do with radical Islam and everything to do with realpolitik.

First, Assad never accepted the legitimacy of Lebanon and considered it southern Syria. Since his troops' intervention during the civil war in the 1970s, his security and intelligence forces had retained effective control of the country. Second, the fall of the Soviet Union had significantly weakened the outside support Assad was used to getting from Moscow. Third, because Syria was largely isolated from both the Arab and Western world, it needed an ally to support it financially, and Iran was happy to please, so long as Assad (and later his successor, his son Bashar) kept a steady flow of arms and aid across the border to Hezbollah. Finally, Hezbollah was a valuable proxy in the war against Israel. Since 1973, Syria had scrupulously avoided violating the armistice agreement for fear of the inevitable counterattack that Assad knew would likely drive him from power.

Nominally independent, Hezbollah generally followed the religious guidance of Khomeini and his successor, Ali Khamenei. The spiritual father of Hezbollah in Lebanon was Sheikh Mohammed Hussein Fadlallah (died 2010), who preached that Islam viewed Israel as illegitimate and occupying land sacred to Islam. He maintained that Israel had no "right to security and peace" because "it is a conglomeration of people who came from all parts of the world to live in Palestine on the ruins of another people."

For Fadlallah and his followers, Israel is a threat because it "wants to establish Jewish culture at the expense of Islamic culture or what some call Arab culture." Echoing the *Protocols*, the sheikh claimed Israel's purpose is to bring "all the Jews in the world to this region, to make it the nucleus for spreading their economic and cultural domination." This was the first step toward their final objective of subordinating and eradicating Islam. "We find that the struggle against the Jewish state, in which the Muslims are engaged, is a continuation of the old struggle of the Muslims against the Jews' conspiracy against Islam." Fadlallah was also an exponent of the view that time is on the side of the Muslims. "When we say that Israel will cease to exist, this does not mean tomorrow or the day after," he said. Israel's elimination might require "one hundred years."[3]

Though its principal mission was to participate in a jihad, Hezbollah understood that it had to win the hearts and minds of the Shiite population. Toward that end, the organization became active in charitable activities and provided education, health care, and social services. This allowed the group to distinguish between its military wing and its social/political activities. Some analysts and countries, especially in Europe, accepted this specious dichotomy—false since the two wings were inextricably entwined—as a means to avoid labeling Hezbollah a terrorist organization and imposing sanctions on its activities. Even the United States refused to designate Hezbollah as a terrorist group until 1997. Meanwhile, with Iran's help, Hezbollah opened training camps throughout Lebanon to instruct recruits how to conduct assassinations, kidnappings, suicide bombings, and guerrilla warfare.

The group literally exploded onto the international stage in April 1983 when a van filled with explosives blew up in front of the U.S. embassy in Beirut, killing 58 Americans and Lebanese. A few months later Hezbollah was allegedly responsible for a truck bomb that detonated in the U.S. Marine barracks, killing 241 American peacekeepers, and a simultaneous truck bombing at the French barracks that killed 58 French soldiers. The death toll in the barracks was the highest suffered by the Marine Corps since the Battle of Iwo Jima in World War II and the deadliest single-day death toll for the United States military since the first day of the Vietnam War's Tet Offensive.[4] These attacks were a major reason President Reagan withdrew U.S. forces from Lebanon a year later.

More ominously, a new breed of terrorist had emerged, motivated by leaders who twisted the teachings of the Prophet, convinced that martyrdom in the service of Islam was an obligation, and that killing Jews to liberate Muslim land would put them on the expressway to Paradise, where 72 virgins would be waiting for them. According to Osama bin Laden, "Your problem will be how to convince your troops to fight, while our problem will be how to restrain our youths to wait for their turn in fighting. . . . These youths know that: if one is not to be killed one will die [anyway] and the most honorable death is to be killed in the way of Allah."[5] And so the age of the suicide bomber was born, yet another step toward turning the conflict into a religious one in which political compromise was unthinkable and any Jew was a valid target.

As the number of Israeli casualties mounted, the public demands to end the war grew louder. In July 1983, the troops began to slowly withdraw. Begin resigned unexpectedly on September 15, 1983, reportedly despondent over the course of the war and the recent death of his wife. A national coalition government made up of representatives of both the Labor and Likud parties took office in 1984, with their leaders rotating as prime minister. The government decided to withdraw from Lebanon in 1985, leaving behind enough troops to patrol a security zone in southern Lebanon along Israel's border.

Israel was prepared to withdraw entirely, but the growing strength and audacity of Hezbollah once again created instability and the threat of renewed terrorist attacks on the northern border. The continued presence of the Israelis stoked Lebanese anger, particularly among the Shiites, who were concentrated in the south, and gave Hezbollah an excuse to attack the soldiers in an effort to drive them out of the country. About the same time, Hezbollah issued a manifesto that made clear the group's objectives: It would not be satisfied with an Israeli withdrawal.

Our primary assumption in our fight against Israel states that the Zionist entity is aggressive from its inception, and built on lands wrested from their owners, at the expense of the rights of the Muslim people. Therefore our struggle will end only when this entity is obliterated. We recognize no treaty with it, no cease-fire, and no peace agreements, whether separate or consolidated.[6]

Israelis had not recovered from the trauma of the war in Lebanon when a conflagration began in the West Bank and Gaza Strip. In December 1987, rumors that four Palestinians killed in a traffic accident in the Gaza Strip had really been murdered by Israelis provoked rioting that escalated and sparked a wave of unrest that engulfed the West Bank, Gaza Strip, and Jerusalem. After initially being caught off guard, Fatah became more directly involved in the activities and planning. This uprising or intifada (Arabic for "shaking off") turned into a nearly four-year street battle in which more than two dozen Israelis were killed by Palestinians in the territories and thousands more were injured. Approximately 1,100 Palestinians died in clashes with Israeli soldiers. Toward the end of the uprising, the battle became an internecine one as Palestinians started to turn on each other to gain political advantage, settle old scores, or punish "collaborators." The violence subsided as the United States–led coalition went to war against Saddam Hussein after his invasion of Kuwait. By the time the intifada flickered out, nearly as many Palestinians had been killed by their fellow Palestinians as died in confrontations with Israeli forces.

The intifada was a landmark because it was the first large-scale revolt by the Palestinians in the territories against Israel. It shocked many Israelis out of their complacency and made them realize that they might need to reach a compromise with the Palestinians because it was unlikely they could remain in control of their lives indefinitely.

The period during the uprising was a milestone for another reason; it marked the reemergence of radical Islamic terrorists. While some apologists for terror try to argue the concept of jihad has nothing to do with violence or terror, the terrorists themselves see things differently. Palestinian Islamic Jihad (PIJ), for example, was established in 1979 by Fathi Shaqaqi and other students in Egypt who thought the Muslim Brotherhood was too moderate. Inspired by the Iranian revolution, PIJ's goals are the destruction of Israel and the liberation of Palestine to unite the Arab and Muslim world in a single great Islamic state. The group began to launch terror attacks against Israel from Gaza in the 1980s. Just as the intifada was heating up, Israel deported Shaqaqi to Lebanon (he was killed in 1995 in Malta by unknown assassins), and his successor, Dr. Ramadan Abadallah Shalah, lacked the charisma and organizational skills of his predecessor. Nevertheless, PIJ became one of two Islamist organizations determined to terrorize Israelis and eradicate Israel.

The second, and, ultimately, larger and more dangerous radical Muslim organization is the Islamic Resistance Movement—Hamas—which emerged as a threat in the early stages of the intifada. An offshoot of the Muslim Brotherhood, Hamas originally was registered in Israel in 1978 as an Islamic Association (Al-Mujamma Al Islami) under the spiritual leadership of Sheikh Ahmed Yassin, who served as the movement's spiritual leader. The intifada was a catalyst for the establishment of a military wing called the Izz al-Din al-Qassam Brigades. The political wing provides charitable and social services to the people, much like Hezbollah does in Lebanon. Yassin created an additional wing called the Majd whose job was to monitor Arabs suspected of "collaborating" with Israel or failing to follow Islamic doctrine.

The media and diplomats often try to distinguish between military and political wings of Islamist organizations such as Hamas and Hezbollah. We're told that it's okay to have contact with the latter because the politicians have nothing to do with violence and run a social welfare network for the benefit of their people. This is utter nonsense. The social welfare activities are primarily a means of winning the loyalty of the people and their assistance in terror activities. Whether all the people understand it or not, there is a quid pro quo for whatever benefits they receive.

For some time Israel was content to allow Hamas to engage in its peaceful activities to improve the lives of the people in Gaza, partly in the hope that it would weaken Fatah. The Israelis began to realize that Hamas was potentially more dangerous than the PLO, however, when they discovered an arms cache in 1984 and jailed Yassin. A year later Yassin was freed in a prisoner exchange between Israel and PFLP-GC leader Ahmad Jibril.

Once Hamas joined the intifada it was clear that Yassin's organization was not content to be a social welfare agency. Hamas made no secret of its intentions, in 1988 publishing its covenant, which explicitly calls for Israel's destruction. Notice also that it is directed at Jews and not just Israel. Here are a few excerpts:

> Our struggle against the Jews is very great and very serious. . . . It strives to raise the banner of Allah over every inch of Palestine. . . . It is one of the links in the chain of the struggle against the Zionist invaders. . . .
>
> The Prophet, Allah bless him and grant him salvation, has said: "The Day of Judgment will not come about until Moslems fight the Jews [killing the Jews], when the Jew will hide behind stones and trees. The stones and trees will say 'O Moslems, O Abdulla, there is a Jew behind me, come and kill him.'" . . . There is no solution for the Palestine question except through Jihad. Initiatives, proposals and international conferences are all a waste of time and vain endeavors. Palestine is an Islamic land.
>
> Our enemies took control of the world media. They were behind the French Revolution and the Communist Revolution. . . . They were behind World War I, when they were able to destroy the Islamic Caliphate, making financial gains and controlling resources. They obtained the Balfour Declaration, formed the League of Nations through which they could rule the world. They were behind World War II, through which they made huge financial gains by trading in armaments, and paved the way for the establishment of their state. It was they that instigated the replacement of the League of Nations with the United Nations and the Security Council to enable them to rule the world through them. There is no war going on anywhere, without [them] having their finger in it.

The principles of the covenant, which Hamas officials and clerics publicly repeat without hesitation, are blatantly anti-Semitic, containing classic conspiracy theories straight out of the *Protocols*. Jews are accused of "undermining societies, destroying values, corrupting consciences, deteriorating character and annihilating Islam." Jews are also "behind the drug trade and alcoholism . . . to facilitate its control and expansion." The covenant also contains a popular refrain that the Zionists seek to expand the boundaries of Israel from the Nile to the Euphrates (a popular myth in the Arab world is that a map showing these borders hangs in the Knesset). Hamas also compares Jews to Nazis, a hallmark of anti-Semites.

According to Hamas, Muslims must combat the threat posed by the Jews through jihad. And this is not just a Palestinian obligation; Hamas expects the entire Islamic world to join the jihad. The bottom line for Hamas—and all the Islamists—is that "no part of Palestine can be surrendered. No single Arab regime or number of regimes acting together has the right to break this trust and give up any of this land, not even the Palestinians themselves. . . . Reconquering the lands is considered a solemn religious duty."[7]

After liberating Palestine, Hamas believes that it can create a model Islamic state, which will "become the vanguard of a larger Islamist movement that will embrace all Muslims, who will eventually shed their respective nationalist convictions and restore the universal Islamic polity and the glories of the past."[8]

Despite the common objective of eradicating Israel, Hamas competes for the hearts and minds of the Palestinian public with the PLO and virulently opposes PLO propaganda suggesting the intention of creating a secular state (even though they don't plan to establish one). Hamas believes the PLO is misguided and calls for its return to Islam, at which time "we will become its soldiers, and fuel for its fire that will burn the enemies." The difference in the organizations' philosophies is apparent in their charters. The PLO Charter does not mention Allah once, whereas his name appears 105 times in the Hamas Covenant. The former is an Arab nationalist document—fitting, given its origins in Nasser's pan-Arabism—while the latter is a religious one. The PLO document is man-made and can be altered, but Hamas considers its covenant to be the immutable word of God.[9]

Although it is a Sunni Muslim organization, Hamas has received substantial support from Iran, including a supply of weapons. The group makes its own crude rockets and mortars while smuggling in more sophisticated missiles from Syria, most of which originate in Iran. Hamas has received support from Sunni-led states and also actively engaged in fundraising in the United States.

Saudi Arabia contributed millions to the families of "martyrs" as well as to the terrorist organizations themselves. By supporting Hamas in the late 1990s and the beginning of the new century, the Saudis helped weaken Fatah at the very time the United States was trying to convince Fatah to negotiate with Israel. At times, the Saudis have played Hamas and Fatah against each other, at one point prompting Mahmoud Abbas, then a deputy to Arafat, to complain to the Saudis for supporting their rivals.

Ironically, in the midst of the intifada, President Reagan made the unexpected decision just before leaving office to lift the long-standing ban on official U.S. contacts with the PLO and recognized the group as the representative of the Palestinians after Yasser Arafat met U.S. conditions to recognize Israel and renounce terror. Five years later secret talks in Oslo led to the mutual recognition of Israel and the PLO and a series of peace agreements that were expected to result in the separation of the two peoples. Arafat was also allowed to leave Tunisia and enter the territories but his return was not universally welcomed. By signing the Oslo agreement with Israel, he created a larger schism with the Islamists, who vehemently opposed the PLO's objective of creating a Palestinian state beside Israel. Hamas insisted that a single Palestinian state under Islamic rule be created in the entire Land of Palestine, which would encompass the Gaza Strip, all of the West Bank, and all of Israel.

The PLO responded to criticism about its lack of commitment to Islam and the growing popularity of Hamas by resorting to more Islamic references and imagery. For example, in a speech in Bethlehem, Yasser Arafat aroused his listeners by chanting "Struggle, struggle, struggle, struggle. Combat, combat, combat, combat. Jihad, Jihad, Jihad, Jihad."[10] Terrorists captured or killed by Israel became martyrs for Islam. Calls to liberate al-Aqsa became more common. In fact, the PLO's "military" arm was named the al-Aqsa Martyrs' Brigade and engaged in suicide bombings and other terror attacks that were no less monstrous than those conducted by Hamas.

Meanwhile, the radical Muslims in the north also remained defiant. Abbas al Musawi became Hezbollah's secretary-general and immediately stated his intention to "wipe out every trace of Israel in Palestine," which he described as "the cancer of the Middle East."[11] A year later, Israeli forces assassinated al Musawi. He was succeeded by the current secretary-general, Hassan Nasrallah. The change in leadership did not alter the organization's rhetoric or hostility toward the Jewish people. For example, Nasrallah said, "If we searched the entire world for a person more cowardly, despicable, weak and feeble in psyche, mind, ideology and religion, we would not find anyone like the Jew. Notice, I do not say the Israeli."[12] In October 2011, Hezbollah's first Facebook posting in English spread the group's message virally: "O Allah, Please Clean This World From Jewish Contamination."[13]

Despite the attacks from Hezbollah and international and domestic pressure, Israeli forces continued to maintain the security zone. As the casualty total grew, Jewish families started vigils outside the Israeli prime minister's home calling for an end to the war. Finally, after 15 years, Prime Minister Ehud Barak decided to unilaterally withdraw all of Israel's troops on May 24, 2000, ending an eight-year war and military occupation that cost the lives of 1,216 Israeli soldiers.

Hezbollah immediately declared victory and took advantage of their increased freedom of movement to create a virtual state within a state in southern Lebanon. The group also focused on acquiring more weapons—in particular rockets from Iran, typically smuggled through Syria—and building a more professional army. Israel had originally hoped the Lebanese government would deploy its army along the southern border, disarm the terrorists, and maintain order, but that did not occur.

No sooner did Israel extricate itself from Lebanon than it became embroiled in yet another uprising by the Palestinians. On September 28, 2000, a few months after Arafat had rejected Barak's offer to create a Palestinian state in roughly 97 percent of the West Bank and 100 percent of the Gaza Strip, Ariel Sharon, leader of the opposition Likud Party, made a controversial visit to the Temple Mount in Jerusalem. The next day, a large number of Palestinians demonstrated at the site, and violence erupted between them and Israeli police. The Palestinians once again turned the issue into an Islamic one by labeling their new uprising the al-Aqsa Intifada.

Though Palestinians said Sharon was responsible for the outbreak of violence, the truth was the Palestinian Authority had given him permission to visit the Temple Mount and he did not go near any of the Muslim holy places. Moreover, documents later proved the entire uprising had been planned much earlier by Arafat.

The honeymoon following the Oslo agreement was now a distant memory. In September 2001, terrorists assassinated Israeli tourism minister Rehavam Ze'evi. In January 2002, Israeli forces stopped a ship bound for the Palestinian Authority; the *Karine-A* was carrying 50 tons of weapons from Iran that were paid for by one of Arafat's top aides. It seemed that hardly a day went by without a new atrocity. Suicide bombers blew themselves up along with Israeli men, women, and children in discotheques, pizzerias, and coffee shops. The martyrs were celebrated afterward with streets and parks and sporting events named in their honor. Israelis were aghast that their neighbors would rejoice over the massacre of innocents and reminded of why they doubted the prospects for peace.

Hypocritically, the leaders of the Islamic groups do not believe martyrdom is important enough for them or their children to commit suicide, but they are happy to send others to do their dirty work. And it was not only men who carried out these massacres; Palestinian women also played a role in the perverse world of Islamic fanaticism. Women who become suicide bombers are viewed as noble and heroic feminists acting out the collective desire of Muslim women to defeat the enemies of Islam. These women, however, are usually pawns of psychotic men who do not have the courage to kill themselves and who instead prey on the vulnerabilities of women who have often already been victimized by the norms of Muslim society.

Sheikh Yassin ruled that women should not become suicide bombers because it was more important for them to "ensure the nation's existence" by reproducing. Nevertheless, he approved suicide actions by women if they had stained their family honor in some way.

Twenty-five-year-old Wafa Idris, an ambulance driver for the Palestinian Red Crescent, was the first Palestinian female suicide bomber. She blew herself up in Jerusalem on January 27, 2002. Idris was divorced by her husband after failing to have children. "Her status as a divorced and barren woman, and her return as a dependent to her parents' home where she became an economic burden, put her in what is a dead end situation in a patriarchal society," according to Professor Mira Tzoreff. Idris believed the way out of her inferior status was by becoming a martyr.[14]

Sadly, Idris was not the only woman to become a human bomb. Roughly 70 women were sent on suicide missions since 2002, including a 60-year-old with more than 40 grandchildren. The grandmother, like most of these women, was lucky to survive; only eight of the women succeeded in blowing themselves up. These are not uneducated women; more than one-fifth, for example, had more than a high school education.[15] Tzoreff notes that women who are childless, divorced, and "unbetrothable" are targets of recruiters. Some younger women are seduced by terrorists and then are blackmailed if they become pregnant. Those who do not become pregnant are still viewed as having shamed themselves and their families by having violated the society's norms regarding modesty. They are then offered the opportunity to redeem themselves by dying for the terrorists' cause.

Not all the Palestinian terrorists were motivated by Islam—some were motivated by personal (such as revenge) and political reasons. But it is telling that only Muslims have turned to violence. Thousands of Palestinian Christians are in the same situation as the rest of the Palestinians in the territories and yet they have not chosen violence or martyrdom.

"The use of suicide bombing is entirely unacceptable. Nothing can justify this," said the UN special representative for the protection of children in armed conflict, Under Secretary-General Olara Otunnu.[16] Nevertheless, apologists for terror constantly offer rationalizations for Palestinian terror. A popular myth, for example, is that Palestinians are driven to terror by poverty and desperation.

It is true that many Palestinians suffer a variety of hardships, see the future as hopeless, and are unhappy with the way they are

treated by Israelis. None of these are excuses for engaging in terrorism. In fact, many of the terrorists are not poor, desperate people at
all (Osama bin Laden was a Saudi millionaire). "There is no clear
profile of someone who hates Israel and the Jewish people. They
come in every shape and from every culture. Demonstrators, riot-
ers and stone throwers do tend to be younger, unmarried males.
But there's a big difference between the young men who participate
in those types of disturbances and terrorists," according to Aryeh
Amit, former Jerusalem district police chief.[17]

A report by the National Bureau of Economic Research concluded, "Economic conditions and education are largely unrelated
to participation in, and support for, terrorism." The researchers
said the outbreak of violence in the region that began in 2000 could
not be blamed on deteriorating economic conditions because there
is no connection between terrorism and economic depression. Furthermore, the authors found that support for violent action against
Israel, including suicide bombing, does not vary much according to
social background.[18]

Arafat typically spoke out of both sides of his mouth when he
criticized Hamas and PIJ. His main objection to their actions was
that they were not carried out under his authority. Even as he condemned the Islamists, he justified their behavior:

> With God's help, next time we will meet in Jerusalem, because
> we are fighting to bring victory to our prophets, every baby,
> every kid, every man, every woman and every old person and
> all the young people, we will all sacrifice ourselves for our holy
> places and we will strengthen our hold of them and we are
> willing to give 70 of our martyrs for every one of theirs in this
> campaign, because this is our holy land. We will continue to
> fight for this blessed land and I call on you to stand strong.[19]

Israel took both offensive and defensive measures to protect its
citizens. In addition to military operations and counter attacks, Israel adopted a policy of targeted killings to eliminate the leaders of
the jihadist groups. In 2004, Israel killed the leader of Hamas, Sheik
Yassin, and his successor, Abdel Aziz al-Rantisi. Israel is sometimes

criticized for these "hits" by countries, including the United States, which was carrying out its own assassination campaign using drones in places such as Afghanistan, Pakistan, and Yemen.

The morality of the policy is debated inside Israel, but the army argues it is effective. First, it places a price on terror: Israelis can't be attacked with impunity anymore, for terrorists know that if they target others, they will become targets themselves. Second, it is a method of self-defense: preemptive strikes eliminate the people who would otherwise murder Israelis. While it is true that there are others to take their place, they can do so only with the knowledge they too will become targets, and leaders are not easily replaceable. Third, it throws the terrorists off balance. Extremists must stay on the move, look over their shoulders at all times, and work much harder to carry out their goals.

"Targeted killings" are sometimes criticized for perpetuating a cycle of violence whereby the terrorists seek revenge. This is probably the least compelling argument against the policy, because the people who blow themselves up to become martyrs can always find a justification for their actions. They are determined to bomb the Jews out of the Middle East and will not stop until their goal is achieved.

Defensively, Israel built a fence to separate Israel and many of the communities in the West Bank from the Palestinians in the territories. A similar fence at the border of Gaza had reduced the number of terrorist infiltrations to practically zero. The security barrier in the West Bank also significantly reduced the number of successful attacks. Prior to erecting the fence, Palestinian terrorists could literally walk from the West Bank into Israel with bombs and wreak havoc.

The Palestinians and their supporters around the world expressed outrage that the Jews would be so audacious as to take measures to defend themselves. It took more than 40 years and nearly 1,000 deaths to finally convince Israelis they needed a physical barrier to separate them from the Palestinians, and while there were claims the fence was illegal, immoral, and unjustified, the truth was that Israel already had fences along its borders with Lebanon, Syria, and Jordan. Moreover, countries around the world, including Ireland, Saudi Arabia, India, Turkey, and the United States have fences.

To call the violence from 2000 to 2005 an uprising (the al-Aqsa Intifada) is to minimize the conflict. This was a war in which Palestinian terror attacks and Israeli counterattacks claimed the lives of more than 1,000 Israelis and 3,000 Palestinians.

The Palestinians learned a lesson from Hezbollah and recognized that Israelis are extremely sensitive to casualties—the country is so small every death impacts the whole country. In response, the PLO, Hamas, and Islamic Jihad hoped to impose such a high cost on Israel, in terms of lives lost, that the Israeli people would demand that their government evacuate the territories in hope of ending the violence. And the terrorists, Hamas in particular, believed they succeeded when Prime Minister Sharon decided to evacuate all of the Israeli civilians and soldiers from the Gaza Strip.

In truth, Israel was not driven from the territories. It made a calculated decision to leave based on its own interests. At the time of the disengagement, Israel had dramatically reduced the level of terror, severely damaged the terrorist infrastructure, and killed or jailed most of the leaders of the major terror groups. The disengagement took place after Israel won the Palestinian War, which the Palestinian Authority had instigated in 2000, and the withdrawal took place from a position of strength, not weakness. And the Palestinian people were not fooled by the terrorists' rhetoric. "Let's be frank," observed Mohammed Ahmed Moussa, a grocer in Jabaliya. "If Israel didn't want to leave Gaza, no one could have forced them out. Those who claim the rockets and attacks made them leave are kidding themselves."[20]

Though uncoordinated, the battlefront for Israel seemed to alternate between the north and south. Even after Israel withdrew from Lebanon entirely (as even the United Nations certified in 2000), Hezbollah continued to attack Israel on the pretext that Israel still occupied an area of Lebanon called Shebaa Farms (which Israel and the United Nations agree is not part of Lebanon) and refused to release Lebanese prisoners in Israeli jails. Israel insisted the area, where Israel had built a series of observation posts on strategic hilltops, was captured from Syria; however, the Syrians supported Hezbollah's claim. The controversy was useful for both Arab parties. "For Syria, it means Hezbollah can still be used to keep the Israelis off balance;

for Lebanon, it provides a way to apply pressure over issues, such as the return of Lebanese prisoners still held in Israeli jails. For Hezbollah, it is a reason to keep its militia armed and active, providing a ready new goal for a resistance movement that otherwise had nothing left to resist."[21]

To pressure Israel, Hezbollah kidnapped three IDF soldiers in October 2000, just months after Israel's evacuation from Lebanon. Though Israel's policy was not to negotiate with terrorists, on several previous occasions, the government agreed to exchanges of Israeli soldiers for prisoners in Israeli jails. It took four years, but Israel ultimately agreed to release 430 Arab prisoners and the bodies of an additional 60 terrorists for the return of Israeli businessman Elchanan Tenenbaum and the three abducted IDF soldiers. They ultimately found themselves negotiating for the bodies of the soldiers, whom, they learned, had been killed.

Table 4.1   Israelis Killed in Terror Attacks Following the Oslo Agreement

1994	65
1995	29
1996	56
1997	41
1998	16
1999	8
2000	43
2001	207
2002	457
2003	213
2004	124
2005	53
2006	29
2007	13
2008	36
2009	6
2010	10
2011	21
2012	9
2013	5
Total	**1,441**

Hezbollah also used the time when Israel was preoccupied with the al-Aqsa Intifada to build up its strength and to import massive amounts of weaponry, especially rockets, from Iran and Syria under the noses of UN peacekeepers who did nothing to prevent the buildup. The Lebanese army also turned a blind eye to the activities of Hezbollah, largely because of the fear that the army would fracture along religious lines, with Shiites unwilling to participate in any campaign against their fellow Shiites.

In addition to the financial and material support from their patrons, Hezbollah has financed its activities through drug trafficking. People associated with the group were arrested in Germany, the United States, and parts of Latin America for drug smuggling and money laundering. Hezbollah was believed to be especially active in the border area abutting Argentina, Paraguay, and Brazil and was also linked to a cocaine smuggling operation in Columbia.[22]

After temporarily pacifying the front with the Palestinians, Hezbollah once again provoked Israel into a war it was not seeking. In fact, following Ariel Sharon's stroke in January 2006, which led to an election that brought Ehud Olmert to power, the expectation was that the new prime minister would continue the process Sharon had started of withdrawing Israeli troops and civilians from the West Bank. Olmert had run for office on a platform that called for essentially a unilateral withdrawal from most of the West Bank. He never had the opportunity to implement his vision because of renewed violence on the border with Lebanon.

On July 12, 2006, shortly after Olmert's election, Hezbollah unleashed a barrage of katyusha rocket and mortar fire aimed at the northern Israeli town of Shlomi. Using this diversion, Hezbollah fighters infiltrated Israel's border and attacked an IDF patrol. The terrorists killed three soldiers, severely wounded three others, and abducted two—Eldad Regev and Ehud Goldwasser. The IDF responded with an artillery barrage and aerial assault before sending ground troops into southern Lebanon to kill as many terrorists as possible and eliminate the rocket threat. Fighting continued for 34 days, during which Hezbollah fired hundreds of rockets indiscriminately into northern Israel. The rockets hit not only Jewish communities but Arab ones as well, and reached as far south as Haifa.

Thousands of Israelis moved to stay with relatives and friends in the south, beyond rocket range, while others hunkered down in bomb shelters.

As the IDF continued their aerial assault over several weeks, Hezbollah used the Lebanese civilian population as shields, placing their rockets among the vulnerable population. Even pinpoint attacks by the IDF could not always ensure there was no collateral damage or loss of innocent life. As the number of Lebanese civilian casualties and refugees grew, Israel came under increasing pressure from the United States (which had initially supported the IDF campaign) and the international community to end the war.

On August 11, 2006, Israel, Hezbollah, and the Lebanese government agreed to a cease-fire. Many analysts, and much of the Israeli public, considered the war a disaster. Israel suffered nearly 200 casualties, its civilian population had been terrorized, and the country was shown to be vulnerable to a non-state terrorist force armed with thousands of rockets. Investigations later found the army had been poorly prepared, soldiers had been sent into battle improperly equipped, and a variety of other shortcomings that embarrassed the IDF. The situation would have been worse if not for the success of the Israeli Air Force in destroying Hezbollah's long-range rockets in the first hours of the war.

Though Hezbollah claimed victory for propaganda purposes, boasting how it had survived the Israeli onslaught, the group lost roughly 600 of its fighters and tons of its weapons were destroyed. In a rare moment of candor, Nasrallah admitted he did not expect the response Israel had to the original kidnapping. "We did not think, even one percent, that the capture would lead to a war at this time and of this magnitude," Nasrallah said in an interview. "You ask me, if I had known on July 11 . . . that the operation would lead to such a war, would I do it? I say no, absolutely not."[23]

One of Israel's principal objectives, the release of the kidnapped soldiers, did not occur until June 2008, nearly two years after they were abducted. Israel again agreed to a prisoner exchange with Hezbollah; this time the bodies of Goldwasser and Regev were returned in exchange for Lebanese terrorist Samir Kuntar (who was in jail for murdering a police officer, a civilian, and a child), four other

Hezbollah guerrillas captured during the war, and the bodies of 200 Hezbollah fighters.

Israel agreed to the cease-fire in part because the United Nations agreed to station a "robust" force in Lebanon to prevent future clashes and to prevent arms smuggling from Syria. Ultimately, the UN force did neither, and Hezbollah replaced the rockets Israel destroyed and built up an even larger arsenal, estimated as high as 100,000 rockets. Nasrallah has remained bellicose and unyielding in his commitment to Israel's destruction. In his longest public remarks since the end of the war, Nasrallah said, "Israel represents a permanent and grave danger to all the countries and all the peoples of this region." Israel, he said, is "a cancer" that must be eradicated.[24]

Many Arabs, especially Sunnis, inside and outside of Lebanon were furious that Nasrallah had brought so much destruction unnecessarily onto the heads of the Lebanese. Nevertheless, Hezbollah's political strength grew in the wake of the 2006 war with Israel and the group's subsequent 2008 takeover of West Beirut. After entering Lebanese politics as a small minority in 1992, it became the dominant faction since at least 2011, when it brought down the government of Saad Hariri, a Saudi-backed Sunni, and replaced him with a more malleable, pro-Syrian prime minister, Najib Mikati. In effect, Hezbollah has taken control of Lebanon through a nearly bloodless coup (the group is suspected of assassinating the former prime minister, Hariri's father).

Once again, Israel had no respite between fighting Islamists in the south and being forced to confront the threat from Gaza. A few months before the war in Lebanon, prodded by the Bush administration, the Palestinian Authority held its first democratic-style election, which was won by Hamas (Israeli analysts and others had warned of this outcome). Most Palestinian voters did not endorse the group's radical Islamist views, but they were fed up with the failure of Fatah to improve their lives and the rampant corruption of its leaders. Hamas spent little time in the new government, however, after disagreements with Fatah over power sharing and negotiations with Israel led to a confrontation in Gaza. In 2007, Hamas supporters overwhelmed Fatah's forces and found themselves ruling Gaza while the Palestinian Authority retained control only in the West Bank.

The Hamas takeover allowed the Muslim extremists to impose their interpretation of Islam on the public. Women were expected to dress modestly and their rights were limited. Hamas enforcers silenced critical journalists through arrests and intimidation and executed suspected collaborators with Israel. The small Christian population was harassed to the point where most either left or were looking for a way out of Gaza.

Despite Hamas leaders' vitriolic rhetoric, some international observers, and even some Israelis, argued that the time had come for Israel to negotiate with Hamas since it now represented a large number of Palestinians and controlled one chunk of what was expected to be a future Palestinian state. Hamas remained defiant, however, and repeatedly reiterated its commitment to destroy Israel. Backed by the United States and other Western powers, Israel imposed a blockade on the Gaza Strip, effectively sealing the entrances from Israel and the sea and limiting goods that could be transferred to the area. Israel was widely criticized for its action and sometimes accused of creating a humanitarian crisis (a "big lie"). In fact the Palestinians did have an opening to the outside world through Gaza's southern border with Egypt, but the Egyptians also effectively closed off access to the Strip, a fact ignored by Israel's detractors.

The possibility that Hamas might enter the peace process was left open. The United States and its allies insisted that Hamas agree to recognize Israel, cease all terror, and honor the agreements signed between the PLO and Israel. The leaders of Hamas refused to do so. Ismail Haniyeh, the prime minister in the Palestinian Authority before the coup in Gaza, declared, "I tell you with all honesty, we will not recognize Israel, we will not recognize Israel, we will not recognize Israel."[25] Later, Haniyeh said, "Palestinians will fight Israel for generation upon generation until victory, and will yet get to dance at the Al-Aqsa mosque in Jerusalem. . . . If Israel is not defeated in this generation, it will be in the next generation."[26]

While Hamas and Fatah fought for supremacy within the Palestinian Authority, both continued to engage in terror attacks against Israel. It was Hamas, however, that dramatically upped the ante, starting with a June 2006 attack on Israeli soldiers that resulted in two deaths and the abduction of Corporal Gilad Shalit. Soon after,

Hamas and PIJ began a steady barrage of rocket fire at towns in southern Israel. Though the deadly rockets were inaccurate, they caused extensive damage, a few fatalities, and created panic and anxiety among citizens who had no more than 15 seconds to find shelter after hearing an alarm indicating incoming rockets.

The bombardments escalated to the point where dozens of rockets and mortars were being fired each day, a total of more than 3,000 between 2006 and the end of 2008. Finally, after roughly 1 million Israelis came within range of the longer-range rockets and life in the south was being paralyzed, the government ordered troops into Gaza for Operation Cast Lead, which lasted 23 days from late December 2008 to January 2009 and temporarily silenced the rocket fire.

The operation failed to rescue Gilad Shalit. It was not until October 2011, after more than five years holding Shalit in captivity, that Hamas agreed to his release in exchange for more than 1,000 Palestinian prisoners in Israeli jails. Some Israelis did not believe one life was worth allowing so many terrorists to go free; others, however, insisted that the Israeli military ethic demanded that every soldier go into battle knowing he would not be left behind or forgotten. Still others argued that the trade represented the difference in how Hamas and Israel viewed human value. Hamas, like Hezbollah, hides behind civilians whereas Israeli soldiers put themselves between the enemy and the people. Moreover, Jews are taught in the Talmud that "whoever destroys a soul, it is considered as if he destroyed an entire world. And whoever saves a life, it is considered as if he saved an entire world."

The calm did not last long, however, as the bombardments resumed in October 2012. Over the course of the next few weeks, approximately 750 rockets were fired from Gaza into Israel. Once again the IDF was called upon to defend the population and mounted Operation Pillar of Defense in Gaza from November 14–21, 2012. Israel believed it did a better job of eliminating the rocket threat than it had during Cast Lead; nevertheless, terrorism continued even after Egypt mediated a cease-fire. Shortly afterward, operatives from Hamas and PIJ bombed a bus in Tel Aviv, wounding 29 people.

In a classic example of Palestinian doublespeak to English-speaking audiences, Hamas's minister of health, Mufid Al-Mukhalalati, said in English, "We are human, we like life. We would like to live like other people living." Hamas spokesman Sami Abu Zahir said something very different in Arabic: "Hamas leaders seek Martyrdom. You scare us with what we love (i.e., death)." A video broadcast on Hamas's al-Aqsa TV station during the fighting expressed a similar sentiment: "The Al-Qassam Brigades love death more than you love life."[27]

Many of Israel's critics were angered by what they considered Israel's "disproportionate" response to the rocket attacks, as if it were possible to devise a proportionate way to terrorize the Palestinian population in the same way Hamas had terrified Israelis. The goal of the IDF is to minimize Palestinian casualties; however, these critics seemed to suggest that Israel was obligated to allow more of its citizens to be murdered to be justified in killing more terrorists. In fact, health officials in Israel discovered the eight years of rocket attacks did a great deal of damage to the survivors: "many residents have to be treated for hearing loss, dizziness, tinnitus, and/or central auditory processing disorders."[28] Children were especially traumatized; one study found that in Sderot (the town closest to Gaza and most often targeted by rockets), between 75 percent and 94 percent of children aged 4–18 exhibited symptoms of post-traumatic stress, and 28 percent of adults, and 30 percent of children in Sderot have post-traumatic stress disorder (PTSD).[29]

To put the impact in more concrete terms, people living in Sderot limit their showers to less than a minute for fear they will literally be caught with their pants down if a warning siren sounds. They also have stopped wearing seat belts so they can get out of their cars more quickly. Some Israelis are afraid to listen to music because they might not hear the siren.[30]

The media and diplomats often divide the Muslim world into moderates and radicals, but those involved in the conflict with the Jews would be more accurately described as radical and more radical. The unwillingness to accept a Jewish state in their midst also is a common thread among Islamists and "moderate" Muslims. Yasser Arafat, for example, was often portrayed as a secular leader, but he was not. The Islamists from the more extreme movements may have seen him as an apostate, but Arafat was a Muslim and he was no more willing to accept Jewish sovereignty over Muslim land than the leaders of Hamas or Islamic Jihad, and that is one reason why he would never end the conflict with Israel.

Mahmoud Abbas is no better than Arafat. Prime Minister Netanyahu has insisted the Palestinians recognize Israel as a Jewish state to put them on the record as acknowledging Israel's right to exist in its homeland. In America's latest peace initiative, Secretary of State John Kerry has reportedly backed this Israeli demand while Abbas has said he will never accept it.

CHAPTER 5

THE ARAB SPRING'S TRANSFORMATION INTO THE ISLAMIC WINTER

The main reason for the bitterness that accumulated in the Arab street and caused the explosion of the Spring was due not only to the chronic problems of poverty, illiteracy, disease, unemployment, hopelessness, corruption, and disparity between the haves and have-nots but also mainly to their despair as, instead of seeing their leaders legitimately elected to sort out their problems and to be accountable for their solution, they were faced with immutable dictators who ruled for life and did not have to account for any misdeed or mismanagement. That was the reason why in all those uprisings, the most strident call of the demonstrators was on their rulers to go.[1]

—Rafael Israeli

Arabs throughout much of the Middle East had good reason to be dissatisfied. Outside the Gulf countries, which could afford to spend oil revenues lavishly to keep the public happy, a significant percentage of Arabs were poor, illiterate, unemployed, homeless, and largely without hope. Their leaders were either disinterested in their plight or unable to cope with the magnitude of the problems. Most were entrenched, some for decades, with no foreseeable opportunity to make any changes given the lack of democracy in the region. For years, the most common means of change in parts of the region were military coups; however, for nearly half a century a handful of authoritarian rulers have dominated the scene, and when any of them died or were replaced, their successors were equally dictatorial. Thus, for example, Khomeini dominated post-revolutionary Iran and was replaced by an equally zealous mullah. Nasser was succeeded by Sadat and Mubarak, who were equally autocratic. Hafez Assad ruled Syria with an iron fist before dying and leaving his son in power.

Given the apparent stability of these regimes, largely by virtue of their ruthless suppression of any opposition, none of the experts or intelligence analysts predicted the earthquake that would shake the region. The upheaval that became known as the Arab Spring did not start because of any change in the political reality; the catalyst came from a completely unexpected direction when a then unknown Tunisian peddler set himself on fire. The horrific act angered the public, provoked nationwide demonstrations against a government that had shown a lack of concern for its citizens, and forced Tunisian president Zine al-Abidine Ben Ali to flee the country after 23 years of repressive rule.

As violence in Tunisia escalated, protests erupted throughout the Middle East, with the most serious unrest occurring in Libya, Yemen, and Egypt. By the end of 2013, regional protests forced rulers from power not only in Tunisia, but also Egypt (twice), Libya, and Yemen; civil uprisings erupted in Bahrain and Syria; major protests broke out in Algeria, Iraq, Jordan, Kuwait, Morocco, and Sudan; and minor protests occurred in Mauritania, Oman, Saudi Arabia, Djibouti, Western Sahara, and the Palestinian Authority.

The Arab Spring was naively viewed by most Westerners, including government officials who should have known better, as a revolutionary breakthrough that brought low several of the more oppressive leaders in the Middle East and North Africa and heralded a new era of freedom and democracy in the region. The press and the Obama Administration focused on the young, idealistic, Western-oriented social media users seeking representative democracy and viewed them as the vanguard for change. In fact, these "young democrats" were mostly too young, inexperienced, unorganized, politically naive, and unprepared to assume power. Middle East experts outside the Obama administration warned that the strongest organizations were Islamic groups that were well organized and funded and had a base of support among the illiterate and the people who had long depended on them for social services and charity. Some of these organizations were prepared to use terror to accomplish their goal, which was not to create Jeffersonian democracies throughout the Middle East but to exploit the fig leaf of democratic elections to assume power and move toward the imposition of Sharia law and the creation of an Islamic theocracy. The problem, the *Telegraph*'s defense editor Con Coughlin observed, is that "Sharia law is the *complete* antithesis of Western-style democracy, as we have seen in Iran these past 30-odd years" (emphasis in the original).[2]

In Islam, Hebrew University history professor Raphael Israeli explains, "If sovereignty belongs to Allah, and he had already dispensed to humanity the most perfect of codes of law, as incorporated in the Qur'an and the sunna, then who would dare to try to improve on it without provoking a blasphemy. . . . Defining divine law as final and unalterable means recognizing that legislation has disappeared from the human world and that all matters of this universe must be arbitrated not by legislators but by jurists who understand and can interpret the laws of Allah."[3]

Many in the West equate holding elections with democracy, but many of the Muslim nations, such as Bashar Assad's Syria and Saddam Hussein's Iraq, held elections in which the ruler received nearly 100 percent of the vote, or in which the vote was for a mostly powerless parliament in a country ruled by a dictator, such as the monarch in Jordan or ayatollah in Iran. Democracy requires more than voting; it is "a collective of individuals who share the same history, territory, culture and language and are willing to surrender voluntarily some of their individual freedoms and pay taxes to the state, which in return keeps peace and order and governs the country according to the will of the people, who periodically choose the government of their taste. Governments come and go, but the structures and institutions of the state still provide continuity, and every individual regards himself as directly linked to the state and its machinery."[4] Or as Israeli minister without portfolio Natan Sharansky expressed it, "Free elections can only take place in societies in which people are free to express their opinions without fear."[5]

The revolution in Tunisia was the catalyst, but anger had been building in Egypt for some time over the state of the economy and 30 years of authoritarian rule under Mubarak. For some, the last straw was the widespread fear and expectation that Mubarak would install his son as his successor in what most Egyptians viewed as an almost Pharaonic abuse of power. The upheaval that began as protests against living conditions escalated to demands for Mubarak's removal as head of state. For the first time, hundreds of thousands of Egyptians went into the streets to demand greater freedom and democracy.

Israel had nothing to do with the protests; yet many of Mubarak's critics, especially from the Muslim Brotherhood, starting calling for the Israel-Egypt peace treaty to be annulled. To show their anger over the treaty, as well as their ability to damage the economy, terrorists attacked the Egyptian oil pipeline that crossed the Sinai Desert and provided Israel (and Jordan) with gas at favorable prices as part of the peace treaty. The arrangement had caused resentment among the critics of Israel and Mubarak's opponents.

The revolutionary fervor in Egypt augured a potential reorientation of the Middle East. As the country that was historically the largest, most populous, most powerful, and most influential in the Arab world, Egypt had remained stable under the dictatorial rule of Nasser, Sadat, and Mubarak. Though Mubarak routinely opposed U.S. policies (for example, he opposed the United States on most UN votes), he was still viewed as an ally who maintained a cold peace with Israel but did not renege on his treaty commitments. He also sometimes played a helpful role in moderating the positions of the Palestinians and had informally collaborated with Israel in the blockade of the Gaza Strip.

Obama's naiveté and inexperience—combined with bad advice from Arabists in the White House, State Department, and Defense Department—led him to make a series of colossal blunders in reacting to the Arab Spring, beginning with the policy he adopted toward Egypt. As protests against Mubarak escalated, President Obama faced a difficult choice: support a longtime ally who was a brutal dictator or throw him under the bus and declare support for the democracy advocates. Obama turned what should have been a serious deliberation into what he considered a no-brainer, that is, to support the "democrats," and he called for Mubarak's ouster even as Middle East specialists outside the administration warned that a democracy would not emerge in the aftermath.

When Mubarak fell, the media created the false impression that his demise was a result of the younger generation of Egyptians using social media to organize large protests that called for the end of tyranny and the beginning of democracy. Unfortunately, the young, inexperienced, and naive protesters were no match for the Islamist groups, particularly the Muslim Brotherhood, which had well-oiled machines that were in a position to field a slate of political candidates (though the Muslim Brotherhood initially said it would not run a candidate for president) and turn out the vote.

Obama repeated the error George W. Bush had made when he pressured Israel to allow Palestinian elections, which led to Hamas assuming power and gaining legitimacy by a democratic vote. By pushing for quick elections in Egypt before building representative political parties, Obama ensured that the one well-organized constituency—the Muslim Brotherhood—would win the election. As most analysts predicted, the Islamists dominated the election, with the Muslim Brotherhood winning 40 percent of the vote in parliamentary elections and the even more extreme Salafists winning 25 percent. A member of the Brotherhood, Mohamad Morsi, was elected president of Egypt on June 24, 2012.

Predictably, Morsi quickly purged the government of Mubarak supporters, sacked the most powerful military figures, and filled positions with cronies from the Brotherhood, many of whom had no experience for the posts they were given. To avoid breaking with the United States and alienating Obama, he did not cancel the peace treaty with Israel, though he was under pressure from his supporters to do so, and some were pushing him to at least modify the terms to make them more favorable to Egypt (e.g., to raise the price of the gas Egypt sold to Israel).

Egyptians had high hopes for Morsi, despite their concern about his association with the Brotherhood. They expected him to address the widespread poverty, illiteracy, and other critical social and economic problems in the country. It became clear early on, however, that he had no experience in dealing with national concerns and that the social service model the Brotherhood practiced locally to gain followers could not be applied across the country.

Besides his failure to address the needs of the people, Morsi began to impose increasingly authoritarian policies that limited the influence of the secular Egyptians who initially led the demonstrations against Mubarak. Additionally, he persecuted minorities such as the Christian Copts (60 Coptic churches and more than 1,000 Coptic homes were destroyed in just the last six months of 2013).[6] Morsi also began to move toward the imposition of Sharia law and cracked down on those young, pro-democracy advocates whom the West had expected would assume power. Over a period of months Morsi succeeded in alienating much of the Egyptian population, provoking new protests against his government. People were angry that the country was moving toward a theocracy rather than a democracy and that Morsi was assuming greater power while his administration was failing to deliver on its promise to the people that it would improve living conditions. The Brotherhood demonstrated it had the power to win elections, but didn't know how to govern. After less than a year in office, Morsi was being unfavorably compared to Mubarak.

Mubarak and his predecessors had held the Islamists in check for decades, often by imprisoning them or outlawing their organizations to prevent them from gaining power and radicalizing the nation. Although Egypt was nominally a Muslim state, like the rest of the Arab countries in the region, it was guided less by religious beliefs than political ideology. The dramatic shift toward an Islamic state based on Sharia and guided by radicals created the potential for a pan-Islamic front composed at least of the Sunni-dominated states.

The election of Morsi also had ominous implications for Israel. Israel had been able to reduce its military deployment on its southern border following the peace treaty with Egypt, but, suddenly, it had to consider the possibility of the border becoming a potential invasion site, as it had been up until the 1973 War.

Israel's other concern was that Morsi would increase cooperation with the Brotherhood's offspring in the Gaza Strip, namely Hamas. The spiritual leader of the Muslim Brotherhood, Yusuf al-Qaradawi, visited Gaza and told Hamas leaders that Muslims would never recognize Israel or make any concessions. "Palestine," he asserted, "was and will remain Arab and Islamic." He added that Muslims were in conflict with Zionism, "which claims to be Jewish, but is far from being so." Al-Qaradawi also erased Jewish history. "Palestine was never a Jewish homeland," he claimed, adding, "Zionism wants to devour the land under false pretexts. Palestine was never Jewish." Al-Qaradawi's Hamas host, Prime Minister Ismail Haniyeh, welcomed the scholar's remarks and added, "We won't give up one inch of the land of Palestine. . . . The land is ours, Jerusalem is ours and God is with us."[7]

While Israel attracted international opprobrium for its blockade of Gaza (with the exception of humanitarian aid, which it allowed to regularly flow across the border), Egypt was nearly equally stringent in keeping its borders sealed from land and sea. The fear, however, was that Morsi would open the borders and allow Hamas to move freely and to assemble an arsenal for a future battle with Israel. Morsi, indeed, moved in this direction.

Morsi tried to project an image of moderation, though his background in the Brotherhood belied his words. For example, in 2010 Morsi described Jews as "bloodsuckers who attack Palestinians" and called them "the descendants of apes and pigs." He added that Egyptians "must not forget to nurse our children and grandchildren on hatred toward those Zionists and Jews, and all those who support them." When a group of senators met with Morsi in Cairo in January 2013, they asked him about his comments; Morsi said he had no prejudice against Jews, but then launched into a diatribe against Israel and Zionism and made a remark the senators interpreted as suggesting that Jews control the media in the United States. A few months earlier, Morsi reaffirmed the importance of martyrdom: "Jihad is our path. . . . And death for the sake of Allah is our most lofty aspiration."[8]

The United States and other countries were willing to give Morsi a chance to prove he could lead and adopt democratic principles, but they quickly realized that Western freedoms were not his priority. Thus, he succeeded in alienating foreign allies and angering the domestic population that had taken to the streets to replace totalitarianism with democracy, not theocracy. Tensions built as the economy and crime worsened and protesters returned to the streets. Even with promises of aid, the unrest further damaged an already weak economy, killing the tourism industry, in particular, which comprises a significant percentage of the country's income and lost $2.5 billion from 2011 to 2013.[9]

Morsi's ambitions became even clearer when he granted himself unlimited powers and the authority to legislate without oversight. Further, he issued an Islamist-backed draft of a constitution that Egyptians feared would result in the creation of an Iranian-style Islamic government. As Morsi abused his power and reacted violently to critics, mass protests by millions of Egyptians erupted throughout the country in late June and early July 2013. At this point, the military stepped in and gave Morsi an ultimatum: he needed to resolve the problems that prompted the unrest or he would be removed. On July 3, 2013, the military staged a coup and arrested Morsi and other members of the Brotherhood. New protests broke out as the Brothers objected to the jailing of Morsi and demanded his reinstatement. The military responded with increasing force, and more than 1,000 Morsi supporters were killed. The Egyptian government, now under the control of Defense Minister Abdul Fatah al-Sisi, outlawed the Brotherhood and designated it a terrorist organization. Morsi was jailed for incitement of murder and violence as well as espionage.

Israel was concerned by the increasing violence in the Sinai, with terrorists from Gaza, including al-Qaeda, attacking primarily Egyptian targets. With Israel's permission, Egypt moved more resources into the area to fight the terrorists. Reversing Morsi's direction, the military government is now trying to destroy Hamas by sealing smuggling tunnels, tightening the blockade of Gaza, and working to strengthen the group's Fatah rivals.

The United States and other countries found themselves in a co-nundrum similar to the one that preceded the Arab Spring: Should they back a military government that can stabilize the country, sup-press the Islamists, and maintain the peace treaty with Israel, or should the military be given an ultimatum to give up power and hold new elections that could lead to the election of religious extremists? The answer to date is a little from column A, a little from column B: the army is being pressured to institute democratic reforms. Rather than allow al-Sisi to wipe out the Brotherhood, Obama said he wants the group included in the democratic process, repeating his earlier mistake. To signal dissatisfaction with the military's behavior, the administration decided to withhold some military aid while keeping economic assistance flowing. In another indication that Obama had not totally abandoned the "democracy exception" and was prepared to work with the military government, he dispatched Secretary of State John Kerry to Cairo in November 2013 and indicated that the United States does not want to lose its longtime ally.

On balance, Egypt appears headed in a more positive direction than under Morsi and the Islamic Winter there has ended—at least for now. A new election has been scheduled for the spring of 2014 with al-Sisi expected to be elected president after resigning from the army.

Obama's abandonment of Mubarak had wider implications be-cause it scared the other conservative leaders, especially in Jordan and Saudi Arabia, who considered themselves U.S. allies but now realized they could not count on American support if the uprising spread to their countries. U.S. officials tried to reassure them, and it soon became clear that the "democracy exception" was still part of America's Middle East policy: that is, while the president was call-ing for democracy and freedom in the countries facing unrest, such as Tunisia, Egypt, Libya, and Yemen, he had nothing to say on the subject with regard to Jordan and the Gulf autocracies that were not moving toward either democracy or freedom but rather were hun-kering down and providing their citizens with a mixture of carrots (in the form of money and programs) and sticks (in the form of brute force) to keep opponents in line.

In retrospect, Obama inadvertently contributed to the Arab Spring by giving his first major foreign policy speech in Cairo. He believed that he could win over the Arabs and Muslims by speaking from one of their capitals about his desire to improve relations. He sent two unintended messages, however, by speaking from Cairo: first, that he was no different than past presidents who stood behind Arab autocrats, and, second, that he did not care about Muslim self-determination, since the autocrat he chose was one who suppressed Muslims. Instead of winning over the Muslims, he alienated them.

The Muslims and Arabs had high hopes for Obama when he was elected. They believed that he would reverse Bush's Middle East policies and would finally use America's leverage to force Israel to capitulate to their demands. He got off on the right track when he immediately declared America's support for a two-state solution, publicly criticized Israeli policy, and demanded that Prime Minister Netanyahu freeze settlement construction in the West Bank and Jerusalem. Obama's attitude and policies toward Israel alienated most Israelis, but they did not play much better in the Arab world, where he thought his tough line would be applauded. He misunderstood the Arabs' position. The Palestinians were not looking for "an honest broker," they were counting on Obama to force Israel to withdraw to the 1949 armistice line, evacuate nearly all the settlements, and support the creation of a Palestinian state with Jerusalem as its capital. Paradoxically, a settlement freeze was not one of their demands. The Palestinians had been negotiating for years without making such a demand, but now that Obama had insisted upon it, the Palestinians could not ask for anything less. Worse, Netanyahu refused to implement any freeze in Jerusalem and only later reluctantly agreed to a ten-month freeze in the West Bank. This was not sufficient, however, because now the Palestinians expected a total and indefinite freeze. Obama's inability to deliver one showed that he was weaker than they thought and no more willing or able to deliver Israel than his predecessors. Abbas, the tin-pot president of a non-state that he didn't even control, then snubbed the president and refused to negotiate for the duration of Obama's first term.

The image of weakness was reinforced by Obama's hat-in-hand approach to the Saudis. He had been convinced that by taking a hard-line toward Israel, the Saudis would step forward and offer an olive branch to the Israelis if they reached an agreement with the Palestinians. The Saudis had no interest in either helping Obama or making any gestures toward Israel.

By the end of his first term, Obama had done what most thought impossible: he had become more unpopular in the Middle East than George W. Bush.

Another consequence of the fall of Mubarak was the change in the attitude of the Gulf States. The states are run by autocrats who viewed America's refusal to support its Egyptian ally as a dangerous precedent should their governments come under similar popular pressure. Their response to the Arab Spring was to monitor and control the use of the Internet and social media. Critics of the regimes were arrested and laws were adopted prohibiting criticism of the rulers. In Kuwait, for example, a Twitter user was given a five-year prison sentence for defaming the ruling prince, the eighth such conviction in 2013.[10]

Most Gulf States, rather than respond with sticks to unrest, offered carrots. Billions of dollars were showered on the people for a variety of economic and social programs. In Saudi Arabia, no democratic reforms were forthcoming; however, the king announced a series of benefits worth $10.7 billion. These included funds to aid young unemployed people and Saudi citizens studying abroad, and to increase the salaries of state employees. The payoffs worked and the Gulf rulers maintained control.

One exception has been Bahrain, where opposition has been much stronger because of its proximity to Iran and relatively large Shiite population. Fearing that the fall of one monarch could upset a series of dominoes, Saudi Arabia sent troops to help Bahrain's leader quell the rebellion. The failure of the United States to support Bahrain further aggravated U.S.-Saudi relations.

Much of the unrest in the Gulf States was provoked by Iran stirring up Shiite communities in those countries. In Saudi Arabia, the Shiite community is relatively small and isolated; nevertheless, they are regarded as a potential threat. Since Saudi Arabia is already an Islamic country that is rabidly anti-Israel, nothing would likely change vis-à-vis Israel even if the Saud monarchy was overthrown by Islamists who simply adhere to a different approach to Islam from the Saudi Wahhabis; nevertheless, the Arabists have convinced successive administrations to view this outcome as catastrophic, so it is not surprising Obama has gone out of his way to reassure the Saudis of his continued loyalty and backed his words with the sale of record amounts of arms that the Saudis don't need and can't use.

The situation in the smaller Gulf States is much different, however, as most of them are not as constrained by Islam as Saudi Arabia. In fact, Israel has had low-level relations with countries such as Qatar, the United Arab Emirates, and Oman in the past because they are driven more by commerce than religious fundamentalism. After having minimal exchanges since the Oslo process collapsed around 2000, Israel in 2013 began to restore quiet interactions with several of these nations.

Though it has attracted little attention, one of the most potentially dangerous consequences of the Arab Spring may be the ultimate destabilization of Jordan. To date, demonstrations in Jordan have been directed primarily at specific issues, such as greater government accountability and transparency, an improvement in the economy, and electoral reform. King Abdullah, following the Saudi model, has attempted to buy off the opposition by investing more money in the economy and social services, firing his government, and promising electoral reforms.

As it stands, Jordan's electoral system is jerry-rigged to maximize the number of pro-monarchy loyalists in the government while minimizing the chance of Islamists winning seats in the Parliament and limiting the number of Palestinian representatives. When Abdullah failed to follow through on the promised electoral reforms, a coalition of disaffected Jordanians was galvanized that included Palestinian Jordanians, the Muslim Brotherhood, and some traditional allies of the monarchy such as the Bedouin; nevertheless, no mass movement has emerged to overthrow the monarchy.

The Jordanian situation has been exacerbated by the flood of tens of thousands of Syrian refugees who have taken refuge in Jordan. Jordan does not have the financial or natural resources to care for this growing population, and the refugee camps, especially those housing Palestinians, could become a powder keg if they continue to grow and Jordan is unable to meet their needs.

Jordan has also suffered the consequences of the upheaval in Egypt. In addition to rousing Islamists in the kingdom, anti-government rebels have repeatedly attacked the gas pipeline in the Sinai Desert that provides cheap natural gas to both Israel and Jordan. The raids, which have damaged the pipeline and reduced the flow of gas, were mainly aimed at the Egyptian government to demonstrate its lack of control and to express the militants' anger over the Egyptian-Israeli peace treaty and what they viewed as too-favorable terms for Israeli gas purchases. Jordan has suffered, however, because of its reliance on the cheap gas, which has exacerbated an already weak economy. The economy has been further damaged by the drastic reduction in tourism caused by the unrest.

One other longtime concern of the monarchy is the possibility of a coup by Palestinians, who comprise an estimated 70 percent of the population. Jordan had long been the only Arab country to grant Palestinians citizenship, but it began stripping away many of their rights in recent years and restricting other Palestinians from obtaining citizenship out of fear that they were becoming a threat. In addition, while Israelis worry that the Palestinians in the West Bank will focus their opprobrium and violence in their direction, Jordanians are equally concerned that they might turn east. This has not yet occurred, but it is a constant threat. The good news for Abdullah regarding Palestinians who have been longtime residents is that most have become very successful in Jordan and have less incentive to bite the hand that has kept them well fed.

In addition to the potential of a Palestinian coup, an even greater danger may be the prospect of a fundamentalist revolution similar to Iran's. As in much of the region, a strong radical undercurrent is present in Jordan, and the monarchy has been very careful to keep a tight rein on the extremists. In April 2006 Jordan arrested several members of Hamas suspected of planning a terrorist attack against senior members of the government on orders from Hamas leaders in Damascus. This followed an earlier threat, uncovered when Jordanian officials learned that Hamas had smuggled weapons, including bombs and rockets, into the kingdom. That discovery led Jordan to cancel a planned visit by Palestinian foreign minister Mahmoud Zahar of Hamas. Radical Muslims are becoming a threat again and Jordan has to worry about the large numbers who have joined the fight in Syria and the possibility that they may turn on Jordan next.

The king is also deeply worried about the Muslim Brotherhood and what he sees as the West's naive understanding of the group. He says U.S. State Department officials dismissed his concerns and were convinced the only route to democracy in Egypt was through the Brotherhood. Abdullah says he tries to convince them that the Brothers are "wolves in sheep's clothing" who want to impose their anti-Western, backward vision of society on the region. This "cult" has a powerful political organization in Jordan, he said, and is determined to replace him.[11]

On Israel's northern border, the Syrian uprising is especially complicated and has potentially serious implications for Israel's security. Syria has remained a part of the rejectionist camp, considering itself still at war with Israel. Nevertheless, prior to the current outbreak of violence, which has escalated to a civil war, no shots had been fired into Israel from Syria since the 1973 War. Moreover, despite the hostility of both Hafez and Bashar Assad, both engaged in peace talks with Israel in hopes of regaining control of the Golan Heights. Those talks ultimately failed because the Assads would not commit to peace in exchange for the land.

In the absence of an agreement, Damascus has served as the headquarters of some of the most dangerous terrorist groups in the world, including Hamas. Damascus has also served along with Iran as the patron and arms supplier for Hezbollah, and it has used that group as its proxy for fighting Israel and undermining Lebanese sovereignty. This relationship is being shaken up and perhaps destroyed, depending on the outcome of the fighting in Syria.

As in other Arab states, the Syrian unrest began with popular protests on March 15, 2011, and then spread nationwide by April. Echoing the first protesters in Egypt, Syrians demanded democratic and economic reform but were not calling for the overthrow of the government. Assad responded with a bloody crackdown in which more than 130 people were killed and many leaders of the movement—students, liberal activists, and human rights activists—were arrested. When the protests continued and spread, the Syrian army was deployed in hopes of bringing the unrest to a quick end. Instead, the brutality of the military, which was killing increasingly large numbers of civilian protesters, sparked new clashes and led to the formation of rebel armies that were determined to drive Assad from power.

During the early fighting many analysts, especially in Israel, predicted Assad's rapid downfall, but he proved to have much greater staying power than expected. He had seen what happened to Mubarak in Egypt, and Assad was determined not to go out the same way. He and his fellow Alawites, already a minority in the largely Sunni country, knew that defeat was not an option, because they feared a Sunni-led regime would persecute or exterminate them. Unlike Mubarak, who refused to deploy the army's full force against Egyptian protesters, Assad gradually intensified his response to include almost his entire arsenal, including attack helicopters, aerial bombers, tanks, artillery, and poison gas.

The West was ambivalent about the war. They knew Assad was a brutal dictator, but they also were accustomed to dealing with him. The Arabists were constantly trying to convince their bosses that Assad was really interested in peace, though the Syrian strongman never agreed to normalize relations with Israel, no matter what territorial concessions Israel offered. For the Israelis, their first inclination was to support the devil they knew rather than risk one they didn't know. They remained on the sidelines, unconvinced that an alternative to Assad would change the situation for the better. As the war dragged on, Assad's departure became less assured, and his brutality resulted in the deaths of thousands and made hundreds of thousands of refugees. In the face of these developments, Israel shifted its view and joined the West in calling for Assad's ouster.

As an increasing number of Syrian officers defected, they began to form a more organized militia, the Free Syrian Army (FSA), which attracted former soldiers and civilians. Infighting among the group made the West nervous and unsure who, if anyone, they should help. This uncertainty meant that the rebel forces had few sources of support, and it was left primarily to the Sunni-led Gulf States, principally Saudi Arabia and Qatar, which had long competed with Assad, to provide aid and weapons to help dispose of Assad. Still, the lack of Western help, especially arms transfers, made the fight asymmetrical: this ragtag band of insurgents was pitted against a modern, well-armed military force armed and funded by Iran and Russia. Assad's troops were also reinforced by the thousands of Hezbollah troops from Lebanon that joined the fighting in 2013.

The entry of Hezbollah into the fighting created a number of new complications. Despite criticism from drawing Israel into a disastrous war in Lebanon, Nasrallah decided, with a push from his Iranian patrons, that Hezbollah's future depended on Assad's survival. Nasrallah declared, "This battle is ours . . . and I promise you victory."[12] Hezbollah also hoped to take advantage of the chaos to smuggle some of Syria's more sophisticated weapons systems back to Lebanon. Israel monitors Hezbollah's activities, however, and Israeli aircraft were believed to have bombed convoys of weapons headed from Syria to Lebanon on several occasions, but there is no way of knowing how many might have reached the terrorists.

Not everyone in Lebanon was happy about Nasrallah's decision to join the Syrian war effort. In fact, even many Shiites began to openly criticize him. As body bags with the fallen Hezbollah fighters began to arrive with increasing frequency (an estimated 500 dead by the end of 2013), dissatisfaction with the war grew. Some Israeli analysts believe that Syria could be Hezbollah's Vietnam and permanently weaken the organization.

Well over 100,000 people have died in the fighting. Thousands more were arrested by the government. In addition, more than 1 million Syrians, and counting, are refugees who have fled across the borders, raising new security challenges for the countries that accept them. The Syrians left behind are caught in a war zone with deteriorating living conditions and shortages of food, drinking water, and medicine. Some Syrians, including fighters injured in the battle, have been allowed into Israel for medical treatment.

Even as the humanitarian crisis worsened, the West remained on the sidelines, unsure of whom to support. Complicated rifts appeared among the rebels, and the uprising was infiltrated by increasing numbers of radical Islamists, some associated with al-Qaeda, who were coming from around the world to expel Assad and create their own vision of an Islamic republic. Toward the end of 2013, out of the 70,000–100,000 estimated rebels in Syria, extremist groups were estimated to comprise as much as 25 percent of the rebel forces, and roughly half of those were linked to al-Qaeda.[13] Hostilities among the rebel groups have impeded the creation of a united opposition to Assad and, worse, have resulted in a three-way conflict.

The introduction of jihadists, including representatives of al-Qaeda offshoots, which had been in decline but now were rejuvenated, complicated the situation for the West. The United States and others face the dilemma of how to oust Assad without allowing radical Islamists to take his place. Israelis face the same dilemma; many have changed their opinions 180 degrees, from hope at Assad's downfall to anxiety over the prospect of having a radical Islamic regime on their border.

In July 2013, reports that Syrian forces had used chemical weapons shocked the West and provoked widespread condemnation. President Obama, whose indecisiveness on what to do about Syria had left U.S. policy in limbo for the duration of the war, suddenly announced that Syrian use of chemical weapons was a red line that would trigger an American response. After an investigation confirmed that on August 21, 2013, at least 635 people were killed in nerve gas attacks, the president was expected to order a military response. Instead, he did nothing, reinforcing his image in the region as a weak amateur with no clue how to conduct Middle East policy.

The Russians, whose last remaining ally in the region was Syria, saw an opportunity to capitalize on Obama's naiveté. They were supplying Assad weapons and political cover and blocking all efforts by the United States to secure a UN Security Council Resolution condemning Syria. Russian president Vladimir Putin took advantage of Obama's dithering and convinced him that Syria would agree to dismantle all of its chemical weapons. Many Americans believed U.S. credibility required a response to Syria's violation of Obama's red line, but the president jumped at the chance to avoid using force and accepted the Russian proposal.

To the surprise of many, Assad agreed to dismantle his stocks of chemical weapons, though some people remain skeptical that he will not hide some of the weapons or transfer them to Hezbollah. By the middle of 2014, most of the arsenal had been transferred out of the country, where it will be destroyed; however, Assad retained some weapons, which he used again in 2014.[14]

Israel is naturally worried that these weapons could fall into the hands of Hezbollah or other extremists. The other fear from the outset of the fighting in Syria is that the violence could spill over into Israel. In fact, a number of incidents have occurred that required Israel to fire across the border to suppress shooting from the Syrian side. While the outcome of the war is in doubt, little hope remains for the emergence of a democratic Syria. The alternatives appear to be that a weakened Assad will remain in power or a more dangerous Islamic leadership will emerge victorious and become a new front in the Islamic-Israel conflict.

As traditional Middle East powers such as Egypt and Iraq have been weakened by the Arab Spring and the U.S. invasion, respectively, Turkey looked to fill the vacuum, and President Tayyip Erdogan had visions of Turkey becoming the hegemon in the region. His plans were upset, however, by several developments. First, Turkey became embroiled in border disputes with Syria. Next, the West backed away from its tough position on Iran's nuclear program, leaving Iran in a position to challenge Turkey for hegemony. Finally, a corruption scandal has forced the ouster of many of Erdogan's government allies and stimulated mass protests that may yet engulf him.

For Israel, the surrounding upheaval has been a mixed blessing. On one hand, the internal struggles its neighbors are facing have distracted them from Israel and forced the leaders to devote all their attention to pacifying their populations. In addition, some of Israel's most dangerous enemies, such as Hezbollah and Assad, have been weakened. At the same time, Israel is stronger than ever militarily.

The instability has also made Israelis wary of making any irrevocable concessions to the Palestinians. They point to the Golan Heights, which the international community has long pressured Israel to return to Syria, and see that had they caved in, a radical Islamic regime in Syria might hold that strategic high ground. Those Israelis who want peace now are frustrated by the distraction of the Islamic Winter, while Israelis who are skeptical see the upheaval as a reason not to take risks for peace. A positive note is that Israel still maintains good relations with Morocco and some of the Gulf nations, and its peace treaties with Egypt and Jordan remain in force.

On the other hand, Israel is in a far more dangerous situation than in the past several decades. No one knows if or when the Islamic Winter will end. Any one of its neighbors could still fall to radical Islamists. Israel could find itself surrounded by radical regimes who believe that Jews have no business ruling over Muslims and that a Jewish state has no place in the Islamic world. In addition, the greatest existential threat to Israel remains Iran's nuclear program.

Meanwhile, the Islamists seeking power face the same fractiousness that prevented Nasser from achieving his pan-Arab goals and earlier Muslim regimes from creating a pan-Islamic identification. Ancient tribal identities were not suppressed by the decades of living within nation-states. Moreover, the strains within Islam among Sunnis, Shiites, Druze, and Alawites remain unresolved, and ethnic groups, such as the Kurds, refuse to sit quietly while their lands and rights are usurped by Muslim rulers. The radicals have another problem, Marwan Muasher observed: "Islamists have lost their 'holiness' in the Arab world. Their once-popular slogan, 'Islam is the solution,' is no longer attractive to wide sectors of the population" who "are starting to embrace the triumph of performance over ideology in the region."[15]

During the Arab Spring a lot of commentaries were written on the subject of whether Muslim states could be democratic. Given the differences in the interpretation of what constitutes basic human rights, it is unlikely any Muslim state will adopt the democratic principles accepted in the West. The United Nations Universal Declaration of Human Rights states that "the inherent dignity and the equal and inalienable rights of all members of the human family is the foundation of freedom, justice and peace in the world." In response, the Organization of Islamic Cooperation issued a Declaration of Human Rights in Islam, which states, "All the rights and freedoms stipulated in this declaration are subject to the Islamic Sharia." On December 7, 1984, nearly three decades before the Arab Spring, Said Rajaie-Khorassami, then Iran's ambassador to the United Nations, said the UN declaration is "'a secular understanding of the

Judeo-Christian tradition' that could not be implemented by Muslims. He argued that 'human dignity could not be reduced to a series of secular norms and that Iran recognized no authority or power but that of Almighty God and no legal tradition apart from Islamic law.'"[16]

The Arab Spring/Islamic Winter should have demolished the Arabist myth that Israel is to blame for all the problems in the Middle East; inter-Arab and inter-Muslim concerns produced instability and turmoil throughout the region and had nothing to do with Israel. Nevertheless, Israel will be deeply affected by the outcome of the unrest. The situation is still evolving and it may take years, if not decades, before some stasis is reached and the full impact is evident. Up until now, however, the direction has not been toward liberal democracy and freedom, as Westerners and many Arabs hoped. Instead, the trend appears toward more traditional Islamic societies, which may adopt the relatively moderate views of a country like Jordan or may turn to the extreme, like Iran. If radical Islamists who reject the values of the West and believe in the restoration of Islamic glory and world domination ultimately come to power, Jews, Christians, Israel, and the Western world will be in danger.

CHAPTER 6

IRAN AND LITTLE SATAN

The Jewish community of Persia, modern-day Iran, is one of the oldest in the Diaspora, and its historical roots reach back to the sixth century BCE, the time of the destruction of the First Temple, when most Jews were sent into exile in neighboring Babylon. Cyrus the Great conquered Babylon in 539 BCE and, over the next two centuries, expanded Persia's influence to the point where it became the largest empire in the world. Cyrus agreed to rebuild the Jews' temple and allowed those who had been expelled to return to the Land of Israel, ending the First Exile. Jewish communities subsequently spread throughout the Persian Empire.

More than 1,000 years later, in 642, Muslims conquered Persia and gradually absorbed most of its territory. Islam was established as the state religion and, over time, many of the Persian elites converted to enable their ascendance to political power. For most of the next 1,500 years, Jews lived under dhimmi status (a protected minority as "People of the Book") and were sometimes forced to convert to Islam. Among the discriminatory practices imposed on the Jews was their exclusion from the government and military, and the requirement that they pay a special tax, wear a special Jewish badge and headgear, and take responsibility as a community for crimes committed by individual Jews.

By the twelfth century, as many as 600,000 Jews may have been living in Iran. Persecution, however, led to a diminution of the population to approximately 50,000 at the beginning of the twentieth century.

During World War I, Russian and British forces occupied parts of Iran. The British were concerned about the possibility of the Bolsheviks gaining a permanent foothold in Iran and threatening Britain's imperial interests in India. The British aided Reza Khan in a coup d'état in 1921, and the new shah succeeded in taking control of the country and reaching an agreement with Russia to withdraw from Iran. The British withdrew and Reza Khan ruled until he was forced to abdicate in 1941. He was succeeded by his son, Mohammad Reza Pahlavi, who broke the power of the Shiite clergy, which had accrued great influence over earlier governments, and created an authoritarian government, which he allied with the West.

By sidelining the clergy, it was possible for the shah to end the persecution of Jews. They were no longer treated as dhimmis and became prominent members of Iranian society. The Persian Jews survived World War II essentially unscathed and began to expand their communal infrastructure, particularly by the construction of new educational institutions designed to strengthen traditional Judaism and Hebrew education. Despite the improvement in conditions, Zionist organizers around the country convinced thousands of Jews to immigrate to the Land of Israel. Many Jews stayed, however, and the Iranian Jewish population eventually reached approximately 100,000, making it the largest Jewish community in the Middle East outside Israel.

Iran voted with the Arab states against the UN partition decision and sided with them in the war as well. Soon after, however, the shah began to look for ways to expand relations with the West, especially the United States, in hopes of getting political, military, and economic assistance. Like other leaders in the region, he may have also believed that having the support of the American Jewish community would smooth the way for building U.S.-Iran ties. He understood that what American Jews cared about was Israel, so it was perhaps no coincidence that in March 1950, shortly after the shah returned from a visit to the United States, Iran recognized Israel.

Israel's early leaders formulated a foreign policy aimed at finding allies to surround their Arab enemies. Turkey and Ethiopia were approached to join an informal alliance. Iran was the other country willing to participate in Israel's "periphery policy" because the shah feared both pan-Arabism and pan-Islamism. Until the revolution in 1979, diplomatic missions were operating in Tehran and Tel Aviv and the two countries maintained discreet diplomatic relations. El Al regularly flew to Tehran and the two countries interacted in fields such as medicine and agriculture. Trade was robust with Israel receiving much of its oil from Iran and engaging in a variety of export-import activities. Israel and Iran also established strong military ties.[1]

Jews also took their place in all aspects of Iranian life. They especially flourished during the economic boom of the 1960s and 70s, when many became wealthy. On the eve of the Islamic Revolution in 1979, 80,000 Jews lived in Iran.

While the shah treated the Jewish community well, he tolerated no opposition to his rule. His secret police force, SAVAK, became much feared and hated by the population because of its use of torture on many of the people who were arrested for real and sometimes false accusations of acting against the state. One of the critics arrested by the authorities was Ayatollah Ruhollah Khomeini, who led demonstrations and riots against the shah. The last straw for the shah was a speech on June 3, 1963, in which Khomeini railed against the dependence of the shah's regime upon the United States and Israel. Khomeini was imprisoned for 18 months. After he was released in 1964, the shah deported him and Khomeini spent time in Turkey and Iraq, and ultimately moved to France where he continued to agitate against the government.

Growing dissent against foreign influence and political repression culminated in the Iranian revolution, which led to the establishment of an Islamic republic on April 1, 1979.

When the Ayatollah Khomeini's followers succeeded in forcing the shah to flee the country, Khomeini returned from exile, instituted Sharia (Islamic) law, and began to purge the country of Western influences. Over time it became clear that Iran had swapped one autocrat for another as Khomeini became the supreme leader of the

nation. Replacing the shah's dreaded SAVAK secret police with revolutionary guards, Khomeini secured his rule and squashed any opposition. Khomeini also sought to export the revolution and enflame
Shiites to replace the Arab governments in the region with Islamic
republics.

The revolution upended Israel's foreign policy overnight as Khomeini immediately began to incite the Muslim world against Israel
and its principal patron, the United States—or, as Iranians refer to
them, the "Little Satan" and the "Big Satan." In the succeeding three
decades, Iran became increasingly belligerent toward the West and,
especially, the "Satans."

Rhetorically, Iran was belligerent toward the United States, but
Khomeini's concern was not just about American power or its relationship with the shah. He was especially worried about the impact on Muslim society of what he considered the immorality and
decadence of the West. Iranians, especially young people who had
become accustomed to wearing Western clothes, listening to Western music, and assimilating Western cultural norms, were seen as a
threat to Islam and the cohesion of the state. Khomeini and his successors ruthlessly cracked down on "deviants," imposed standards
of modesty, and did everything possible to block access to Western
ideas, a task that grew increasingly difficult with the spread of the
Internet and social media.

Iran also rejected Western notions of human rights founded on
the belief that freedom, peace, and security are grounded in the "inherent dignity and the equal and inalienable rights of all members
of the human family." Iran's response to this Universal Declaration
of Human Rights issued by the United Nations was expressed by
its ambassador, Said Rajaie-Khorassami, who said the UN language
represented the secular Judeo-Christian tradition and could never
be accepted by Muslims, who, he said, "recognized no authority or
power but that of Almighty God and no legal tradition apart from
Islamic law."[2]

For Khomeini, Western imperialism was part of the confrontation between the House of Islam and the House of War. He argued
the division of the Middle East into nation states was a deliberate
attempt to weaken the Muslim world by splitting it into pieces that

could be gobbled up or controlled by the non-believers. Even while he was limiting progress within Iran, and advocating a return to a more insular Islam, Khomeini was blaming the West for misleading Muslims and tempting them with depraved Western culture. "The imperialists, the oppressive and treacherous rulers, the Jews, Christians, and materialists," he said, "are all attempting to distort the truth of Islam and lead the Muslims astray."[3]

Following the overthrow of the shah and the declaration of an Islamic state in 1979, Iran severed relations with Israel. Approximately 60,000 Jews left Iran during the first ten years of the Islamic regime; most (35,000) went to the United States; 20,000 moved to Israel, and the rest lived mostly in Europe.[4] Many of these Jews were wealthy but, like the rest of the fleeing Jews, had to leave their property behind.

The once strong and proud Iranian Jewish community continued to decline and now is believed to be around 10,000, but it is still the largest number of Jews in the region outside Israel. The remaining Iranian Jews are largely isolated from the rest of the Jewish world and have to tread carefully. Jews who apply for a passport to travel abroad are put under surveillance and the government usually does not allow all the members of a family to travel abroad at the same time, essentially keeping hostages to ensure the traveler(s) return to Iran.

Virtually every Jew who still lives in Iran is under suspicion of treachery, especially for spying for the United States or Israel, a crime punishable by death. A number of Jews have been accused of spying for the "Zionist entity"; at least 13 have been executed for either religious reasons or their connection to Israel.

Jews were impelled to leave Iran by the change in leadership and, more important, its attitude toward Jews. The demonization of Jews that took place for centuries in the Islamic world returned with a vengeance under Khomeini, who believed Jews were the "embodiment of evil," seeking Jewish dominance over Muslims and, ultimately, the destruction of Islam.[5] He warned:

We see today that the Jews (may God curse them) have meddled with the text of the Qur'an. . . . We must protest and make people aware that the Jews and their foreign backers are opposed to the very foundations of Islam and wish to establish Jewish domination throughout the world. Since they are a cunning and resourceful group of people, I fear that—God forbid!—they may one day achieve their goal, and that apathy shown by some of may allow a Jew to rule over us one day.[6]

The regime says it allows Jews to worship freely as an example of the distinction it makes between the Jewish religion and Zionism. Iranian officials say they do not have anything against the Jews, only the Zionists. For example, Ayatollah Ahmad Khatami said on August 17, 2012, "We differentiate between the Jews who live in Iran, who are law-abiding and participate in Qods Day, and the Zionists, whose history attests to their murderous nature."[7]

The aforementioned quotations from Khomeini, however, make clear no such distinction exists. This is reinforced by various comparisons made between the situation today and the battles between Jews and Muhammad. For example, in a speech on January 9, 2012, Supreme Leader Ali Khamenei said Iran's struggle with the infidel United States and its Zionist allies was similar to the battles in 628 when the Prophet and his followers massacred the Jews of Khaybar.[8]

The Iranian media and officials also spread anti-Semitic messages denouncing Jews, attributing them with a range of undesirable characteristics and portraying them as the root of all evil. Another example of the government's official view is reflected by its publication of the *Protocols of the Elders of Zion*. The government's propaganda is broadcast domestically as well as abroad, so the Iranian people are fed a steady diet of anti-Semitism.

After the Iranian revolution, many people predicted that this was the first of many dominoes to fall in the Middle East. Iran was determined to export its revolution and American policy makers feared other pro-Western leaders would fall as militant Islam spread. It did not happen.

Iran never gave up its campaign; however, only Syria, among the Arab states, allied with Iran. In many ways, this is a peculiar alliance because the ruling Assad family is not deeply religious. Worse, from the Shiite perspective, the Assads are part of the Alawite sect, which is considered heretical by other Muslims. Not only that, Hafez Assad suppressed radical Muslims in Syria, most famously when he razed the town of Hama to quash a rebellion by the Muslim Brotherhood and killed an estimated 20,000 people, perhaps the largest massacre of Arabs in the twentieth century. Iran's leaders may have been less disturbed by the mass murder because the Brotherhood is associated with Sunni Muslims.

Assad's calculation in allying with Iran was all about realpolitik and not Islam. Assad wanted to maintain pressure on Israel but knew he could not do it directly, so he was able to use Iran's creation, Hezbollah, to harass the Israelis from Lebanon. Syria was largely isolated from both the Arab and Western countries, making his need for a regional ally acute. Furthermore, the fall of the Soviet Union also meant Syria lost its main patron—even though Russia continued to provide support—and needed financial help, which Iran was prepared to provide in exchange for Assad's loyalty and assistance in the Iranian agenda.

Since Iran was unsuccessful in spreading its revolution to its neighbors, the regime decided to use other means of persuasion and became the spiritual and financial patron for most of the region's Islamists. It is the Iranian model of revolution, its institution of Islamic law, and its anti-Western philosophy that characterize the rhetoric of many extremist groups. Much of the weapons, training, and literature that are the backbone of Islamist violence are bankrolled by Tehran.

Iran gradually became the world's second leading sponsor of terror (after Saudi Arabia), most of which was directed at American or Jewish targets and, occasionally, its Arab rivals. The attacks are sometimes carried out directly by Iranian agents and other times through proxies such as Hezbollah. Iran has been linked to numerous terrorist attacks, ranging from taking hostages and hijacking airliners to carrying out assassinations and bombings. Some of these incidents include the taking of more than 30 Western hostages in Lebanon between 1984 and 1992, the bombings of the U.S. embassy and the French-U.S. Marine barracks in Beirut in 1983, and the bombings of the Israeli embassy and the AMIA Jewish community center building in Buenos Aires.

Deadly weapons were also smuggled to Hezbollah and used against Israeli civilians in commando-style raids. During the 2006 war, the sophistication of these weapons became apparent when the Israeli Air Force destroyed long-range missiles that could reach Tel Aviv and when an anti-ship missile disabled one of the Israeli Navy's ships. Hezbollah is now using the cover of the Syrian civil war and the UN peacekeeping force's ineptness to smuggle advanced guided-missile systems into Lebanon piece by piece. Iran and Hezbollah fear that their supply chain will be broken if the Assad regime falls. Iran also hopes that upgrading Hezbollah's arsenal will deter Israel from attacking Lebanon or Iran's nuclear program. Today, it is estimated that Hezbollah has 100,000 or more rockets with ranges capable of reaching virtually every city in Israel.[9]

The Iranians also see the Palestinian issue as part of the larger campaign to purge the region of infidels. According to Khomeini:

> Israel on the land of the Palestinian people is a cancerous growth that is hatching schemes within the kingdom of Islam, and the fear is that it will take over [additional] Islamic lands. Therefore, it is incumbent upon all the Muslims to foil its schemes by all means available, and to prevent the spread of Israeli influence.[10]

To help fight this cancer, Iran has been willing to provide funding and arms for both Hamas and Islamic Jihad despite the fact that their members are Sunni rather than Shiite Muslims. In January 2002, for example, Israeli forces intercepted a Palestinian-owned freighter carrying 50 tons of Iranian- and Russian-made weapons. In October 2005, a senior Palestinian intelligence official revealed that Iran promised a reward of $10,000 to Islamic Jihad if it launched rockets from the West Bank toward Tel Aviv.

Harassing Israel from afar is a low-cost affair, since the Israeli reactions are directed at the terrorists rather than Iran. Using Palestinian and Lebanese proxies is just one way that Iran is pursuing its goal of destroying Israel. Iran also hopes to checkmate Israel by keeping up a steady drumbeat of criticism of Israeli policies in an effort to drive a wedge between Israel and its allies, especially the United States. Stripped of American protection, Israel can be isolated and, ultimately, destroyed, either by military means or the type of international political and economic campaign that was used to change the government in South Africa. Iran also hopes to rally the Muslim world behind it to remove the "cancer" from the Islamic body.

Since Israel has no territorial dispute with Iran, the basis for Iran's hostility comes from its leaders' interpretation of Islam. Like Hitler, the Iranians and other detractors of Israel have spent decades conditioning not only Muslims but Westerners that the "Zionists/ Jews are the embodiment of evil" and "Israel must be destroyed."

The most immediate way that Iran can threaten Israel is by developing nuclear weapons. Israeli officials have been debating whether to strike Iran's nuclear facilities or to wait and see if sanctions and negotiations put a halt to Iran's program. If sanctions fail, there is also the possibility that the United States will take military action. Rhetorically at least, the Iranians believe that Allah will protect Iran from an Israeli or American military strike.

Though Iran's leaders have focused their public threats on Israel, the nuclear program was not initiated with the Israelis in mind. Iran's interest was in developing the means to deter its principal rival, Iraqi president Saddam Hussein, who it feared had resumed his nuclear weapons program after Israel destroyed the Osirak nuclear reactor in 1981. The two nations are historical rivals from ancient times, and Saddam Hussein was viewed as the principal impediment to Iranian hegemony in the region. Worse, he was a Sunni Muslim whose co-religionists dominated the Iraqi government, military, and economy at the expense of the Shiite minority. Partly motivated by the fear that Iran would inspire an insurgency by the Shiites, Iraq attacked Iran in September 1980. For the next eight years Iran and Iraq fought a war that killed approximately 1 million people and still ended essentially in a stalemate.

The outcome of the war did not change the enmity between the countries, but the balance of power began to change when Hussein made the mistake of invading Kuwait in 1990 and threatening Saudi Arabia. The U.S.-led coalition subsequently defeated Iraq and weakened its capacity to challenge Iran. When George W. Bush decided to attack Iraq a decade later and drive Hussein from power, one of the unintended consequences was to significantly strengthen Iran's position. Once Iraq was eliminated as a counterbalance to Iran, Iranians could rally Iraqi Shiites to either seize power or at least bring about an improvement in relations between the two countries. Iraq has indeed moved closer to Iran, and Shiites and Sunnis have been fighting since the U.S. invasion. The battle of religious factions for supremacy intensified after U.S. troops withdrew and the outcome of the civil strife is still in doubt.

Even though the United States failed to find weapons of mass destruction in Iraq, Iran continued its own secret weapons program with the assistance of the father of Pakistan's bomb, Dr. Abdul Qadeer Khan, and North Korea. Iran might have built a bomb before anyone knew about it if not for the blustering of Mahmoud Ahmadinejad, who became president of Iran in 2005. Unlike his subtler predecessors, Ahmadinejad was bombastic and his public statements gave the impression he was an unstable, anti-Semitic, anti-American Muslim fanatic. Ahmadinejad brought attention to Iran's nuclear ambitions by publicly talking about the right of Iran to nuclear power and the progress it was making in the enrichment of uranium, while simultaneously threatening to wipe Israel off the map.

Ahmadinejad displayed an obsession with Israel and the Jews and seemed to take delight in enraging Jews around the world with anti-Semitic remarks and statements questioning the veracity of the Holocaust. In 2005, for example, he spoke at "A World Without Zionism" conference and declared, "Our dear Imam [Khomeini] said that the occupying regime must be wiped off the map and this was a very wise statement. We cannot compromise over the issue of Palestine."[11] Jews and Israelis were especially angered by his use of the UN as an international platform for anti-Israel diatribes, as in 2008, when he used the General Assembly rostrum to rail against "Zionist murderers" and the "Zionist network" that dominates "an important portion of the financial and monetary centers as well as the political decisions-making centers of some European countries and the U.S."[12]

The nuclear program began long before Ahmadinejad became president, and he was never in control of its development. In fact,

Ahmadinejad was never the real problem, and it was a mistake for those concerned with Iran's nuclear program to focus so much attention on him rather than on the supreme leader, who was the true ruler of Iran. Genocidal threats did not originate with Ahmadinejad; they came from the top, first from Khomeini and then from his successor, the current supreme leader, Ali Khamenei. For example, in one of Khomeini's speeches echoing the *Protocols*, he said:

> Regardless of [the] occupation of Palestine, it is crystal clear and never has been denied by the heads of the fake regime of Israel that they want to gain control of other Muslim countries, and want to expand their occupied territory to include the other parts of [the] Islamic entity between [the] Nile River [and the] Euphrates. Every day they plan how to achieve this evil goal. It is a must [for all Muslims] to defend the Islamic countries by all means.[13]

In 2000, Khamenei's New Year's greeting included the declaration that "there is only one solution to the Middle East problem, namely the annihilation and destruction of the Jewish state." More recently, in February 2012, Khamenei gave a sermon in which he referred to Israel as a "cancerous tumor . . . that must be removed."[14]

Irwin Cotler, a Canadian member of Parliament, former justice minister, and human rights attorney, has called on the international community to hold Iran accountable for these statements. "As the Foreign Affairs Committee of the Canadian Parliament unanimously concluded," Cotler said, "Iran has already committed the crime of incitement to genocide prohibited under the Genocide Convention . . . State Parties are obliged to undertake the legal measures to hold Iran accountable."[15]

Cotler's call for action has been ignored. The fact that public genocidal threats can be made without anything more than mild rebukes from the West sent a strong message to the Israelis that no one else was taking them seriously, and Israel was on its own to confront the danger.

Iranians and their supporters ask why Iran should be prevented from acquiring nuclear weapons when it is acceptable for other countries. The idea has been floated that a nuclear Iran can be deterred from using a bomb the way the United States deterred the Soviet Union—with the threat of retaliation. The Soviets, however, were not interested in destroying the United States or any other country. They were also afraid of the consequences of an American first or second strike. Iran is different because its leaders base their decisions on their religious beliefs, not an ideology.

Shiites look forward to an apocalyptic battle in which the warriors of Islam defeat the forces of evil and usher in a new era in which Islam is the dominant religion throughout the world. At that time, the Twelfth Imam, the Mahdi or "divinely guided one," will return after disappearing in 874 and bringing an end to Muhammad's lineage. Like the believers of other faiths waiting for the Messiah, the Shiites have looked forward to the Mahdi's appearance for more than a thousand years. Ayatollah Khomeini said, "Either we all become free, or we will go to the greater freedom, which is martyrdom. Either we shake one another's hands in joy at the victory of Islam in the world, or all of us will turn to eternal life and martyrdom. In both cases, victory and success are ours."[16]

Deterrence also works in two directions. It may be true that Iran would not attack Israel out of fear of Israel's second-strike capability, but it is also possible that a nuclear Iran could deter Israel from attacking Iran's allies. For example, what would happen if Iran threatened a nuclear strike on Israel if it assaulted Hezbollah or Islamic Jihad or Syria? Could Israel's leaders take the risk that the Iranians were bluffing?

It has become a cliché in the West to say that no one wins in a nuclear war, but the Iranians do not necessarily believe this. In fact, Iran's former president Akbar Hashemi Rafsanjani said that "Israel is much smaller than Iran in land mass, and therefore far more vulnerable to nuclear attack." Since Iran has 70 million people and Israel only has 8 million, Rafsanjani believes Iran could survive an exchange of nuclear bombs while Israel would be annihilated. Furthermore, Iran could wipe out Israel by dropping nuclear bombs on Tel Aviv, Haifa, and Jerusalem. Some would argue that Rafsanjani is "irrational"; however, acting according to their faith is perfectly rational for Muslims.

While the media has focused on tensions between Israel and the Obama administration over the Iranian issue, Iran's Arab neighbors are especially alarmed by the prospect of a nuclear Iran on their doorstep. The "Little Satan," is a target because it is the home of the Jews, but Iran also has theological and political reasons to target its Arab neighbors. The Gulf States, in particular, fear that a nuclear Iran will galvanize Shiite minorities and help them overthrow the monarchies in the region. Economics also motivate Iran, which believes that countries such as Saudi Arabia have kept oil prices artificially low to deprive Iran of revenue.

Former Saudi ambassador to Washington Turki Al-Faisal complained in 2013 about the "Iranian leadership's meddling and destabilizing efforts in the countries with Shia majorities, Iraq and Bahrain, as well as those countries with significant minority Shia communities, such as Kuwait, Lebanon and Yemen." Saudi Arabia is another of those countries, and the Saudis have accused the Iranians of trying to provoke their Shiite community to destabilize their regime. Iran also interferes in the affairs of the Palestinians, Iraq, and Morocco.[17]

Since 2006, at least 13 Arab countries have either announced new plans to explore atomic energy or revived pre-existing nuclear programs in response to Iran's nuclear program.[18] While these agreements are all supposed to be for peaceful purposes, the Saudis have made no secret of their intentions. "If Iran develops a nuclear weapon," an official close to Saudi prince Turki al-Faisal said in June 2011, "that will be unacceptable to us and we will have to follow suit."[19] Since then, reports have suggested the Saudis have made arrangements to purchase bombs from Pakistan.[20]

The common interests of Israel and the Gulf States, especially, have created a temporary alliance based on the idea that the enemy of my enemy is my friend. This explains reports of cooperation between the Israelis and Arab states, including rumors that Saudi Arabia has developed a joint plan with Israel and given the Israelis permission to transit Saudi airspace should it need to do so for a military strike on Iran.[21]

Curiously, the Arab public is much less worried about Iran and may be more impressed than their leaders by the fact that the Iranians are standing up to the West and to Israel. One poll, which includes 14 countries, representing 89 percent of the population of the Arab world, found that about one-third of the people in Saudi Arabia, Yemen, Iraq, and Kuwait are worried about Iran, but, overall, only 6 percent of the Arab public viewed Iran as the single biggest threat to their home country, while 52 percent said Israel and 21 percent the United States. It is an indication of the degree of anti-Semitism that pervades these countries that more than one-third of the people fear Israel even though the Jewish state has not fought a war with any of their nations since 1973 and has never been in conflict with most of the countries surveyed.

The West views Iran as a serious threat because it could coerce its neighbors to raise oil prices, interfere with oil shipments through the Persian Gulf, sponsor terrorism, and acquire the capability of hitting U.S. military targets and European cities with its increasingly long-range missiles. Iranians believe that once they have the bomb, they will be insulated from any attacks by the West or its neighbors out of fear of an Iranian nuclear retaliation.

The West finally acted to stop Iran's program, but not because of the threats against Israel or the Arab states. By raising the profile of the Iranian nuclear developments, while simultaneously presenting the image of a leader just crazy enough to use the bomb, Ahmadinejad drew international attention, especially from the United Kingdom, France, and Germany. The Europeans recognized that their economic and security interests in the Middle East were at risk if Iran got the bomb. Initially the United States had to be dragged along because President Obama came to office hoping to engage Iran. He mistakenly believed the mere force of his personality would be enough to restore U.S.-Iran ties and dissuade the Iranians from their nuclear quest. Iran's intransigence convinced Obama he was wrong, and the United States joined the European campaign to impose international sanctions on Iran.

As early as 2004, the Europeans attempted to convince Iran to suspend work on uranium enrichment and submit to inspections from the International Atomic Energy Agency (IAEA). The Iranians rejected the offer. After several more abortive attempts to reach a diplomatic agreement, the issue was referred to the UN Security Council, where eight resolutions were adopted from 2006–2012, placing a variety of sanctions on Iran for failing to halt its enrichment and reprocessing activities. The sanctions were partially watered down because of veto threats from China and Russia, which wanted to limit the damage to Iran because both had significant political and economic relations with Tehran (ironically, the Islamic fundamentalists have no hesitancy about being in bed with the godless Communists). Over the next several years, however, the United States and individual European countries imposed their own stricter sanctions.

In a rare case of international consensus, almost the entire world agrees that Iran should not be allowed to develop nuclear weapons. Since the military option to stop Iran is a scenario everyone wants to avoid, the hope has been that Iran can be convinced to comply with the world's wishes by forcing the Iranians to choose between continuing the nuclear program and letting their economy and citizens suffer. Iran ignored each of the resolutions and continued its steady march toward development of a bomb.

Former CIA director Leon Panetta said that while sanctions carry the possibility to create serious economic problems and weaken the Iranian government, they would probably not deter Iran's "ambitions with regards to nuclear capability."[22] Israeli prime minister Netanyahu complained that sanctions have not done nearly enough to effect a change in Iran's nuclear program, and, in testimony before a Senate intelligence committee in February 2012, CIA director James Clapper said, "The sanctions as imposed so far have not caused [Iran] to change their behavior or their policy."[23]

Clapper's view was reinforced by a speech on February 3, 2012, by Khamenei, which reaffirmed Iran's commitment to acquire nuclear weapons and called Israel a "cancerous tumor" that "needs to be removed and will be removed" from the Middle East.[24]

Nevertheless, Israel, despite public misperceptions, has not been the advocate of military action. The country clamoring for an attack on Iran is Saudi Arabia, and the Saudis have been furious with President Bush and President Obama for failing to use force to eliminate the nuclear danger.

Obama repeatedly said that the United States was not interested in containing Iran and that all options were on the table, but Iran did not seem to take the threat of American military action seriously. And for good reason. They recognized the last thing Obama wanted was a war in a third Muslim country, especially after improving relations with Muslims had been one of his top priorities coming into office. Administration officials in the Pentagon and other national security agencies made numerous remarks that either no military option existed or that any operation would lead to some type of world catastrophe. Many of the same officials emphasized that Israel was also incapable of destroying Iran's nuclear facilities and that if they even tried, the implications would be calamitous.

Secretary of Defense Leon Panetta, for example, warned that a strike against Iran could be disastrous for the world economy. The impact on the economy would apply to any country attacking Iran, but his remarks were clearly directed at Israel because he made them just before meeting Israeli defense minister Ehud Barak and amid a flurry of reports that Israel was considering an imminent attack. Meanwhile, the Saudis have no concern about the impact on the world economy or U.S. forces. They care only about the survival of the Saud dynasty.

Panetta's comments unintentionally reinforced the Iranian anti-Semitic narrative that Jews are responsible for the world's ills, especially economic ones. He also appeared to be setting Israel up to be the scapegoat for any negative consequences that might follow their actions. Panetta's suggestion that Jews defending themselves from extermination should then be held responsible for any resulting damage to the world economy was a classic case of blaming the victim. Panetta did not stop there, however; he also suggested an attack on Iran would have "a serious impact on U.S. forces in the region." This comment echoed others made by administration officials, such as the suggestion in a Pentagon report that the "perception of U.S. favoritism for Israel" is responsible for anti-American sentiment. The truth is that U.S. troops are targets of Islamic extremists and other anti-American elements in the Middle East because of who they are, what they represent, and their presence in the region, not because of anything Israel says or does. Shouts of "Death to America" in Tehran, Iranian aid to insurgents in Iraq, and plots to kill a Saudi diplomat in Washington have nothing to do with Israel.

The prospect of the world economy being damaged, Iranian counterstrikes, terror attacks, oil price spikes, and other potential negative consequences of a military operation placed great international pressure on Israel's leaders to have faith that the big boys—the P5 + 1, comprised of the five permanent members of the UN Security Council (the United States, Germany, France, Russia, China) plus the United Nations—will take care of the problem and that they should stay out of the way.

Given the fact that Iran could be the first country with the capability to carry out its genocidal threats against the Jews, it should come as no surprise that Israelis refuse to sit quietly in the corner. As the only country that Iran repeatedly threatened to attack and destroy, Israel is uncomfortable trusting its security to others, even its close ally the United States. Israel will not "leave our fate in the hands of other countries, even the best of our best friends," Netanyahu said.[25] Jews have experience with genocidal threats and the failure of the international community to respond to them, so they should be forgiven if they are not willing to risk their future on the decisions of the United Nations, the Europeans, or the United States.

Doubt is widespread, even among some Israeli experts, as to whether the Israel Defense Forces has the capability to carry out an effective strike that would, at a minimum, set the Iranian nuclear program back several years if not destroy it entirely. Israel's chief of staff, Lieutenant General Benny Gantz, however, said the country's military was capable of attacking Iran on its own without foreign support. If necessary, Israel could fight alone without the help of the United States or other countries. "We have our plans and forecasts. . . . If the time comes we'll decide" on whether to take military action, he said.[26]

The conventional wisdom that Israel is incapable of eliminating Iran's nuclear facilities is just that, conventional, and Israel has repeatedly proved that it has the daring and creativity to disprove the skeptics. As early as 1948, Israel surprised U.S. officials, including

Secretary of State George Marshall, by defeating the combined Arab forces that invaded the newly independent country. In 1967, no one anticipated that Israel would surprise their neighbors, destroy their air forces on the ground, and rout their enemies in six days. In 1976, Israel shocked the world when it rescued 102 hostages in Entebbe. In 1981, Israel flew through Arab air space and destroyed Iraq's nuclear reactor. In 2007, an Israeli raid destroyed a suspected Syrian nuclear facility.

A number of military options have been discussed in the press, including the aerial bombardment of Iranian nuclear facilities, the launch of Jericho or submarine-based cruise missiles at Iranian targets, the use of electromagnetic pulses to disable communications, or the use of commandos to storm the enrichment facility housing Iran's centrifuges, remove the enriched uranium, and destroy the facility.[27]

Israel and its allies have not been idle while waiting for sanctions to have an effect. A variety of covert operations were conducted, including the sabotage of equipment used in nuclear facilities, the use of cyber warfare to introduce viruses into Iranian computers to damage centrifuges, and the alleged assassination of at least four nuclear scientists.

Public discussions of the military option assume Iran will respond to any attack; however, Israel attacked both Iraqi and Syrian nuclear facilities and neither country counterattacked Israel. The Iranians know that if they strike back, Israel can respond in devastating fashion. If Iran attacks American targets or interferes with oil supplies, they would provoke an overwhelming U.S. response and might bring other Western powers into the fight.

A military strike on Iran would potentially have serious negative consequences, but Netanyahu argues the cost of *not stopping* Iran's nuclear program is higher.[28] Moreover, as the country on the front line, Israel has far more at stake than the United States, which is a safe 6,000 miles away. Netanyahu faces excruciating choices: If he waits too long to act he puts Israel at risk; if he acts too soon he alienates the world, which wants a peaceful solution; and if he does nothing, he leaves his nation's security at the mercy of the decisions of others.

The Israeli public's view of Israel's options reflect the difficulty of Netanyahu's decision. They would prefer a peaceful, negotiated solution, but most Israelis do not believe that sanctions will stop Iran's nuclear development; fewer than four in ten say Israel can rely on the United States to prevent Iran from obtaining a nuclear weapon, while 57 percent believe Israel has to defend itself. Another poll found that only 22 percent of likely Israeli voters agreed with the statement, "I trust U.S. President Barack Obama to ensure that Iran does not achieve a nuclear weapon"; 64 percent disagreed.[29]

Netanyahu has been widely criticized for harping on the Iranian threat before and during negotiations to reach a diplomatic solution to the problem. A *Washington Post* editorial, however, said proponents of diplomacy over war with Iran should thank Netanyahu for setting a "red line" because it "appears to have accomplished what neither negotiations nor sanctions have yielded: concrete Iranian action to limit its enrichment." The *Post* added, "The credible threat of military action has to be part of any strategy for preventing an Iranian nuclear weapon, and clear red lines can help create the 'time and space for diplomacy.'"[30]

For the moment, the debate regarding the wisdom of a military strike is moot because of an agreement negotiated by the P5+1 and Iran in Geneva on November 24, 2013. The deal was made possible by the June election in which Hassan Rouhani was elected president in what the media interpreted as a shift toward moderation in Iran, which raised hopes that negotiations can finally resolve the stalemate over Iran's nuclear program.

The Geneva agreement is only an interim deal, set for six months, to give world powers time to reach a permanent solution to the nuclear crisis with Iran. Key points of the deal include:

- Iran will stop enriching uranium beyond 5 percent and "neutralize" its stockpile of uranium enriched beyond this point.
- Iran will give greater access to inspectors, including daily access at Natanz and Fordo nuclear sites.
- There will be no further development of the Arak plant, which, it is believed, could produce plutonium.

- In return, there will be no new nuclear-related sanctions for six months if Iran sticks by the accord.
- Iran will also receive sanctions relief worth about $7 billion on sectors including precious metals.

Immediately afterward, Rouhani claimed victory by saying "Iran's right to enrichment has been recognized."[31]

Many people, including a large number of members of Congress, expressed skepticism of the agreement and suspicions about the Iranians. Secretary of State John Kerry told Congress sanctions would not be lifted in a way that reduces the pressure on Iran; nevertheless, 59 senators said they wanted Obama to impose *stiffer* sanctions on Iran to maintain pressure on Tehran to comply with the agreement and UN resolutions. The Senate's skepticism reflected that of the American public. By nearly two-to-one, Americans who heard at least a little about the agreement do not believe Iran's leaders are serious about satisfying international concerns regarding its nuclear program. A plurality of 43 percent disapproved of the agreement while 32 percent approved.[32] Nevertheless, Obama threatened to veto any new sanctions and led a full-court press to derail the legislation, which he said would give Iran an excuse to abandon the negotiations and renege on the agreements they signed. Lacking a veto-proof majority, the senators said they would closely monitor the talks and would move the legislation forward over Obama's objections if Iran does not fulfill its obligations.

Netanyahu called the agreement a "historic mistake." He added, "For years the international community has demanded that Iran cease all uranium enrichment. Now, for the first time, the international community has formally consented that Iran continue its enrichment of uranium." Netanyahu called the steps required of Tehran "cosmetic" and said Iran could easily reverse them.[33]

Critics also fear the Iranians are just going to drag out the negotiations. The precedent was set during the years of talks between the Europeans and Iranians, which achieved nothing except giving Iran time to make further advances in their nuclear program. Ironically, Rouhani was then the chief Iranian negotiator, and he admitted in 2004: "While we were talking with the Europeans in Tehran, we were installing equipment in parts of the [uranium conversion] facility in Isfahan. . . . In fact, by creating a calm environment, we were able to complete the work in Isfahan."[34]

The prospect of Rouhani using a similar tactic has not been lost on the administration. During the 2012 campaign Obama said he will not let the Iranians drag out talks and continue to develop their nuclear capability. "The clock is ticking," the president said. "We're not going to allow Iran to perpetually engage in negotiations that lead nowhere. And I've been very clear to them, you know . . . we have a sense of when they would get breakout capacity, which means that we would not be able to intervene in time to stop their nuclear program, and that clock is ticking."[35]

One reason Rouhani may have agreed to more serious negotiations is in response to Iranian public opinion. While there is no evidence the Iranian leadership responded to the public, it is worth noting that most Iranians are concerned about improving the economy, advancing democracy, protecting political and civil rights, increasing the rights of women, ending corruption, and reforming the government. Surprisingly, the lowest priorities were improving relations with the West, continuing the nuclear enrichment program, and resolving the nuclear confrontation to end sanctions. Despite this order of priorities, polls have also shown that most Iranians believe their country should have a nuclear capability, primarily for nationalist reasons; that is, Iran has the same right to nuclear weapons as any other country. Two-thirds of Iranians support the nuclear effort because they believe they need a deterrent against their enemies and that the country should have the bomb because Iran "is a major nation."[36]

Negotiations resumed weeks later, and the P5+1 and Iran agreed January 12, 2014, on how to implement November's Geneva agreement. "Beginning January 20th, Iran will for the first time start eliminating its stockpile of higher levels of enriched uranium and dismantling some of the infrastructure that makes such enrichment possible," President Obama said. "Iran has agreed to limit its enrichment capability by not installing or starting up additional centrifuges or using next-generation centrifuges. New and more frequent inspections of Iran's nuclear sites will allow the world to verify that

Iran is keeping its commitments. Taken together, these and other steps will advance our goal of preventing Iran from obtaining a nuclear weapon."[37]

More specifically, Iran agreed to take the following steps:

- From January 20, Iran will start diluting its stockpile of 20 percent–enriched uranium.
- All 20 percent–enriched uranium will be gone within six months.
- Daily access will be provided to the Fordo uranium enrichment site near the holy city of Qom.
- Monthly inspections will be allowed at the Arak heavy water reactor.

In exchange, the P5+1 agreed to "modest relief" from sanctions. The United States agreed to release $7 billion of Iranian funds that were frozen and to temporarily suspend sanctions on Iran's imports of goods and services for autos, oil, gold and precious metals.

On January 20, 2014, both sides took the promised steps, and the IAEA verified that Iran stopped producing 20 percent–enriched uranium, disabled the configuration of the centrifuge cascades Iran used to do the enrichment, began diluting its stockpile of 20 percent–enriched uranium, and refrained from installing new centrifuges at Natanz and Fordow. The administration hailed the actions as the first time in nearly a decade that Iran verifiably took steps to roll back some aspects of its nuclear program and halt progress toward further development. A subsequent meeting in February led to an agreement on the framework for continuing talks, but little progress was made afterward when it became clear that the parties could not make a deal by the July deadline and they agreed to extend negotiations another four months.

While Obama boasted of the progress made in the talks, Iranian officials continued to say in public that they have no intention of giving up uranium enrichment or shutting down their nuclear facilities. "Dismantling (the) nuclear program is not on the agenda," said Deputy Foreign Minister Abbas Araghchi.[38]

Commentator George Will is among the critics who believe the agreement does not go far enough to prevent Iran from building a nuclear weapon. "The president says I'm not just unwilling to contain Iran, I'm committed to preventing a nuclear Iran, and he goes beyond that. He said on November 23rd [2013] he wants to be able to verify that Iran cannot build, not that it's not building, but cannot build. Trouble with that is as long as they have the right to enrich, the capacity to enrich, and the stock of low enriched uranium, they can build a weapon. That is why Iran is claiming victory, and I think probably rightly so."[39]

If Iran does indeed cease its nuclear weapons program, this does not mean Israel no longer is in danger. The existential threat will be gone; however, Iran's proxies will continue to conduct terror attacks against Israel and the regime will not change its ideology or attitude toward Jews. The Iranians and other Muslims do not see the campaign to destroy Israel and to pursue a global jihad as a short-term goal; they are patient and prepared to wait for as long as it takes to achieve their objectives. The power of faith should not be underestimated, or the commitment of Iran to restoring its former glory and working toward the creation of a worldwide caliphate. Iranians also believe they have an advantage over the infidels because they love death, whereas the Jews love life. Daniel Goldhagen suggests the Iranians are convinced "the lovers of life can hold out for only so long against people willing to die and to kill for their ultimate goal: Israel and its Jewish people's destruction."[40]

CHAPTER 7

THE GLOBAL JIHAD

The war against Israel is not restricted to the Middle East; it is waged on a global scale. Approximately 1.6 billion Muslims live around the world, and while not all have hostile attitudes, many do express an animus toward Jews. Having bigoted attitudes does not necessarily lead to anti-Semitism or acts of violence; still, the Islamization of the conflict has made not just Israelis but all Jews targets because they represent the evils of Zionism, infidels, and enemies of Allah. Even before the shift from a political to a religious conflict, terrorists targeted Jews worldwide in the 1960s and 1970s (e.g., the hijacking that precipitated the Entebbe operation). These attacks were usually launched on nationalist grounds to draw attention to the Palestinian cause, to coerce governments to release other terrorists, and to create anxiety in Israel and make Jews around the world feel unsafe so long as Palestinian demands were unmet. These terrorists saw their actions as a means to a political end, unlike the Islamist terrorists who seek martyrdom, believe the killing of Jews is a route to Paradise, and see the destruction of Israel as their goal.

Today, threats against the Jews come from Muslims around the world, even from places with few Jews. In Chechnya, for example, where the census found only two Jews, a rebel said, "Whoever does not . . . prepare himself for the liberation of Al-Aqsa is distant from the Muslim nation and will die. . . . The Jews are dispersed and visible, Allah be praised, and it is possible to carry out military actions against them."[1] The threat against Jews in Europe, where the approximately 54 million Muslims outnumber Jews roughly 36 to 1, is especially acute.

Muslim anti-Semites and their apologists sometimes make artificial distinctions between Jews and Zionists, mostly for appearances, since anti-Semitism is considered morally unacceptable in most non-Muslim countries whereas anti-Zionism is widely tolerated as a legitimate expression of distaste for Israeli policies. It's not Jews they oppose, these prevaricators claim, only the evil Zionists who "stole" the land of the Palestinians and perpetrate all manner of crimes against them.

Radical Muslims can be distinguished by their unabashed admission that they are talking about Jews. Purveyors of Jew-hatred and their apologists claim that they are not anti-Jewish, but in word and deed Jews are implicitly and explicitly targeted. In fact, it is not only the Islamists who focus their hatred on Jews. For example, the Arab League announced a Jewish boycott in 1945, nearly four years before Israel won its independence. The wording is explicit: "*Jewish* products and manufactured goods shall be considered undesirable to the Arab countries." All Arab "institutions, organizations, merchants, commission agents and individuals" were called upon "to refuse to deal in, distribute, or consume *Zionist* products or manufactured goods." The terms "Jewish" and "Zionist" were used synonymously to declare an economic boycott against the Jews of Palestine.

The Koran, written hundreds of years before the establishment of Israel, naturally has nothing to say about Zionists but a great deal to say about Jews. For centuries Muslims did not have any reason to see Jews as a threat since they were stateless, powerless, and despised as the descendants of apes and pigs. The radical Muslims we are discussing here use the words *Jew* and *Zionist* interchangeably as "generic slurs" and often criticize both Jews and Zionists in the same sentence.[2] As historian Daniel Goldhagen observes, this conflation has global implications: "Arab and Islamic anti-Semitism has relentlessly provided the general political orientation, and the specific orientation about the need to destroy the Jews *politically*, that fundamentally shapes global anti-Semitism's new nature" (emphasis in the original).[3]

Detractors of Israel often complain that anyone who condemns Israeli policy is labeled an anti-Semite; however, this is rarely true. Nevertheless, explained British author Howard Jacobson, critics of Israel have created the following syllogism to argue that they cannot be anti-Semites: "Not all critics of Israel are anti-Semites. I am a critic of Israel. Therefore I am not an anti-Semite." Using this logic, Jacobson says, anti-Zionism becomes an "inviolable space" and cannot be questioned.[4]

Despite such verbal calisthenics, it is not difficult to distinguish between legitimate criticism and anti-Semitism. The determining factor is the intent of the speaker.

- Legitimate critics accept Israel's right to exist, whereas anti-Semites do not.
- Anti-Semites use double standards when they criticize Israel, for example, denying Israelis the right to pursue their legitimate claims while encouraging the Palestinians to do so.
- Anti-Semites deny Israel the right to defend itself and ignore Jewish victims while blaming Israel for pursuing their murderers.
- Anti-Semites rarely, if ever, make positive statements about Israel.
- Anti-Semites describe Israelis using pejorative terms and hate-speech, suggesting, for example, that they are "racists" or "Nazis."

Critics of Israel are not silenced; to the contrary, they are given platforms at the United Nations, in the media, on college campuses, and on social media. The most outspoken critics of Israeli policies are Israelis themselves, who use their freedom of speech to express their concerns every day. Anti-Semites, however, do not share Israelis' interest in improving the society; their goal is to delegitimize the state in the short run, and destroy it in the long run. There is nothing Israel could do, short of national suicide, to satisfy these critics.

Around the world, anti-Semitism and related anti-Jewish attacks have been increasing. Much of this alarming trend has nothing to do with Islam and is rooted in traditional anti-Semitism. In addition to neo-Nazis, a number of countries have anti-Jewish ultra-nationalist parties, some of which are gaining political strength. As Yossi Melman observed, however, "more and more, the hatred is also surfacing among the growing Muslim communities in various parts of the world, drawing inspiration from the al-Qaeda notion of 'world jihad' against the 'Crusaders (Christians) and Jews,' as decreed by Osama Bin Laden."[5] Thus, Islamists outside the Middle East are motivated to physically attack and harass Jews and Israelis as well as to politically threaten Israel.

The changing demographics of Europe are having a dangerous impact on European Jewry as well as European-Israeli relations. These ties have long been hampered by Europe's dependence on Middle East oil and determination that supporting Israel would alienate their oil suppliers. This remains a problem; however, it is amplified by the growing Muslim populations on the continent.

The influx of Muslims from North Africa and the Middle East occurred at the end of the twentieth century as European birth rates were falling. The shift means that Muslims will have increasing political clout to drive a wedge between Europe and Israel as they become larger percentages of the population (France is 7.5 percent Muslim, Germany 5 percent, the United Kingdom 4.6 percent, and Denmark 4 percent). In France, for example, the Muslim population is ten times larger than the Jewish community, which means, at the very least, Muslims will become a formidable political force that might influence future French policy.

The situation is likely to grow worse if current trends continue with the non-Muslim population declining and the Muslim population growing exponentially. For example, a Pew forecast said that by 2030:

- The total Muslim population in Europe will increase from approximately 18 million to nearly 30 million.
- Muslims are projected to make up more than 10 percent of the total population in ten European countries: Kosovo (93.5

percent), Albania (83.2 percent), Bosnia-Herzegovina (42.7 percent), Republic of Macedonia (40.3 percent), Montenegro (21.5 percent), Bulgaria (15.7 percent), Russia (14.4 percent), Georgia (11.5 percent), France (10.3 percent), and Belgium (10.2 percent).

- Russia will continue to have the largest Muslim population (in absolute numbers) in Europe in 2030. Its Muslim population is expected to rise from 16.4 million in 2010 to 18.6 million in 2030.

- France had a net influx of 66,000 Muslim immigrants in 2010, primarily from North Africa. Spain was expected to see a net gain of 70,000 Muslim immigrants. The United Kingdom's net inflow of Muslim immigrants was nearly 64,000.[6]

The West does not even recognize that it is sowing the seeds for its own possible destruction. One of the few politicians who understands the global threat posed by radical Islam is former British prime minister Tony Blair. "The threat of this radical Islam is not abating," according to Blair. "It is growing. It is spreading across the world. It is destabilizing communities and even nations. It is undermining the possibility of peaceful co-existence in an era of globalization." Look around the world, he says: "There is not a region of the world not adversely affected by Islamism and the ideology is growing." Blair is especially concerned with Europe's 40 million Muslims. "The Muslim Brotherhood and other organizations are increasingly active and they operate without much investigation or constraint. Recent controversy over schools in Birmingham (and similar allegations in France) show heightened levels of concern about Islamist penetration of our own societies." Worse, Blair says, "in the face of this threat we seem curiously reluctant to acknowledge it and powerless to counter it effectively."[7]

While Western countries are open to Muslims and the free practice of their religion. non-Muslims are not welcome in most Muslim countries. This one-sided flow of Muslims, including extremists, has allowed the radicals to find havens in European countries where they can recruit jihadists, plan attacks domestically and abroad, and take advantage of Western democracy to create bases of operations. In Great Britain, for example, Prime Minister David Cameron ordered an investigation to determine whether the Muslim Brotherhood is planning attacks in the Middle East from Britain. Officials are concerned that London has become a hub for the Brotherhood's extremist activities.[8]

Though the percentage of Muslims in Europe has increased, it is not likely to grow to anywhere near a majority. Still, Cameron's actions, as well as those of other European leaders, illustrates their concern about the potential negative impact of Muslims, especially radical Islamists, on their societies and their willingness to respond to the threat.

The impact of demographics is not merely political; it also poses a physical threat to Jews in Europe, where anti-Semitism has become a growing concern for Israel and Diaspora Jewry. A poll of Jews in Belgium, Britain, France, Germany, Hungary, Italy, Latvia, and Sweden conducted in 2013 by the Fundamental Rights Agency (a European Union agency that monitors discrimination and other violations of basic rights) found that nearly one-third of European Jews are considering emigration because they don't feel safe. Two-thirds said they considered anti-Semitism to be a major problem, and 76 percent said the situation had grown worse in the last five years. The Jewish respondents said the threats came from Muslim extremists (27 percent), people with left-wing political views (22 percent), and people with right-wing views (19 percent).[9]

Even American Jews worry about anti-Semitism in Europe, with 38 percent reporting it is a "very serious problem" and another 52 percent calling it "somewhat of a problem." Thus, 90 percent of American Jews believe anti-Semitism is flourishing in Europe. By comparison, 81 percent of American Jews said anti-Semitism is a problem in the United States (14 percent said it is a serious problem). Almost every American Jew (98 percent) in the poll said anti-Semitism is a problem in the Arab/Muslim world; 88 percent said it was very serious.[10]

Clearly, Muslims are not the sole source of anti-Semitism in Europe. Actually, the traditional Christian anti-Semitism of Europe, the ideological extremists on both ends of the political spectrum, and the Muslim radicals are mutually reinforcing. The European environment is vulnerable to anti-Semitic propagandists and provides a nurturing environment for Islamists. The Muslim extremists, meanwhile, provide ammunition and Middle East street cred to the far right and far left. To give one example, Muslim propaganda often accuses Israel of Nazi-like crimes. This charge finds surprisingly fertile ground in Europe, where people rationalize that if the Jews are now behaving like Nazis, they do not need to feel guilty about complicity in the Holocaust.

The danger of the growth of radical Islam in Europe is that it is:

> a philosophy and a way of life that reject democracy, the open society, and, needless to add, Jews. Islamists see Europe as an Islamic-society-in-the-making; attempts by ethnic Europeans or by democratically-minded Muslims to reverse that process, or to reconcile Islam with European and democratic values, are regarded prima facie as "Islamophobia": i.e., a Western war on Islam. Indeed, in the radical Islamic view, any objection or opposition to Islam or to the transformation of Western secular democracy into Islamic theocracy vindicates jihadism as a legitimate form of self-defense.[11]

Public opinion polls present an alarming picture of the attitudes of Muslims in Europe. A Pew study in 2006, for example, asked Muslims and non-Muslims if they have a "favorable or unfavorable opinion of Jews." In the United Kingdom, 7 percent of the general public said they had an unfavorable attitude toward Jews compared with 47 percent of Muslims; in France, the corresponding figures were 13 percent and 28 percent; and in Germany, the results were 22 percent and 44 percent.

The Anti-Defamation League's 2013 study of 100 countries, representing nearly 90 percent of the world's population, created an index of anti-Semitism based on responses to 11 statements that reflect negative stereotypes about Jews. Respondents who said at least 6 out of 11 statements are "probably true" are considered to harbor anti-Semitic attitudes. Overall, 26 percent of the world's population was found to hold anti-Semitic views using this measurement. By far the highest levels of anti-Semitism were found in the Middle East and North Africa (MENA)—74 percent—with the next highest found in Eastern Europe (34 percent) and the figure for English-speaking countries was 13 percent.

The two most widely accepted stereotypes in MENA were "People hate Jews because of the way Jews behave" (75 percent) and "Jews are more loyal to Israel than to this country/the countries they live in" (74 percent). Even Christians in that region ranked far higher than on the index (64 percent) than those in other areas (the next highest is 35 percent in eastern Europe).

The ADL study also found that Muslims are more likely to harbor anti-Semitic views than members of other religions: Muslim (49 percent), Christian (24 percent), no religion (21 percent), Hindu (19 percent). Where they live, however, makes a big difference in the scale of Muslim antipathy toward Jews. Muslims in MENA (75 percent Index Score) are much more likely to harbor anti-Semitic attitudes than Muslims in Asia (37 percent Index Score), Western Europe (29 percent Index Score), Eastern Europe (20 percent Index Score), and sub-Saharan Africa (18 percent Index Score).

ADL also found that the source of information has an impact on attitudes on attitudes toward Jews. Muslims who get their information about Jews from the Internet are much more likely to harbor anti-Semitic views than those who get their information from other sources—Internet (73 percent), religious leaders (54 percent), television (54 percent), newspapers (49 percent), word of mouth (40 percent).

The ADL survey does not distinguish between radical and non-radical Muslims, so these statistics either reflect the views of a cross-section of the Muslim world, only the radicals, or some combination. The bottom line is that roughly half of all Muslims worldwide hold anti-Semitic views. This should send shivers down the necks of Jews, especially those in the Middle East and other countries with high percentages of Muslims.

We must be careful, of course, to distinguish between thoughts and actions. Not everyone will behave in a way that reflects their bigotry. Unfortunately, in the case of radical Muslims, all too many do frequently act violently. Moreover, these statistics indicate that there is a very large pool of Muslims who hold anti-Semitic views and could be radicalized under the right conditions.[12]

A 2005 study found that 46 percent of "religious" Muslims in France had anti-Jewish prejudices, compared to 30 percent of non-practicing Muslims.[13]

In Germany, a 2010 survey of students in four different cities found that anti-Semitic views were significantly higher among Muslims than non-Muslims. When asked if their religion believes that it is "Jews who drive the world to disaster," 16 percent of Muslim students with a Turkish background agreed, as did 26 percent of those with Arab backgrounds.[14]

Günther Jikeli, a visiting scholar in Jewish Studies at Indiana University, interviewed 117 Muslims, with an average age of 19, in London, Paris, and Berlin. He said many openly expressed "classic" anti-Semitic stereotypes about Jews and sometimes expressed the desire to attack Jews in their neighborhoods. They also conflated Jews and Israelis and approvingly made statements such as "Muslims and Jews are enemies." The Muslims indicated their views were common in their social milieu. From the discussions, Jikeli observed: "We know that anti-Semitism is never rational. Yet some Muslim youngsters do not even try justifying their attitudes. For them, if someone is Jewish, that is sufficient reason for their loathing."[15]

Studies in Britain also found that Muslims were nearly eight times more likely to hold unfavorable opinions of Jews than the general population. More than one-third of British Muslims in a second study said Jews were legitimate targets in the struggle for justice in the Middle East.[16]

A Belgian sociologist published a study in 2011 on Dutch-language elementary schools in Brussels and found that 50 percent of Muslim students in second and third grade expressed anti-Semitic views.[17] In 2013, another Belgian study was released that found anti-Semitism was seven times more prevalent among Muslim high school students than among non-Muslim students. More than 50 percent of the Muslim teenagers agreed that "Jews foment war and blame others for it," while 45 percent said "Jews seek to control everything," and 35 percent said "Jews have too much clout in Belgium."[18]

While the surveys in Europe show alarming levels of anti-Semitism, they still are light years away from the hostility of Muslims in the Middle East where, for example, favorable opinions of Jews among Turks, Egyptians, Jordanians, Lebanese, and Pakistanis was in the single digits in Pew's 2008 poll. Looking strictly at the Arab countries in the Middle East, on average, more than 95 percent of respondents had unfavorable impressions of Jews.[19]

Pew surveys found that substantial minorities in several countries believe violence against civilians in the name of Islam is at least sometimes justified, including 40 percent of Muslims in the Palestinian territories, 39 percent in Afghanistan, and 29 percent in Egypt. This survey was conducted in 39 countries that collectively are home to approximately 67 percent of the world's 1.6 billion Muslims.[20]

Anti-Israel Muslim terrorist organizations also enjoy widespread support in the Middle East, but much less support from Muslim countries removed from the Islamic-Jewish conflict (e.g., Pakistan, Malaysia, Nigeria, and Senegal). For example, support for Hamas ranged from 32 percent in Lebanon to 48 percent in the disputed territories to 55 percent in Egypt (before the military coup and crackdown on Hamas). Support for Hezbollah is significantly lower, with support at 19 percent in Egypt, 25 percent in Jordan, 41 percent in Lebanon, and 43 percent in the territories. Support for al-Qaeda is virtually non-existent, with most countries showing support in the single or low double digits, with the exception again of the Palestinians, 34 percent of whom have a somewhat favorable or favorable opinion of the group. Paradoxically, even while expressing sympathy for radical Islamic organizations, respondents also said they were concerned about Islamic extremism in their countries (Egypt, 69 percent; Jordan, 54 percent; 81 percent in Lebanon, and 64 percent in the disputed territories). This poll also found relatively low levels of support for suicide bombing, with the exception of the Palestinians, 62 percent of whom said suicide bombing and other forms of violence against civilian targets is often or sometimes justified to defend Islam from its enemies. The figures for Egypt (25 percent), Lebanon (33 percent), and Jordan (12 percent) were troubling but considerably lower.[21]

The media and apologists for Muslim extremism often try to distinguish between moderates and radicals, but those who are part of the Islamic-Jewish conflict should be termed radical and more radical. The Pew study cited above indicates widespread support for terrorism among Muslim countries in the Middle East. This view was challenged by John Esposito and Dalia Mogahed, authors of a worldwide study conducted by Gallup that claimed to represent 90 percent of all Muslims and reported that only 7 percent are "radicals," which they defined as people who believed that the September 11 attacks were "completely" justified and hold unfavorable opinions of the United States. Consider, however, that 7 percent represents approximately *115 million* Muslims. The report actually significantly underestimated the number of Muslims holding extreme views; the proportion expressing a "radical" view was actually 13.5 percent. Another 23.1 percent said the 9/11 attacks were in some way justified, which means that nearly one-fourth of all Muslims expressed some support for the terror bombings. Middle East analyst Robert Satloff notes that a "moderate" Muslim, according to Esposito and Mogahed, is "a Muslim who hates America, wants to impose Sharia law, supports suicide bombing, and opposes equal rights for women but does not 'completely' justify 9/11."[22]

The situation has become so bad in Europe that historian Robert Wistrich believes the Jewish community there has no future: "The increasingly isolated Jewish communities have become the targets of militant Muslim rage in much of Western Europe. Their synagogues, communal institutions and even cultural centers have steadily been turned into fortresses—for whose maintenance Jews have, in most cases, to bear the cost. No other ethno-religious group in Europe has had to take such drastic measures for its communal security."[23]

Statistics back up Wistrich's concerns. A report by the EU Monitoring Center on Racism and Xenophobia concluded:

It can be said that the anti-Semitic incidents in the monitoring period [2002] were committed above all by right-wing extremists and radical Islamists or young Muslims. . . . Physical attacks on Jews and the desecration and destruction of synagogues were acts mainly committed by young Muslim perpetrators mostly of an Arab descent in the monitoring period. Many of these attacks occurred during or after pro-Palestinian demonstrations, which were also used by radical Islamists for hurling verbal abuse. In addition, Islamic circles were responsible for placing anti-Semitic propaganda in the Internet and in Arab-language media.[24]

Interestingly, this report was leaked but not released by the European Union, presumably because it points out significant Muslim involvement in European anti-Semitism.

In 2012, a report on anti-Semitism in France found that 55 percent of all racist attacks were directed specifically at Jews. Moreover, a majority of the violent attacks against Jewish citizens were being perpetrated by Muslims rather than by neo-Nazis."[25]

In 2012, the European Union's Fundamental Rights Agency (FRA) surveyed self-identified Jews from eight European countries and found that 65 percent believed anti-Semitism was a big or very big problem in their country, and 76 percent said it's gotten worse in the last five years. French Jews were second only to Hungarian Jews (89 percent) in their concern about anti-Semitism, with 85 percent describing it as a "big problem." By comparison, the figure for British respondents was high, 48 percent, but still far below the figure for French Jews. French Jews also see the problem getting worse, with 88 percent of respondents saying it has grown worse the last five years. The everyday fear is reflected in the survey's finding that 20 percent of Jews always avoid publicly wearing, carrying, or displaying anything that would identify them as Jews. The figure jumps to 34 percent in Sweden, 29 percent in France, and 25 percent in Belgium.[26] Nearly one-third (29 percent) have considered emigrating in the past five years because they don't feel safe. The figure is closer to one-half in Hungary (48 percent), France (46 percent), and Belgium (40 percent).

Europeans fear the spread of radical Islam and are especially concerned about threats posed by the growing Muslim communities in their midst. Finding new demons, however, has not freed Europeans from their tradition of Jew-hatred. A poll released in 2012 by the Anti-Defamation League, for example, found that anti-Semitic attitudes in ten European countries (Austria, France, Germany, Hungary, Italy, the Netherlands, Norway, Poland, Spain, and the United Kingdom) were at disturbingly high levels. Since 2009, levels of anti-Semitism increased most dramatically in Hungary, the United Kingdom, and Spain; Austria was the only country in which there was a slight decline.[27]

The negative attitudes toward Jews in Europe carry over to feelings about Israel. Still, the degree of hostility is shocking. In an annual poll of 22 countries conducted by the BBC, Israel was rated as one of the worst countries in the world. In 2012, Israel was rated negatively by 50 percent of respondents, equating it with North Korea, and placing it only ahead of Pakistan (51 percent) and Iran (55 percent).

This is the milieu in which European Jews live. It is difficult to break down how much hostility toward Jews and Israel is due to historic anti-Semitism, Israeli policies, and Muslim and pro-Palestinian propaganda. The problem is not restricted to Europe. Out of 22 countries, the only countries where at least 50 percent of the respondents had a positive view of Israel were the United States and Nigeria. The overall global average was 21 percent positive and 50 percent negative.[28]

While views of Jews are negative, those of Muslims are even more unfavorable. For example, a Pew poll in 2008 found that attitudes toward Jews had grown worse since 2006 in most countries surveyed. They were not as negative, however, as opinions of Muslims, which were also on the upswing.

In Europe, officials may be reluctant to speak out against Muslim anti-Semitism, or violence against Jews, but they are much less hesitant to take measures to restrict Muslim activities and force them to conform to the society. This is especially true in France, where the Muslim population has not assimilated into French culture; one response of the government has been to ban face coverings, a law apparently directed at Muslim women. In Switzerland, Muslims were banned from building new minarets. Intelligence agencies have also been unsparing in their analysis of the terror threats posed by Muslims in their countries. In the United Kingdom, for example, the director-general of MI5, Jonathan Evans, said in 2008 that the Saudi government's multimillion-dollar investments in British universities have led to a "dangerous increase in the spread of extremism in leading university campuses."[29]

Table 7.1   Views of Israel's Influence (%)[30]

Country	Mainly Positive	Mainly Negative	Net Positive/ Negative
USA	50	35	+15
Canada	25	59	−34
Chile	21	34	−13
Mexico	19	44	−15
Brazil	17	58	−41
Peru	11	35	−24
Russia	25	26	−1
France	20	65	−45
UK	16	68	−52
Germany	16	60	−46
Spain	12	74	−62
Nigeria	54	29	+25
Kenya	45	31	+14
Ghana	19	19	0
Egypt	7	85	−78
China	23	45	−22
South Korea	20	69	−49
Australia	18	65	−47
India	17	29	−12
Pakistan	9	59	−50
Indonesia	8	61	−53
Japan	3	45	−42
Global Average	21	50	−29

Table 7.2   Negative Views of Muslims and Jews in Europe (%)[31]

Country	Jews	Muslims	Difference
Spain	46	52	−6
Russia	34	50	−16
Poland	36	46	−10
Germany	25	50	−25
France	20	38	−18
Britain	9	23	−14
USA	7	23	−16

As the European country with the highest Muslim population, it is not surprising that France has the most serious problem with Muslim-Jewish violence. As journalist Bernard Edinger reported, "Spontaneous, unprovoked attacks against Jews, overwhelmingly carried out by young Arabs, have traumatized French Jewry. Young

religious Jews on their own have been officially advised by the rab-
binate to wear baseball caps instead of kippas when using public
transport or in the street."[32]

The most heinous incident was the murder of three French-
Jewish children and a rabbi in the Otzar Hatorah School in Toulouse in 2012; however, a number of other incidents were recorded
throughout the country in 2012:

- January 22: A 16-year-old Jewish girl carrying documents
  with Hebrew letters was attacked exiting the metro in the
  Paris suburb of Montreuil. She was hit, slashed with a knife,
  and taunted with anti-Semitic insults.
- February 16: A young man was mugged in the nineteenth
  arrondissement by four men who stole his wallet and coat.
  When they realized he was Jewish, one mugger said, "This is
  what Israelis do to the Palestinians," and then punched and
  kicked him.
- March 8: Three teens stopped a young Jew on a Montreuil
  street and said they didn't like his kippa or Jews before
  spraying tear gas in his face.
- March 26: An 11-year-old wearing tzitzit was called a "dirty
  Jew" and punched in the face outside her school in the
  thirteenth arrondissement.
- April 30: A young Jew in Marseille was assaulted by a
  group that called him a "dirty Jew" and said they supported
  Palestine and were going to kill him. He was severely beaten
  and the Star of David chain around his neck was stolen.

The attacks on Jews did not begin in 2012; others were recorded
earlier, including:

- A 1982 attack on the Israeli Goldenberg restaurant in Paris
  carried out by Arab terrorists from abroad left six people dead.
- In 2003, a Jewish disc jockey was killed by his Muslim
  neighbor.
- In 2006, a young Jewish man was kidnapped and tortured
  for 24 days before being murdered by a Muslim gang. The

gang leader was brought to trial in 2009 and shouted "Allahu
Akbar," "God is Great."[33]

The danger is being exacerbated by the Islamic Winter, especially
the civil war in Syria. Approximately 3,000 Westerners are fighting
in Syria, and security officials worry that their citizens will return
home radicalized and battle-tested and become active in terrorism.
Jews worry they will be prime targets, and for good reason. On May
24, 2014, a French citizen returning from Syria, where he fought
with an al-Qaeda offshoot, attacked the Jewish Museum in Brussels,
killing three people.[34] Threats do not only come from Syria; a Rand
study reports a 58 percent increase in jihadist groups worldwide.[35]

The entire Muslim community cannot be blamed for the violence, but France's interior minister, Manuel Valls, said the vast majority of anti-Semitic incidents in France were attributable to young
Muslims. "Salafism has bred a new brand of anti-Semitism born
from hatred for Jews, for Israel and for France and its values," Valls
told a TV interviewer in March 2013.[36]

Valls's remarks were consistent with polls showing that eight
out of ten French people believe Islam is trying to impose its views
on others, and 74 percent think Islam is "incompatible with French
values." Whereas 66 percent of respondents consider Jews tolerant,
74 percent see Islam as intolerant. A *Le Figaro* survey found that 43
percent of the French people think that Muslims are a threat to their
national identity.[37]

Roger Cukierman, president of the Conseil Représentatif des Institutions juives de France (Representative Council of French Jewish
Institutions, or CRIF) umbrella group of French Jewish communities, observed that most French-Jewish parents enroll their children
in private schools because of anti-Semitism. "Most of them go to
Jewish or Christian private schools," he said.[38] The situation has
become so serious that 25 percent of French Jews have expressed a
desire to emigrate.

Cukierman noted that the discomfort of Jews around Europe is
not due solely to the growing Muslim population and violence against
Jews. The economy has had an impact, as have government initiatives
in parts of the EU to ban circumcision and kosher slaughter.

Despite the perceptions of danger, and the feeling among many French Jews that there is no future for them in France, immigration to Israel has remained remarkably stable. In 2013, immigration from France jumped 63 percent from 1,916 to 3,120, and the figures at the beginning of 2014 were up 312 percent from the comparable period in 2013.[39] However, Cukierman said, "These figures fluctuate between 1,500 and 3,000 every year, and at their highest represent half a percent of French Jewry. So this is not such a big figure."[40] Nevertheless, wealthy French Jews and other Europeans are buying luxury apartments in Tel Aviv, Jerusalem, and other desirable areas of Israel (and driving up home prices for Israelis), which they rarely inhabit, but apparently see as havens if the situation in France deteriorates.

The United Kingdom has had fewer cases of anti-Jewish violence than France, and British Jews feel safer. While 70 percent of French Jews fear becoming the victim of a hate crime, 28 percent in the United Kingdom are concerned with verbal abuse and 17 percent physical threats. Nevertheless, London is the principal hub for the campaign to delegitimize Israel. Since most British Muslims came from former colonies in Asia, they are more concerned with issues such as the conflict over Kashmir than the Middle East; however, the community has been radicalized over the last two decades by an influx of Middle Eastern Arabs, including several leading activists and thinkers, and organizations such as the Muslim Association of Britain, which is affiliated with the Muslim Brotherhood.[41]

Today, anti-Semitic literature is widely available in the British Muslim community and disseminated through libraries, mosques, and bookstores. One study found that Muslims were responsible for 30 percent of the anti-Semitic incidents in Britain even though they comprise only 3 percent of the population. Another study found that 37 percent of British Muslims believe British Jews are legitimate targets as part of the struggle for justice in the Middle East.[42]

Smaller communities throughout Europe seem to be especially vulnerable. In Norway, a country that has grown increasingly hostile to Israel, the largest anti-Semitic riots in the country's history took place during Israel's Operation Cast Lead in Gaza in 2009. The participants were all Muslims. Ironically, the demonstrations occurred in Oslo, the birthplace of the first Palestinian-Israeli peace agreement.

Approximately 700 Jews, mostly descendants of World War II refugees from Poland and Germany, live in Malmö, Sweden's third-largest city, whose population of 300,000 is now estimated to be nearly one-fifth Muslim. Unlike larger communities, the Jews of Malmö feel isolated and receive little support from outside organizations or the local government. Now considered "the capital of European anti-Semitism," Jews are targets of physical and verbal attacks, primarily by Muslims, and have reported record numbers of hate crimes. In 2010 and 2011, those complaints did not result in a single conviction. The city's synagogue has guards and rocket-proof glass in the windows, while the Jewish kindergarten can only be reached through thick steel security doors.

Judith Popinski, an 86-year-old Auschwitz survivor, told the *Daily Telegraph* that she is no longer invited to schools that have a large Muslim presence to tell her story of surviving the Holocaust. "Muslim schoolchildren often ignore me now when I talk about my experiences in the camps," she said. "It is because of what their parents tell them about Jews. The hatreds of the Middle East have come to Malmö. Schools in Muslim areas of the city simply won't invite Holocaust survivors to speak any more." She was especially shocked when a small demonstration supporting Israel during its operation in Gaza in 2009 was attacked by "a screaming mob of Arabs and Swedish leftists, who threw bottles and firecrackers as the police looked on." This was the worst incident, Popinski said. "I haven't seen hatred like that for decades," she recalled. "It reminded me of what I saw in my youth. Jews feel vulnerable here now." Not surprisingly, Jews have started to leave Malmö for Israel and other countries.[43]

Also in 2009, Israel was scheduled to play Sweden in a Davis Cup tennis match in Malmö, but critics of Israeli policy wanted to cancel the tournament, which would have resulted in an automatic forfeit and elimination from the Cup tournament. It was too late to move the match, so the event went on as scheduled, but, due to security concerns, the three-day match was played in an empty stadium, during which Israel eliminated the Swedish team. More than 6,000 pro-Palestinian protesters, one of the largest demonstrations against Israel in Swedish history, came to the stadium, and subsequent riots led to violent clashes and multiple arrests. Malmö was subsequently banned from hosting any further Davis Cup matches, fined $25,000 by the International Tennis Federation, and forced to pay an additional $15,000 to recoup revenues lost when spectators were barred from the match.[44]

Robert Wistrich notes that countries such as Belgium and "rabidly anti-Israel" Norway, which have small Jewish communities already outnumbered by Muslims, are under siege from "the hostile attitude of many of the elites, and a remorseless anti-Zionist incitement in the media that inevitably inflames latent anti-Semitic reflexes." Hostility to Israel, he adds, has "become the daily bread of European public discourse." Wistrich believes the situation in Europe is becoming so dangerous that "any clear-sighted and sensible Jew who has a sense of history would understand that this is the time to get out."[45] Former Dutch defense minister Professor Frits Bolkestein, was equally adamant talking specifically about Jews in the Netherlands. "Jews have to realize," he said, "that there is no future for them in the Netherlands and that they best advise their children to leave for the United States or Israel."[46]

It is noteworthy that the shifting demographics, Muslim terror, growing anti-Semitism, media bias, and tendency to blame Israel for all the Middle East's problems has not had much impact on European-Israeli relations. If anything, Israeli-European ties have grown stronger in the last decade. The EU is Israel's largest trading partner and a variety of agreements have enhanced cooperation in trade, diplomacy, science, and other areas. In January 2014, for example, Israel was invited to become the twenty-first member of CERN, the European Organization for Nuclear Research. Israel's ties with NATO have also expanded, with Israel increasingly being included in joint exercises, counterterrorism, and other areas of military cooperation. The settlement issue remains an irritant, but leaders of Italy, Germany, England, and France have been very pro-Israel in recent years.

Muslim anti-Semitism outside the Middle East has multiple roots. Inspiration can be found in the Koran, the media, sermons, the Internet, and the policies of Israel. It is also taught to Muslims in schools and mosques throughout the world, financed primarily by Saudi Arabia. The Saudis budget more than $4 billion annually for Islamic activities with the objective of indoctrinating Muslims with their Wahhabi beliefs and the conviction that Islam "is the superior religion and must always be so."[47]

In 2012, a Canadian Islamic school lost its license to use Toronto District School Board property after it was discovered the curriculum disparaged Jews and encouraged boys to keep fit for jihad. Jews were referred to as "crafty" and "treacherous," and Islam was contrasted with "the Jews and the Nazis." Children were taught that Islam was the "best" religion and given a list of "unclean things" that included pigs, dogs, and people who do not believe in Allah. According to the FBI, the materials were taken from books supported by the Iranian government.[48]

At the Islamic Saudi Academy in Fairfax, Virginia, maps of the Middle East were missing one country. Students were taught that the "Jews conspired against Islam," and an eleventh-grade textbook said that on the Day of Judgment, the trees will say, "Oh Muslim, Oh servant of God, here is a Jew hiding behind me. Come here and kill him." A twelfth-grade Islamic studies textbook quoted a Koranic verse: "It is said: The apes are the people of the Sabbath, the Jews. The swine are the unbelievers of Jesus' table, the Christians." Students told a *Washington Post* reporter that in Islamic studies they were taught that they should shun or dislike Christians, Jews, and Shiite Muslims. A revised textbook called jihad "the pinnacle of Islam" and extolled the virtues of martyrdom.[49]

The situation in Britain isn't much better. Textbooks found in 2010 in more than three dozen British Islamic schools and clubs "promoted dehumanizing and demonizing anti-Semitism, including the notion that Jews descended from 'monkeys' and 'pigs,' and tasking the schoolchildren to list the 'reprehensible qualities of Jews.'"[50]

If these are the lessons that have gotten through the educational system's filters in Canada, Britain, and the United States, you can imagine how much worse the Saudi-produced textbooks must be in other countries and, especially, in the 1,500 Saudi-funded madrassas. Actually, you don't have to use your imagination as the following are examples of lessons disseminated by the Saudis:

- "The clash between this [Muslim] nation and the Jews and Christians has endured, and it will continue as long as God wills."

- "In Islamic law, however, [jihad] has two uses: One usage is specific. It means to exert effort to wage war against the unbelievers and tyrants." "In its general usage, 'jihad' is divided into the following categories: . . . Wrestling with the infidels by calling them to the faith and battling against them."
- "As cited in Ibn Abbas: The apes are Jews, the people of the Sabbath; while the swine are Christians, the infidels of the communion of Jesus."
- "You can hardly find an example of sedition in which the Jews have not played a role."[51]

The Center for Religious Freedom report on Saudi textbooks notes that "Wahhabi teachings . . . are murderously intolerant toward the Shi'a, Jews, Baha'i, Ahmadiyya, homosexuals, apostates and 'unbelievers' of all kinds, and horribly repressive with respect to everyone else, especially women. The ultimate Wahhabi objective is quite clear from a wide range of their writings—the establishment of a world-wide theocratic dictatorship, the caliphate. These are essentially the same basic beliefs as those expressed by al-Qaeda."[52] Even the U.S. State Department conceded that the Saudi textbooks "contain some overtly intolerant statements against Jews and Christians and subtly intolerant statements against Shi'a and other religious groups."[53]

It is much more difficult to find out what lessons are being taught in mosques, except for when imams make vitriolic sermons in public. British filmmakers in London, however, went undercover at the London Central Mosque, considered one of the most prestigious in Britain, and their subsequent documentary reportedly exposed imams teaching "the faithful that God orders them to kill homosexuals and apostates; that they should curtail the freedom of women; and that they should view non-Muslims in a derogatory manner and limit contact with them."[54] Similarly, a study of Islamic schools in Britain found that some of the 166 full-time institutions taught the rejection of Western values and hatred of Jews.[55]

The Internet and social media now allow radical Islamists to spread their messages around the globe. Thousands of web sites, blogs, Facebook pages, and Twitter accounts are available to extremists to share information, terrorist know-how (e.g., bomb building), and anti-Semitic propaganda. Videos on YouTube spread virally to reach far more people than anti-Semites could ever hope to have reached in the past. In fact, "one person knowing four languages, or three people each knowing two of the four—English, Spanish, Arabic and French—can post an anti-Semitic article or video, or cartoon or image, or accusation in those languages, potentially reach more than two billion people, and readily seed the entire world for translations or transcriptions into every language and for every community in the world."[56]

Calling out the Muslim extremists leaves one vulnerable to the charge of being "Islamophobic," a term invented to mirror the word "anti-Semitic" and portray all those who criticize Muslims as bigots. Even as Muslims continue to be arrested for attempted and actual terror attacks, the Arab lobby uses this smear to insulate radical Muslims from scrutiny, incite anger among Muslims, and make non-Muslims feel guilty. Undoubtedly, some people hold bigoted views toward Muslims; however, it is not an irrational fear (i.e., a phobia) to worry about the threat of radical Islam given that its adherents are indeed dangerous and have given non-Muslims legitimate cause to be afraid (e.g., 9/11).

In the United States, since a brief but relatively limited outburst of anti-Muslim incidents following 9/11, apologists for terror and radicalism propagate the myth of widespread Islamophobia and use the slur to intimidate and silence any critics. The FBI's annual hate statistics, however, consistently show that incidents targeting Muslims are a small fraction of those directed at Jews, who remain the number one target of hate crimes in America. Hate crimes against Muslims peaked at 481 in 2001 (26 percent of all religious hate crimes compared to 57 percent committed against Jews) but declined significantly afterward. Of the 1,322 incidents of anti-religious hate crimes reported in 2012, 887 or 67 percent were anti-Jewish; 130 incidents or 10 percent involved Muslim victims.

Muslim anti-Semitism, meanwhile, gets a pass outside the United States. For human rights organizations, the UN, and leftist Europeans it is an "unmentionable prejudice,"[57] so they remain silent on the subject out of fear of alienating Muslims, having their progressive anti-racist credentials questioned, losing access to the

Muslim world, risking commercial relations, and provoking terror attacks in their cities.

Ironically, Jews are targeted by anti-Semitism and charged with Islamophobia for speaking out against Muslim extremism. This is doubly strange because polls show that Jews in Western nations are more tolerant than other groups.[58]

Jews are not only subjected to anti-Semitism; they are also targets of terrorism. Since the mid-1990s, Muslim-inspired attacks outside the Middle East have become the norm. From 2002–2010, 51 attacks and failed plots targeted Jews and Israelis; 39 were conducted by al-Qaeda, its affiliates, Lashkar-e-Taiba, and others associated with the global jihad movement.[59]

The principal sponsors of Islamic-based terrorism are Iran and Saudi Arabia. In the war against the Jews, both have supported terror groups targeting Jews and Israelis. The former primarily supports Shiite terror groups such as Hezbollah, while the latter backs Sunni groups. Osama bin Laden and 15 of the 19 hijackers on 9/11 were Saudis, and a report to the United Nations on terror financing concluded that Saudi bankers and businessmen had transferred as much as half a billion dollars to al-Qaeda in one decade.[60]

European Muslims are a heterogeneous group with representatives from around the world, many of whom do not agree on interpretations of Islam or Middle East politics. Because of their colonial ties, France has a large population of Arabs from North Africa, for example, while Britain's Muslims come mostly from Asia. A minority regularly worships at mosques, and no Muslim organizations represent a significant percentage of the Muslims in any European country. The most influential group—though, again, it represents a limited number of people—is the radical Muslim Brotherhood. On a pan-European basis, the European Council of Fatwa is well known because of its leader, Yusuf al-Qaradawi, an ideologue for the Muslim Brotherhood and a purveyor of anti-Semitic propaganda.

Though bin Laden had little interest in Jews prior to 9/11, his successor, Ayman al-Zawahiri, has called for attacks against Israelis and Jews. In one of his videotapes, al-Zawahiri responded to a question about why al-Qaeda had not attacked Israel:

Does the person asking the question not know that al-Qaeda struck the Jews in Djerba, Tunisia [on April 11, 2002, a truck full of explosives was detonated near the synagogue, killing 21 people and wounding over 30], and Israeli tourists in their hotel [on November 28, 2002, a truck blew up killing 13 and injuring 80] in Mombasa? We promise our Muslim brothers that we will do our best to strike the Jews both inside and outside Israel and, with the help of Allah, we will succeed.

Al-Zawahiri could have also mentioned a number of other attacks by Muslims from various organizations, including:

- In 2002, *Wall Street Journal* reporter Daniel Pearl was kidnapped and beheaded in Pakistan.
- Economic development expert Warren Weinstein, 72, was kidnapped in Pakistan in 2011 and remained in captivity as of June 2014.
- Six Jews were murdered at the Chabad center in Mumbai, India in 2008.
- Assaults were carried out on the El Al ticket counter in Los Angeles (2002), the Jewish Federation in Seattle (2006), synagogues in the Bronx (2009), and a rabbi's house in Nashville (2010).
- One of the six Muslim terrorists who planned to kill U.S. soldiers at Fort Dix, New Jersey, told an informant that his first choice was to kill Jews in Israel. "I love to kill Jews," he said. "I tell you this, in all honesty, it is a dream of mine."[61]

Even before 9/11, Iran was engaged in terror attacks against Jews and developed especially close ties with several nations in South America, providing another base from which to pursue their jihad against Israel. The most heinous attacks were carried out in Buenos Aires, Argentina.

On March 17, 1992, the Israeli embassy in Buenos Aires was the target of a car bomb that killed 29 people and injured more than 250 others. Among the victims were Israeli diplomats, children, clergy from a church located across the street, and other passersby. The investigation languished for more than two years until July 18, 1994, when the Asociación Mutual Israelita Argentina (AMIA) Jewish community center in Buenos Aires was bombed, killing 87 people and wounding more than 100.

Later in 1994 came the first of several breakthroughs in the embassy bombing case. Six Lebanese citizens and one Brazilian, arrested for operating a drug cache, were found to be members of Hezbollah. The Argentine government immediately announced that the men were tied to the embassy bombing; however, after several days the supposed suspects were released due to a lack of evidence. In 1998, a telephone call intercepted from the Iranian embassy in Argentina demonstrated conclusively that Iran had been involved in the attack on the embassy. Argentina expelled six Iranian diplomats from the country, but that was the extent of their action and it was never determined which individuals were culpable for the attack.

For a number of years the case remained dormant, but in 2005 a 21-year-old Lebanese citizen, Ibrahim Hussein Berro, was identified as the suicide bomber who blew up the Jewish community center in 1994. A year later prosecutors accused top officials within the government of Iran with orchestrating the bombing and Hezbollah for carrying it out. Their indictment stated that the decision to approve the bombing was ultimately made by Iranian supreme leader Ali Khamenei, but other senior government members were also part of the discussion, including then-president Ali Akbar Hashemi Rafsanjani, Foreign Minister Ali Akbar Velayati, Intelligence Minister Ali Fallahijan, and National Security Council secretary Hassan Rouhani (now Iran's president). In 2007, Argentine authorities secured Interpol arrest warrants for five Iranians and a Lebanese over the AMIA attack, but they were never apprehended.

In March 2012, an Argentinian judge accused former president Carlos Menem and other former officials of concealing evidence and protecting accomplices in the bombing. That year, the Argentine government also issued arrest warrants for Iranian defense minister Ahmad Vahidi and former president Akbar Hashemi Rafsanjani. Despite these developments, not one person has been convicted for either bombing.

Shockingly, in January 2013, Argentine foreign minister Héctor Timerman signed a memorandum of understanding with Iran intended to resolve the cases surrounding the two terrorist bombings. Argentinian Jewish leaders were outraged at the decision to involve Iran in a "truth commission" investigating a crime that Iran was accused of orchestrating.

Though Islamic Jihad claimed responsibility for the 1992 bombing, Argentine, Israeli, and U.S. officials believe the AMIA attack was carried out by Hezbollah terrorists backed by Iran.

Iran and Hezbollah have also been implicated in a variety of other attacks, both before and after the bombings in Argentina. These include:

- The bombing of Jewish communal institutions in Paris in 1986.
- A failed car bombing at a Jewish community building in Bucharest in 1992.
- A failed ambush of a Turkish Jewish leader in 1993.

More recently, attempted terrorist attacks were thwarted in Hungary, India, Turkey, Thailand, and Azerbaijan. In 2012, local law enforcement and intelligence agencies foiled a terror plot in Cyprus, where a Hezbollah operative was arrested and later convicted for his role in a plan to attack Israeli tourists. On July 18, 2012, Hezbollah terrorists were involved in bombing a bus carrying Israeli tourists in Burgas, Bulgaria, which killed five Israelis and injured 32, as well as killed the Bulgarian bus driver. It is likely that many other plans are uncovered without any publicity.

It was only after Hezbollah's complicity in the Bulgaria attack was proven that the European Union, after great debate, finally designated Hezbollah's "armed wing" as a terrorist organization. The decision came after roughly two decades of terror attacks and still maintained the specious distinction between Hezbollah's armed and political wings. Meanwhile, two Hezbollah terrorists (a third, Imad Mughniyah, was believed to be assassinated by Israel) remain on the FBI's list of most wanted terrorists for the hijacking of TWA Flight 847 in 1985 during which a U.S. Navy diver was murdered.

As Iran has become more isolated by the West because of its nuclear program, it has found willing allies in Latin America, especially in Hugo Chavez and his successor in Venezuela, who is helping Iran to obtain arms, identification documents, bank accounts, and routes to transfer operatives and equipment between the two countries and elsewhere in the region. Iran also increased the number of its embassies in Latin America from 5 to 11, doubled its trade with the region, and launched a Spanish-language channel. Furthermore, drug traffickers with links to Iran are reportedly operating a cocaine network in Colombia, Venezuela, and Panama that is providing funds to Hezbollah.[62] Iran is also recruiting students from all over Latin America to a madrassa for Hispanics in the city of Qom, where they are being taught about Islam, encouraged to convert, and indoctrinated with anti-American propaganda.[63]

Iran did not get into the terror business until after the revolution in 1979; however, the Saudis have funded terrorists for decades. "The Saudis are active at every level of the terror chain, from planners to financiers, from cadre to foot soldier, from ideologist to cheerleader," Rand Corporation analyst Laurent Murawiec told the Defense Policy Board on July 10, 2002.[64] In June 2003, David Aufhauser, general counsel for the U.S. Treasury Department, told the Senate Judiciary Committee that Saudi Arabia is the "epicenter" of terrorist financing. On the sixth anniversary of the 9/11 attacks, Undersecretary of the Treasury for Terrorism and Financial Intelligence Stuart Levey said, "If I could somehow snap my fingers and cut off the funding from one country, it would be Saudi Arabia," and, in April 2008, he reiterated that Saudi Arabia remained the world's leading source of money for al-Qaeda and other extremist networks.[65]

Saudi support for terror against Jews has been primarily focused on Israel, with Saudi officials and individuals backing Hamas at times and Fatah at others. Saudis have not been directly involved in attacks in Israel, but they have financed the terrorists as well as the families of "martyrs."

The Islamist war against Israel is not limited to a violent jihad; it is also conducted in the political and economic arenas. In addition to the campaigns conducted by individual Muslim countries, the prime mover behind the international effort to isolate and ultimately destroy Israel is the Organization of Islamic Cooperation. The OIC, originally called the Organization of the Islamic Conference, was founded in 1969 following the humiliation of Arab armies in the 1967 War and the arson attack on the al-Aqsa Mosque on August 21, 1969. Israel was naturally blamed by the Muslim world for the attack, which reinforced the "al-Aqsa is in danger" libel, but the perpetrator was actually an Australian citizen who was arrested, tried, and found to be insane.

The OIC "is the collective voice of the Muslim world," which works "to safeguard and protect the interests of the Muslim world in the spirit of promoting international peace and harmony."[66] It is the largest international organization outside the United Nations, has 57 members, and, as a permanent delegation to the UN, effectively multiplies the influence of Muslim countries in international forums. As a bloc, the OIC nations represent 30 percent of the voting members of the UN. This means that on any Israel-related issue that comes before the General Assembly, and to some degree the Security Council, non-Muslim nations have a strong incentive to vote with the OIC bloc because opposing the Muslim countries will alienate at least 57 countries while winning the gratitude of only Israel and, usually, the United States. Most countries are afraid to take such a stand knowing that when an issue of importance to them arises, they may find the OIC as a roadblock.

Though it is not a wholly Islamic campaign, the Islamic countries have led the onslaught on Israel at the UN, typically with the support of the feckless Europeans, whose fear of antagonizing Muslims and oil producers, as well as risking potentially lucrative arms sales, shapes their attitudes at international forums. These concerns have been a motivating force for UN votes since the debate over partition, decades before the creation of the OIC.

In the years following the partition vote, a decision the Arabs rejected by force, Israel has routinely been condemned by the UN and many of its affiliates. Most years, more resolutions condemning Israel are introduced than for all other countries combined. Expensive bureaucracies (funded largely by U.S. taxpayers) have been created for the sole purpose of promoting the Palestinian cause and implicitly or explicitly attacking Israel. In 1975, the UN established the Committee on the Inalienable Rights of the Palestinian People, which is essentially a propaganda organization that issues stamps, organizes meetings, prepares films, and drafts resolutions in support of Palestinian "rights." The committees are primarily Israel-bashing entities, none of which are interested in rights such as freedom of speech, religion or assembly, let alone women's rights or gay rights, all of which are denied to Palestinians by *their* leaders.

Millions of dollars support approximately 20 committees and organizations dedicated to the Palestinian issue, including the United Nations Relief and Works Agency for Palestine Refugees in the Near East; the Division for Palestinian Rights; the Special Committee to Investigate Israeli Practices Affecting the Human Rights of the Palestinian People and Other Arabs of the Occupied Territories; and the Committee on the Exercise of the Inalienable Rights of the Palestinian People. Most of these organizations exist primarily for the purpose of vilifying Israel rather than promoting peace between Israel and the Palestinians. The UN declared 2014 the "International Year of Solidarity with the Palestinian People" even as thousands of Africans and Syrians were being slaughtered and people in countries such as Saudi Arabia, China, Russia, and Cuba are being deprived their human rights.

The OIC has worked with nongovernmental organizations and member states to demonize and delegitimize Israel. In 1975, the General Assembly approved Resolution 3379, which slandered Zionism by branding it a form of racism. Seventy-two nations, a majority from the Islamic bloc, voted to deny the Jewish people the same right to self-determination granted to other peoples. Only 35 members, including Israel, opposed this anti-Semitic resolution.

Israel is the only country whose right to exist is challenged. Even bigots who hate Germans, Argentines, Poles, Vietnamese, or any other people do not question the legitimacy of their countries. Abba Eban, a former Israeli ambassador to the UN, dismissed the efforts to delegitimize his country. "Nobody does Israel any service by proclaiming its 'right to exist,'" he said. "Israel's right to exist, like that of the United States, Saudi Arabia and 152 other states, is axiomatic and unreserved. Israel's legitimacy is not suspended in midair awaiting acknowledgement. . . . There is certainly no other state, big or small, young or old, that would consider mere recognition of its 'right to exist' a favor, or a negotiable concession."[67]

The Zionism resolution was repealed in 1991 by a wide margin, 111–25; however, 13 of the 19 Arab countries, including those engaged in negotiations with Israel—Syria, Lebanon, and Jordan—voted to retain the resolution, as did Saudi Arabia. Six, including Egypt—which lobbied against repeal—were absent. No Arab country voted for repeal. The Arabs "voted yet once again to impugn the very birthright of the Jewish State," the New York Times editorialized. "That even now most Arab states cling to a demeaning and vicious doctrine mars an otherwise belated triumph for sense and conscience."[68]

The repeal did little to erase the stain on the liberation movement of the Jewish people, and the specious equation stuck and remains a staple of anti-Israel propaganda.

The vote on Zionism also made no impact on the onslaught of anti-Israel resolutions. Less than a week before repealing the measure, the General Assembly approved four new one-sided resolutions on the Middle East. In fact, the same day the Zionism resolution was repealed, the UN voted 152–1, with the United States abstaining, to call on Israel to rescind a Knesset resolution declaring Jerusalem its capital; demand Israel's withdrawal from "occupied territories," including Jerusalem; and denounce Israeli administration of the Golan Heights.

The OIC and its allies increasingly found that UN-affiliated groups provided easy opportunities to criticize and isolate Israel. For example, in October 2013, the United Nations Educational, Scientific and Cultural Organization (UNESCO) voted in favor of at least six resolutions singling out Israel for condemnation at the instigation of the Arab and Islamic bloc. UNESCO censured Israel over a variety of issues, including the preservation of archaeological sites in the Old City, the construction of a visitors' center, plans to build an elevator by the Western Wall, accusations of archeological excavations said to be damaging Muslim sites atop the Temple Mount, the alleged deterioration of educational and cultural institutions in the West Bank and the Gaza Strip, and plans to invest in places it considers national heritage sites, such as the Tomb of the Patriarchs.

The worst example of how the UN is used by the anti-Semites rather than standing against them is the Human Rights Council. The HRC was established in 2006 to replace the former Commission on Human Rights, which had become a travesty after allowing some of the worst human rights violators to participate in deliberations and to adopt a steady stream of one-sided condemnations of Israel. The General Assembly created a new body ostensibly to erase the stain on the UN left by the original organization. In the first months of operation, however, the new council proved to be worse than the original. Of the 47 members, 17 were members of the Organization of the Islamic Conference, and repressive dictatorships such as China and Cuba were members. The council still has human rights abusers, such as China, Saudi Arabia, Russia, and Cuba as members.

While Western nations struggled to focus the HRC's attention on international crises in Africa and elsewhere, the majority of council members prefer to produce reports criticizing Israel. For example, the HRC did not criticize Hezbollah for attacking Israel, kidnapping its soldiers, indiscriminately firing missiles at Israel, or using Lebanese civilians as shields, but it did condemn Israel for "violations of human rights and breaches of international humanitarian law in Lebanon." When a report was produced that criticized Hezbollah as well as Israel, the Muslim members of the HRC rejected it.

After these embarrassing votes, UN secretary-general Kofi Annan warned the council that it might be discredited, as was its predecessor. He noted that in its first five months the council had focused heavily on the Arab-Israeli conflict, holding three special sessions to approve resolutions condemning alleged violations by the Jewish state. "There are surely other situations, besides the one in the Middle East, which would merit scrutiny at a special session," he said. "I would suggest that Darfur is a glaring case in point."[69]

The situation only grew worse when Richard Falk became the UN's monitor of human rights violations by Israel in the Palestinian territories. He was given no mandate to investigate Palestinian human rights abuses against Israelis and showed no interest in them. Falk took the position with a well-known bias, having compared Israel's treatment of Palestinians with the Nazi's treatment of Jews during the Holocaust.[70] After taking the position, Falk repeatedly made spurious accusations against Israel and drew strong U.S. State Department condemnation in December 2013 for suggesting that Israel is "genocidal." U.S. State Department spokeswoman Jen Psaki said, "The Administration has repeatedly condemned in the strongest terms his despicable and deeply offensive comments, particularly his anti-Semitic blog postings, his endorsement of 9/11 conspiracy theories, and more recently, his deplorable statements with regard to the terrorist attacks in Boston."[71]

Following Israel's Cast Lead Operation in Gaza in December 2008–January 2009, the HRC appointed a fact-finding mission to investigate whether any violations of international humanitarian law took place during the conflict. No one was surprised when the four-person panel, led by Judge Richard Goldstone, issued a report highly critical of Israel, which based virtually all of its conclusions on unverified accounts by Palestinians and NGOs. The Goldstone Commission fixated on Israel's incursion into Gaza while failing to adequately address the provocation—three years of Hamas rocket bombardment of Israeli towns and villages—that led to the Israeli operation.

Ironically, Hamas undermined claims by Goldstone and other critics of Israel who insisted the victims of the war were mostly innocent civilians when Hamas interior minister Fathi Hammad admitted in 2010 that it lost more than 600 fighters during the war. This is consistent with the figure of 709 calculated by the Israel Defense Forces.[72]

Goldstone later retracted the report's accusations that Israel intentionally targeted civilians and was guilty of war crimes. He also admitted the work used by Israel's detractors to vilify Israel was based on incomplete information and falsely accused Israel of wrongdoing. Goldstone conceded that "if I had known then what I know now, the Goldstone Report would have been a different document."[73]

The report, which inaccurately asserted that Israel led a "deliberately disproportionate attack designed to punish, humiliate and terrorize a civilian population," became a tool for Israel's detractors to demonize the Jewish state and denigrate its right to self-defense. Goldstone subsequently acknowledged that "civilians were not intentionally targeted [by Israel] as a matter of policy" and that in the aftermath of having thousands of rockets and missiles fired at its cities, Israel had the "right and obligation to defend itself and its citizens against such attacks."[74] In fact, as Colonel Richard Kemp, former commander of British forces in Afghanistan, testified to the Goldstone committee in 2009, "The IDF did more to safeguard the rights of civilians in a combat zone than any other army in the history of warfare."[75]

Goldstone later emphasized that the attacks by Hamas were war crimes regardless of the number of Israeli casualties. "That comparatively few Israelis have been killed by the unlawful rocket and mortar attacks from Gaza," Goldstone acknowledged, "in no way minimizes their criminality."[76] He added that Hamas's actions during the conflict were intentional and "purposefully indiscriminate." Goldstone also criticized the Human Rights Council for taking a position that was "skewed against Israel."

Even UN secretary-general Kofi Annan admitted that Israel is often unfairly judged at the United Nations: "On one side, supporters of Israel feel that it is harshly judged by standards that are not applied to its enemies," he said. "And too often this is true, particularly in some UN bodies."[77]

None of the UN's anti-Israel activities come as a surprise anymore. The General Assembly resembles a convocation of the flat-earth society rather than a deliberative body of world leaders seeking peace. The UN is also saturated with anti-Semitic and anti-Zionist sentiment. The following comments illustrate how ugly the atmosphere has become:

- "The Talmud says that if a Jew does not drink every year the blood of a non-Jewish man, he will be damned for eternity."—Saudi Arabian delegate Marouf al-Dawalibi before the 1984 UN Human Rights Commission conference on religious tolerance.[78]
- At a 1991 meeting, a similar remark was made by the Syrian ambassador, who urged delegates to read *The Matzah of Zion*, which insisted Jews killed Christian children to use their blood to make matzos.[79]

- On March 11, 1997, the Palestinian representative to the UN Human Rights Commission claimed the Israeli government had injected 300 Palestinian children with the HIV virus.[80]
- In July 2005, Jean Ziegler, the UN special rapporteur on the Right to Food, called the Gaza Strip "an immense concentration camp" and compared Israelis to Nazis.[81]
- In April 2012, the Palestinian Authority's minister for prisoner's affairs told a UN committee that "there was a call at the highest level of the Israeli state for concentration camps to be set up for the rounding up and extermination of Palestinian people."[82]

In 2003, the first resolution explicitly condemning anti-Semitism was offered in the General Assembly, but its sponsor, Ireland, later withdrew it due to lack of support.

While anti-Semitism is considered acceptable, the OIC has actively lobbied for the adoption of new laws around the world protecting Islam from criticism. In 2009, the Human Rights Council passed a resolution supporting the OIC position, though it was framed as seeking the protection of "religion" in general. This did not fool members of the HRC, and 11 mostly Western nations opposed the proposition and another 13 abstained. The goal of the OIC was to criminalize any portrayals of Islam they find objectionable, such as cartoons depicting the Prophet Muhammad, anything they regard as "Islamophobia," and criticism of Islamic beliefs. "Islam is frequently and wrongly associated with human rights violations and terrorism," the resolution said, making clear that criticism of the human rights practices of Muslim states or discussion of Islamic extremism or Muslim involvement in terrorism should be outlawed. The resolution, sponsored by Pakistan, also was meant to encourage and justify Islamic Sharia-based blasphemy laws like those in Pakistan.

Philosopher Austin Dacey observed that the UN is engaged in an "Inquisition" to silence criticism of extremist organizations, religions, and sacred persons. He said the organization "conflates peaceful criticism of Islam with anti-Muslim bigotry and seeks to stifle free speech in the name of 'respect for religious beliefs.'"[83]

Another key forum in which the OIC and its allies successfully demonized Israel was the 2001 UN World Conference against Racism in Durban, South Africa. The United States and Israel walked out of this Israel-bashing festival, which inspired an international campaign to delegitimize Israel. The NGO forum's final declaration described Israel as a state that was guilty of "racist crimes including war crimes, acts of genocide and ethnic cleansing." The declaration established an action plan—the "Durban Strategy"—promoting "a policy of complete and total isolation of Israel . . . the imposition of mandatory and comprehensive sanctions and embargoes, the full cessation of all links (diplomatic, economic, social, aid, military co-operation and training) between all states and Israel."[84]

Proponents of these views are Israel deniers. Like Holocaust deniers who ignore facts, the Israel deniers invent their own narrative, which precludes Jews from exercising the same rights as other peoples and ultimately rejects the Jewish right to self-determination in its homeland, Israel.

The Israel deniers want to convince the world that the Jews are evil, they have no historical connection to any part of the Holy Land, they are not a people, they have no right to a state, and they pose a danger to others; therefore, it is justifiable to destroy Israel and the Jewish people. The first step, however, is to turn Israel into a pariah.

The effort to isolate Israel and to link its policies to those of the former regime in South Africa has spread around the world and manifests itself in efforts to convince unions, universities, artists, companies, and others to boycott Israel, divest from companies doing business in or with Israel, and impose sanctions on Israel. The hope is that the international community will put sufficient pressure on Israel to force it to capitulate to Palestinian demands and, ideally, to bring about its destruction. The Boycott, Divestment and Sanctions (BDS) campaign, which would more accurately be called the Bigotry, Demonization and Slander movement, has had some success in damaging Israel's image as a democratic bastion that protects human rights; however, the movement has had virtually no impact on Israel's diplomatic or trade relations. In fact, for all the talk of boycotts, Israel's trade with Europe, the United States, and Asia is booming.

BDS activities are indiscriminate: They harm those Israelis who are most actively campaigning for peace and strengthen those who are more skeptical of peace initiatives. BDS reinforces the views of the cynics who do not believe that any compromise will satisfy the Palestinians, and undermines the peace activists who believe the Palestinians would trade peace for land. Rather than encourage compromise, efforts to isolate Israel only make its citizens feel more vulnerable and raise the already high level of risk associated with evacuating additional territory.

Moreover, the BDS activists have made it clear they have no interest in promoting peace or helping the Palestinians achieve independence. They oppose a two-state solution and advocate the creation of one state that will replace Israel. A founder of the movement, Omar Barghouti (who called for boycotting Israeli universities even while attending Tel Aviv University), explains the BDS agenda:

The two-state solution for the Palestinian-Israeli conflict is finally dead. But someone has to issue an official death certificate before the rotting corpse is given a proper burial and we can all move on and explore the more just, moral and therefore enduring alternative for peaceful coexistence between Jews and Arabs in Mandate Palestine: the one-state solution.[85]

Barghouti is referring to one Islamic state replacing Israel.

As two members of the American Jewish Committee in Europe noted, there are moderate Muslims who speak out against radicalism and try to steer young Muslims away from extremism and anti-Semitism, but too few are willing to do so in Europe or elsewhere. Moreover, their voices are drowned out by the more numerous and affluent Saudis, Qataris, and other Middle Eastern Muslims who fund mosques and schools that spread extremist brands of Islam, and are now supporting Islamist groups seeking to overthrow the regimes in Iraq and Syria. Furthermore, the surfeit of radical Muslim Internet sites, Facebook pages, and other social media has made it impossible to stem the flow of venom emanating from the Middle East and Israel deniers around the world.[86]

Criticism of Islam is already largely squelched through intimidation, violence, and threats of violence. While it's been said that in response to anti-Semitic attacks Jews will talk you to death, Muslims have demonstrated they will actually kill their critics. Evidence of this includes the fatwa calling for the murder of Salman Rushdie after Ayatollah Khomeini deemed his book *Satanic Verses* blasphemous; the worldwide outbreak of violence and threats against the Danish artist and publisher of cartoons depicting the Prophet; and the murder of Dutch film director Theo van Gogh after he made a movie dealing with violence against women in some Islamic societies (the film's writer, Ayaan Hirsi Ali, received death threats and spent time in hiding).

What makes the Islamic-Jewish conflict unique, disturbing, and dangerous is that it is indeed global. As Goldhagen explains:

> Even during the Nazi period, when the threat facing Jews in the Germans' orbit was far more acute, and certainly the prospect of a German military victory mortally imperiled all Jews, in most of the world Jews did not have to walk around fearing physical assault. Global anti-Semitism—with the substantial exception of the United States—equals a global, if variable physical threat.[87]

CHAPTER 8

JERUSALEM

GROUND ZERO OF THE CONFLICT

Anyone who doubts the conflict is rooted in religion need look no further than Jerusalem. Every aspect of the dispute is on display in discussions about Jerusalem. The holy city is the place where all the elements of Middle East conflict intersect: politics, history, psychology, and geography. All of those factors, however, are trumped by the role of religion.

Geographically and strategically, Jerusalem is roughly in the center of Israel. It is built on a hilltop with a strategic view of the valleys below. Today, most of Israel's population and industry live within a narrow belt in the center of Israel, which would be in rocket range of terrorists based in or near Jerusalem. For Palestinians, the city is also in the center of their hoped-for state and has strategic value for defending that state against Israel.

Psychologically, Jews feel that Jerusalem is a source of strength and symbol of their ancient connection to the land of Israel. The Muslims find it unimaginable that Jews should control their holy places.

Politically, Jerusalem has become the capital of Israel and no Israeli is willing to change that status, though some are willing to find a compromise that cedes the Palestinians part of the city and some degree of control.

Religiously, Jerusalem is the place where the holy temple once stood, the place Jews still consider the holiest in Judaism, and the place where many believe the Messiah will arrive. Many Arabs/ Muslims do not acknowledge any Jewish connection to the city, and yet they are aware of the Jewish tradition that the Messiah will enter Jerusalem through the Golden (or Mercy) Gate (located on the far side of the Temple Mount opposite the Western Wall). Constructed in the post-Byzantine period around 640, Muslims during the rule of Suleiman the Magnificent (1520–1566) sealed the gate to prevent the Jewish Messiah from coming, and also placed a cemetery outside the city wall because of the tradition that the Messiah will be from the priestly caste of kohanim, who are not permitted to enter cemeteries.

While Jews trace their connection to Jerusalem back more than 3,000 years, the Muslim connection dates back less than 1,500 years. Jerusalem is not mentioned once by name in the Koran, and, in fact, it is not the city that is revered by the Muslims; it is only the al-Aqsa Mosque (built in 705) where they believe Muhammad took his night flight to heaven in the year 620. According to Muslim tradition, Muhammad went to visit the Farthest Mosque (which many Muslims believe is the al-Aqsa Mosque in Jerusalem) on the back of Al-Buraq, a winged creature (portrayed often as Pegasus-like) and then ascended to heaven with the angel Gabriel. Some Muslims believe Muhammad left from the holy rock that is now within the Dome of the Rock (a shrine built in 691).

The city is also important to Christians because it is the place Jesus lived and died. This religious significance makes Jerusalem important not only for the Jews, Christians, and Muslims who live in and around the city, but it makes the city important to the people of those faiths around the world. This international sense of ownership makes the city unique and leads people from around the world to believe they should have a say in its final status.

For centuries under Arab rule, Jerusalem was a backwater, neglected except during times of conflict when the city became a prize for invaders. Small numbers of Jews always lived in the city, and larger numbers began to arrive in the nineteenth century. From 1844 on, Jews have comprised the majority of Jerusalem's population,

Table 8.1   Jerusalem's Population[1]

Year	Jews	Muslims	Christians	Total
1844	7,120	5,000	3,390	15,510
1876	12,000	7,560	5,470	25,030
1896	28,112	8,560	8,748	45,420
1922	33,971	13,411	4,699	52,081
1931	51,222	19,894	19,335	90,451
1948	100,000	40,000	25,000	165,000
1967	195,700	54,963	12,646	263,309
1987	340,000	121,000	14,000	475,000
1990	378,200	131,800	14,400	524,400
2000	530,400	204,100	14,700	758,300
2012	660,200	310,700	16,500	987,400

growing from around 7,000 to nearly 700,000 today (two-thirds of the city's total).

Anyone who has seen a picture of the Western Wall today would not recognize the same place 100 years ago. Instead of a large, spacious plaza for worshippers, Arab homes nearly abutted the wall, and only a narrow alleyway was open for Jewish prayer. The Jews had to bribe local authorities to allow them to bring benches to sit on or arks with Torah scrolls to conduct prayers. Jews attempted to buy land near the wall and, at one point, sought permission to repair part of the wall, but were unsuccessful. The efforts did, however, frighten the Muslims, who thought the Jews were plotting to take over the Temple Mount and rebuild their temple. This was never the Jews' intention, but it marked the beginning of a repetitive charge against the Jews that continues to this day.

This first of many subsequent battles over the Western Wall and Temple Mount also led the Palestinians away from nationalism and toward Islamism. The controversy "moved a nascent Palestinian national movement from a discussion of self-determination and majority rights—concepts borrowed from the political vocabulary of Europe—to a more familiar defense of Islam and Islamic territory against the Jews."[2]

This sense of international ownership, combined with the irreconcilable positions of Jews and Muslims, led the UN to exclude the city from both the Jewish and Arab states when it introduced the partition resolution in 1947. The city was to be a demilitarized zone, not a part of either the Jewish or the Arab state, and under the governance of a trusteeship council administering the city on behalf of the United Nations.

The Arabs rejected the entire partition resolution and considered the Jerusalem decision an additional insult. For the Jews, cutting the heart out of the new state was devastating. It also left 100,000 Jews isolated in the Old City, surrounded by the Arab state. The Jews, nevertheless, agreed to the partition plan because they recognized partition would not pass otherwise, and, at that point, the most important step was to establish an internationally recognized state as soon as possible, even if it was not quite the state they had been promised in the Balfour Declaration. David Ben-Gurion swallowed the internationalization of Jerusalem because the partition resolution stipulated that the inhabitants of Jerusalem would decide the city's future in a plebiscite after ten years, and he was confident the Jews, who formed the majority of the population, would win the election and vote to incorporate the city into the Jewish state.

The one Arab force the Jews did not succeed in expelling in their war for independence was the British armed, trained, and commanded Arab Legion. Consequently, the war left Transjordan in control of the West Bank and roughly one-third of Jerusalem, including the Old City. None of the Arab states recognized King Abdullah's annexation of the territory. He ignored them and all criticism over his illegal and illegitimate action.

The surviving inhabitants of the Jewish Quarter were evacuated to the New City, the four-fifths of the capital the defenders had succeeded in holding. Losing the Old City was bad enough, but the defeat was compounded by Abdullah's decision to bar Jews from their holy places. The United Nations, the Vatican, and others who had expressed great concern over the future of the city and the freedom of all to worship there quickly lost interest in their commitment to internationalization and acceded to Jordan's occupation for the next 19 years.

The international community also turned a blind eye to Jordan's desecration of Jewish holy places. Hundreds of Torah scrolls and other holy books were stolen, defaced, and burned. Synagogues were

Table 8.2   The Population of Jerusalem Prior to Partition

Year	Jews	Percent	Muslims	Percent	Christians	Percent	Others	Percent	Total
1922	33,971	54.3	13,413	21.4	14,699	23.5	495	.8	62,578
1931	51,222	56.6	19,894	22.0	19,335	21.4	52	.0	90,503
1944	97,000	61.7	30,630	19.5	29,350	18.7	100	.1	157,080
1946	99,320	60.4	33,680	20.4	31,330	19.1	110	.1	164,410

razed or plundered before their interiors were used as hen houses and stables, filled with dung-heaps, garbage, and carcasses, or as sites for latrines and sewage canals. Even the Jewish dead were not safe as graves were defiled and bones scattered; tombstones from the ancient Mount of Olives were broken and used for stepping stones and to build roads, walls, and latrines, while part of the cemetery was converted into parking lots and a filling station. Neither Jews nor Israeli Christians were allowed into the occupied areas to pray at their shrines.

This all happened on the international community's watch after the king had promised to protect the holy places. The world only became concerned with the status of Jerusalem when Israel captured the city in 1967.

After centuries of neglect, Muslims began to pay closer attention to the part of Jerusalem Israel made its capital in 1949. David Ben-Gurion told the UN on December 5, 1949:

> Jerusalem is the "heart of hearts" of Israel. . . . A Nation which over 2,500 years has always maintained the pledge vowed by the banished people on the rivers of Babylon, not to forget Jerusalem—this nation will never sanction its separation. [Moreover], Jewish Jerusalem will never accept foreign rule after thousands of her sons and daughters have freed, for the third time, their historic homeland and delivered Jerusalem from destruction. . . . Israelis are ready to sacrifice themselves for Jerusalem no less than the English for London, the Russians for Moscow, and the Americans for Washington.[3]

Jerusalem never served as the capital for any Arab or Muslim state; nevertheless, the Muslims and Arabs were determined to prevent the city from remaining part of Israel. To head off opposition, Israel quickly moved to solidify its claim to the city by holding the first Knesset meeting in the city on February 14, 1949.

The formal decision to make Jerusalem Israel's capital was made on December 11, 1949, spurred by a UN General Assembly resolution two days earlier reaffirming the partition plan to internationalize the city. The Vatican was particularly angered by Israel's actions, the division of the city, and the loss of control over its holy places, and it led the effort in the years after 1948 to convince the UN to vote anew to internationalize the city. Votes were taken in 1948, 1949, 1950, and 1952, but only the first two were adopted, and the others failed to win the necessary two-thirds majority.

Israel categorically rejected any change in the status of the city. Ben-Gurion said that because the partition decision was never implemented, "'the decision of 29 November on Jerusalem is null and void.'"[4]

After 1952, the UN lost interest in Jerusalem, and no other votes were held until after the city's reunification during the 1967 War and Israel's decision to annex the city on June 11, 1967. Despite Israel's assurances regarding freedom of access to the city and freedom of worship for all faiths, censure was quick. Arab and Muslim states— which never recognized Jordan's control of the West Bank and Jerusalem, but also never condemned its occupation at the UN—began to introduce resolutions condemning Israel's actions and calling for them to be rescinded. After 1971, the United Nations Educational, Scientific and Cultural Organization (UNESCO) became the primary forum to attack Israel's annexation of Jerusalem. The General Assembly did not return to the issue until 1981, when annual resolutions denouncing Israel resumed. The Security Council first addressed the issue in 1968, calling on Israel to cancel a planned military parade in Jerusalem. Later, another resolution was adopted demanding that Israel desist from taking any action to alter the status of Jerusalem. Similar language was repeated in subsequent UN resolutions.

All of Israel's government ministries moved to Jerusalem except the Defense and Foreign ministries. When the Foreign Ministry shifted to the capital in 1953, Israel was subject to a new round of condemnations, led by the United States and the United Kingdom, which boycotted the ministry. Eventually, the uproar faded and diplomatic missions began setting up in Jerusalem. By 1972, 23 of the 47 diplomatic missions in Israel, most from Latin America and Africa, were in Jerusalem. In 1974, however, under pressure from the Arab oil-producing states, all of the embassies in Jerusalem were closed and relocated to Tel Aviv. Even after the oil embargo ended, only Costa Rica and El Salvador reopened embassies in Jerusalem.

In 2006, both decided to move their embassies back to Tel Aviv after the UN passed a resolution saying that Israel's declaration of Jerusalem as its capital violated international law.

In 1990, Congress passed a resolution declaring that "Jerusalem is and should remain the capital of the State of Israel" and "must remain an undivided city in which the rights of every ethnic and religious group are protected." Five years later, Congress overwhelmingly passed the Jerusalem Embassy Act of 1995, which reiterated that Jerusalem should be Israel's capital and required that the U.S. embassy in Israel be established in Jerusalem no later than May 1999. The law also included a waiver, however, that allowed the U.S. president to ignore the legislation if he deemed doing so to be in the best interest of the United States. Every president has invoked that waiver since it was adopted, and so, more than 15 years later, the embassy remains in Tel Aviv, creating the anomaly that of the more than 180 nations with which America has diplomatic relations, Israel is the only one where the United States does not recognize the capital or have its embassy located in that city. The U.S. embassy in Tel Aviv is 40 miles from Jerusalem. The United States maintains a consulate in East Jerusalem that deals with Palestinians in the territories and works independently of the embassy, reporting directly to Washington. Thus, we have the incongruous situation whereby American diplomats refuse to meet with Israelis in their capital because Jerusalem's status is negotiable, but they do business with Palestinians who claim Jerusalem as their capital.

The position of repeated administrations reflects the Arabist mentality that has dominated U.S. Middle East policy-making for decades. Arabists are so afraid of the Muslim reaction to any U.S. recognition of Jerusalem that the U.S. State Department rejected a passport application from an American Jew born in Jerusalem who wanted his birthplace listed as Israel. Congress passed a law to allow this, but the courts backed the administration and ruled it unconstitutional.

If the U.S. embassy moved to Jerusalem, would the Muslim world rise up against America? Certainly many Muslims would be upset, but the populations are mostly controlled by autocratic rulers who would have to allow them to demonstrate. In light of the Arab

Spring, the last thing the dictators want is a large number of protesters in the streets who might turn their ire from Israel and the United States toward their own leaders.

The United States might face new terrorism threats from radical Muslims in reaction to the embassy's relocation, but the terrorists don't need any new excuse to target America; they do it already. Another possibility is that Muslim countries will try to blackmail the United States and any other country that considers moving its embassy. We know of at least one instance where this already occurred. In 1979, the Canadian government announced it would move its embassy to Jerusalem; shortly thereafter Saudi Arabia and Kuwait canceled more than $400 million worth of contracts with Canadian firms and threatened to withdraw their deposits from Canadian banks. The value of the Canadian dollar sank and the country faced a potential economic crisis. The government subsequently decided to postpone the embassy move indefinitely.

While countries such as Saudi Arabia can blackmail most countries to stay away from Jerusalem, the Saudis and others need the United States more than we need them, and, though the Arabists would raise the alarm that we must cave in to these countries, the reality is that we do not have to. There would be the requisite condemnations at the UN, but eventually they would get used to the facts on the ground, just as they have been forced to accept Israel's control of the city. More important, perhaps, by moving the embassy and leaving no doubt as to U.S. recognition of Jerusalem as the united capital of Israel, the seemingly intractable issue of meeting Palestinian and Israeli demands would be solved. The Palestinians would have to accept the fact that they will not rule over Jerusalem.

Once Israel captured and reunited the city in 1967, the government could have fulfilled the prayer Jews recite calling for the Temple to be rebuilt speedily in our days. Instead, General Moshe Dayan immediately ordered that the Israeli flag placed on the Temple Mount by Israeli paratroopers following the battle over the Old City be removed. Dayan also told his men to ensure that no harm come to any of the holy places of the Christians or Muslims. The Protection of Holy Places Law passed later by the Knesset criminalized any acts against shrines or interference in the freedom of worship.

Dayan also decided that Jews should not be permitted to pray on the Temple Mount. He understood that as important as the city was to the Jewish people, if the sensitivities of other faiths, especially Islam, were not respected, Jerusalem could be the catalyst for turning the political conflict instantly into a religious one. Dayan recognized that the Temple Mount was primarily a historical site for Jews, but it was a sacred place for Muslims. According to Nadav Shragai, the defense minister believed:

> Islam must be allowed to express its religious sovereignty—as opposed to national sovereignty—over the mount; that the Arab-Israeli conflict must be kept on the territorial-national level; and that the potential for a conflict between the Jewish religion and the Muslim religion must be removed. In granting Jews the right to visit the mount, Dayan sought to placate the Jewish demands for worship and sovereignty there. In giving religious sovereignty of the mount to the Muslims, he believed he was defusing the site as a center of Palestinian nationalism.[5]

Dayan's view was sensitive, compromising, evenhanded, and wrong.

The Palestinians never showed any special interest in the city during the Jordanian occupation; their concern only arose when Israel reunited Jerusalem in 1967. Even then, Israel's expectation was that any compromise regarding the city would be with Jordan rather than the Palestinians.

Today, outside Israel (and even among some Israeli Jews), it's taken for granted that the Palestinians are entitled to make Jerusalem—or at least the eastern part—the capital of a future Palestinian state. It may be the first time in history that a people has obtained international support for taking control of an area where few of their people live, where they do not own the land, and where they have no legitimate claim to sovereignty. Boiled down, the Palestinian claim to Jerusalem amounts to a childlike bully's demand—I want it, and if I don't get what I want, I will hurt you.

Though typically ignored today, the basis for all peace discussions since 1967 has been UN Resolution 242, which intentionally omitted any reference to Jerusalem and certainly did not foresee or mandate Palestinian control over any part of the city. In fact, the Palestinians are not mentioned at all in the resolution because they were not viewed as having any national claims and were expected to be absorbed back into Jordan where most had lived under occupation since 1949.

So where does this totally indefensible claim that the Palestinians should be entitled to a state with Jerusalem as its capital arise? And why does anyone accept it?

The explanation can be found in a combination of politics, religion, and bigotry. For Muslims, Jerusalem, like the rest of Israel, rests on Islamic territory that cannot be held by non-Muslims and is inhabited by Muslims who cannot be ruled by Jews. Palestinians can argue that they should control the Temple Mount because they are Muslims; however, the Palestinians do not just want sovereignty over Muslim holy places, they want the entire Old City and the rest of East Jerusalem to be the capital of a Palestinian state. They claim that East Jerusalem is fundamentally Arab; however, this is untrue. The main reason that the area is predominantly Palestinian today is because Jordan prevented any Jews from entering that part of the city during its 19-year occupation. Before 1865, however, the entire population of Jerusalem lived behind the Old City walls, which today is considered part of East Jerusalem. At the time of partition, a thriving Jewish community was living in the area, which included the Jewish Quarter that had to be evacuated following the Jordanian takeover. This part of the city also has the most holy place in Judaism, the Western Wall, as well as the City of David, the Mount of Olives Cemetery, and the Temple Mount.

Despite the historical facts, the international community has backed Palestinian demands for a state with Jerusalem as its capital for pragmatic political reasons. Many Western countries are afraid of the backlash from Muslim countries, especially the oil producers, if they were to recognize Israel's sovereignty over the city. In addition, because the Palestinians insist they will not compromise on their demands, the international community believes it must support their position as the only way to achieve peace. No country, including the United States, can imagine a scenario that would allow Israel to retain control of the entire city. Since Israel insists that Jerusalem remain the undivided capital of Israel, the future of the city is a matter of controversy, and resolution of the issue is believed by many to be the biggest impediment to a comprehensive peace. This ignores more fundamental obstacles, such as the unwillingness of the Palestinians to agree to end the conflict under any circumstances and the radical Islamic rejection of the legitimacy of a Jewish state.

In 2000, Israeli prime minister Ehud Barak offered to withdraw from roughly 97 percent of the West Bank and establish a Palestinian state with certain rights in Jerusalem, including full sovereignty over the Temple Mount. Nevertheless, Arafat refused to concede anything because he was afraid to be seen compromising on a holy spot of Islam. He also would not admit that Jews had any right to the city; in fact, he went so far as to deny the Jewish connection to the city, insisting that no Jewish Temple ever existed on the Temple Mount. Arafat's opinion was consistent with that of many Muslims who consider the idea of a Jewish Temple a figment of the Jews' imagination. One poll found that 72 percent of Palestinians deny "that Jews have a long history in Jerusalem going back thousands of years."[6] Today, it is Palestinian Authority policy to negate Jewish history by using the term "alleged Temple."[7]

Denying the Jewish connection to Jerusalem typically takes three forms: It is said that Jews were present in the city for a short period and therefore they have no claim to sovereignty over the city; that the Temple of Solomon was actually an ancient Muslim building or did not exist at all; and that the Western Wall is sacred to Muslims and did not become a place of veneration for Jews until the nineteenth century. These are recent Palestinian propaganda points designed to erase the Jewish connection to the city, but the Supreme Muslim Council published a guide to the Temple Mount in 1924 that acknowledged it was the site of Solomon's Temple.

For now, Jerusalem remains a rallying point for Palestinians and other Muslims. The "al-Aqsa is in danger libel," as Nadav Shragai calls it,[8] dates back at least to the 1920s, when the mufti of Jerusalem used the lie to incite the masses. Even more secular Palestinians recognize the use of Islamic imagery as a sure way to unite the masses. Beyond the manipulation, however, the connection between Palestinian nationalists and terrorists and Islamism is evident in the repeated use of the al-Aqsa Mosque for political purposes. For example, Fatah's terror organization is called the al-Aqsa Martyrs' Brigade. The second intifada, which was planned by the PLO but blamed on Ariel Sharon's September 2000 visit to the Temple Mount, is referred to as the al-Aqsa Intifada.

Eighty years after Haj Amin el-Husseini challenged the Jews' right to live in their homeland and their connection to Jerusalem, the mufti of Jerusalem, Sheikh Akrama Sabri, made similar claims. He complained that Muslims hadn't sacrificed enough to liberate al-Aqsa. Like the former mufti, Sabri is a rabid anti-Semite who said that he is "filled with wrath toward the Jews," who he believed were scheming to take over not only Palestine but the whole world, and that he "never wished a Jew peace."[9]

It is not surprising that Muslims outside Israel have also used al-Aqsa as a rallying point. The Muslim Brotherhood's Sheikh Yusuf al-Qaradawi, for example, said "the danger to al-Aqsa is now greater than ever . . . and hence the Muslims of the world must arise and defend it because it is not the property of the Palestinians alone but of the whole Muslim nation."[10]

One of the most frequent uses of the al-Aqsa libel occurs when Israel engages in any archaeological activity in Jerusalem. Dating back more than 3,000 years, the city has a rich past that was unexplored for centuries. In fact, prior to 1967, few excavations were done in the city. After the Muslim Wakf was given responsibility for the Temple Mount, this policy was continued. The authorities are concerned about damage to the Muslim sites, but given the care taken by archaeologists to protect the area, the more likely objection is the fear that researchers will make discoveries that support existing evidence of the longstanding Jewish association with Jerusalem and the Land of Israel, which would contradict Muslim propaganda claims denying such a connection.

Due to Muslim objections to archaeological research, we know relatively little about the history of the Temple Mount. Worse, actions by the Wakf have contributed to the destruction of evidence from the past and, ironically, have created the greatest threat to the stability of the Temple Mount. This was especially true when, in the mid-1990s, the Israeli Islamic Movement began the process of converting an area in the southeastern corner of the mount known as Solomon's Stables (so named because the Crusaders had used the area as stables and believed it was located near Solomon's Temple) into a mosque.

This area had never been used as a Muslim prayer area; nevertheless, Israeli officials allowed Muslims to pray there and to renovate it. Today, it is a huge mosque that can hold 10,000 worshippers.

Israel's decision to allow the Muslims to use the area for a mosque was not as controversial in the end as the careless way the excavation was conducted. Because it is nearly impossible to walk anywhere in Israel without stepping on a spot with some historical meaning, all building projects are undertaken cautiously to protect anything that might have archaeological significance. This includes not only artifacts but layers of earth that can sometimes tell the story of different time periods and civilizations. None of this concerned the Wakf, which ordered trucks to carry the dirt and rocks from the work site and dump it outside the city in the middle of the night. Israeli archaeologists later sifted through the debris and found relics and other evidence of the past, but were upset when they realized how much they might have discovered if they had been involved in the excavation.

Israel has done extensive research along the length of the Western Wall and a short distance from the southern side of the Temple Mount. Whenever Israel engages in any excavations, however, the Muslims inevitably protest. The most serious brouhaha arose in 1996 after Israel completed digging along the entire length of the Western Wall, revealing 2,000-year-old stones where the street had once been. The entire project was completely outside the Temple Mount and nowhere near the mosques. Nevertheless, the Muslim authorities claimed the Jews were digging under the mount with the intention of destroying the mosques or at least undermining their foundations. While the work had been going on for some time, the spark that led to widespread rioting and international condemnation was Prime Minister Netanyahu's decision to open an exit from what is now referred to as the Western Wall tunnel, at a point along the Via Dolorosa in the Muslim Quarter of the city. Prior to opening the exit, visitors to the tunnel had to walk from the end back the way they came and, in narrow spaces, barely could fit past people coming from the other direction. The new exit made it possible to avoid backtracking so thousands more visitors could enjoy the site.

The exit was opened in the middle of the night in the hope of minimizing the reaction, but Arafat and others criticized Israel, and the Arab League repeated the libel by claiming "Israel's aim in opening this gate is to cause the collapse of the al-Aqsa Mosque, so that it can build the Third Temple in its stead."[11] Palestinians rioted and attacks on soldiers and civilians resulted in the deaths of 15 Israeli soldiers and dozens of injuries. Forty Palestinians died in the melee, and hundreds more were injured.

The libel has been extended to provoke riots even when Israeli excavations and construction are nowhere near the Temple Mount. This was the case, for example, when Israel rebuilt the Hurva Synagogue in the center of the Jewish Quarter. This synagogue had been destroyed in 1948 by the Jordanians and finally rebuilt by Israel in 2010. Despite its remote location from the Mount, repetition of the libel led to two days of rioting.

Muslims have not let up in perpetuating the al-Aqsa libel or in contending that every Israeli action in the area of the Temple Mount is an affront to Islam. In 2004, for example, the only access for non-Muslims to the Temple Mount, a ramp leading to the Mughrabi Gate, partially collapsed. After several years of planning, Israel decided the old ramp should be replaced with a sturdier permanent one. Once again, Palestinian and Muslim officials accused Israel of destroying a "historical pathway to the al-Aqsa Mosque" and new plots against the mosque itself even though the ramp was outside the mount. Israel brought in experts, including representatives of UNESCO to testify to the fact that a new ramp would not cause any damage to the Mount; nevertheless, the uproar led Israel to make a number of compromises regarding excavations in the area. The date for replacing the ramp was delayed, and when the Arab Spring began, it was postponed indefinitely out of fear that it might provoke a reaction from Muslims in Egypt and Jordan and further destabilize the two countries with whom Israel shared a peace treaty. Ultimately, the old ramp was renovated and fortified, but the plan for replacing it was delayed indefinitely.

In 2013, tensions escalated when Palestinians began to protest and, in some cases, attack Jews visiting the Temple Mount with stones, bottles, and other projectiles. They claimed Jews desecrate Islam's holy place and plan to build the third temple on the site. On February 25, 2014, the PA minister of religious affairs, Mahmoud Al-Habbash, told a television interviewer that Israel plans to destroy the al-Aqsa Mosque and the Dome of the Rock.[12] The repetition of the libel rarely has anything to do with the behavior of Jews; it inevitably is used for a political purpose, such as rallying the masses, provoking violence, or diverting attention from some unpopular action taken by Palestinian leaders, such as returning to peace talks before Israel satisfies their preconditions.

Jews, like other non-Muslims, have been visiting the Temple Mount since 1967. The Israeli government limits visits by non-Jews to specific times and also insists that visitors show sensitivity to Muslims by dressing modestly and refraining from bringing any Jewish sacred objects or conducting any public prayers. The Israeli Supreme Court has ruled that Jews may pray at the Temple Mount, but police were given the discretion to prevent any provocative activities. Most Orthodox Jews do not go to the area because their rabbinical authorities have said they should not step foot in an area where the Ark of the Covenant may have been kept (no one knows for sure where the inner sanctum of the Temple was located on the Temple Mount) and only the high priest was permitted to enter. Israeli politicians have on occasion been barred from going to the area when security officials anticipate the visits might cause disturbances. Extremist Jewish groups suspected of plotting against Muslim shrines are either prohibited from the Temple Mount altogether or escorted by police. When plots against the mosque have been uncovered, the schemers have been arrested.

Occasionally, for security reasons, Israel bars or limits Muslim visitors to the Temple Mount. The rest of the time the area is accessible to Muslims, even those who come from countries that are technically at war with Israel, such as Anwar Sadat, who prayed at the al-Aqsa Mosque on his visit to Jerusalem. On major Muslim holidays, especially Ramadan, tens of thousands of Muslims pray on the Temple Mount.

In September 2013, Jordan condemned Israel for building a platform for women and other non-Orthodox worshippers who wanted
a place to pray according to their own customs. Ultra-Orthodox Jews
control the Western Wall plaza and impose restrictions on worshippers there. They insist, for example, that men and women pray on
separate sides of a barrier and bar women from singing or wearing
prayer shawls or yarmulkes. Jordan claimed the platform was built
in the courtyard of the al-Aqsa Mosque complex and represented a
"flagrant" attack on historical Islamic sites and should be removed.
In fact, the platform was built in an archaeological park south of the
Temple Mount and is nowhere near the mosque or any other Islamic
sites or places of prayer.[13]

To show how far the libel extends, it is sometimes applied to
places that are merely in the vicinity of the Temple Mount and not
even within the walls of the Old City. For example, an Islamic group
protested Jewish activities in the nearby village of Silwan because it
is "the gateway to al-Aqsa Mosque." The group also believed that
the Jews planned to destroy the mosque and rebuild the Temple.[14]

Earlier that summer, Palestinians complained about Israeli excavations that were, again, no danger to the Temple Mount but were
labeled as an attempt "to Judaize Jerusalem and the collapse of al-
Aqsa Mosque to build the so-called third temple on ruins of it."[15]

Protests based on the libel are not restricted to Jerusalem. For
the past 18 years, Israeli Muslims have held an annual "al-Aqsa Is
in Danger" festival. Thousands of people attended the 2013 rally in
Umm al-Fahm, where they heard a vitriolic speech by Sheikh Raed
Salah, the former mayor of the Israeli Arab town. "Anyone who
gives away one stone from al-Aqsa, or one meter of east Jerusalem,
or whoever gives up the right of return or the right to free prisoners,"
Salah thundered, "is a traitor."[16]

Salah leads the northern branch of the Islamic Movement, a pro-
Palestinian, anti-Zionist organization that has called for violence
against Jews at the Temple Mount and warned Palestinian leaders in
the West Bank not to make any concessions to Israel. He is a provo-
cateur who served a prison sentence for funding Hamas and meeting
with an Iranian intelligence agent. He was also held for five months
after assaulting an Israeli police officer and inciting violence. He was

convicted of incitement again in November 2013 because of a statement he made calling for all Arabs to use violence in support of the Palestinians and to "initiate an Islamic intifada from sea to sea, in support of the holy Jerusalem and the blessed al-Aqsa mosque." Protesters listening to his speech subsequently attacked police and chanted, "With blood we will redeem you, al-Aqsa." His conviction was, more specifically, for his use of the ancient blood libel: he referred to children in Europe, "whose blood was mixed in with the dough of the holy bread."[17]

As the mufti attempted nearly a century earlier, Palestinian Islamic extremists today continue to stoke the religious war between Muslims and Jews. They hope to incite a new Palestinian uprising and, ideally, to inspire Arab and Islamic armies to go to war to prevent the Jews from destroying the Dome of the Rock and the al-Aqsa Mosque.

Meanwhile, the Temple Mount and the mosque are used for propaganda and to raise funds. For example, inside al-Aqsa, glass display cases exhibit tear gas shells used by the Israeli police to quell riots during the first intifada. An Arab security guard said they were used "to make visitors sympathize and give donations." Despite large amounts of contributions, the area is not well maintained, raising questions about where the money from individuals and Muslim countries actually goes. Other members of the security staff pointed out scaffoldings that are not really used for maintenance, but are instead shown to donors to suggest that money is needed for repairs. "Look at the donation boxes here; they collect an average of one million shekels ($284,000) per month. We have no idea where that money goes. The poor and the needy never see any of it."[18]

The Israeli-Palestinian Declaration of Principles, or the Oslo agreement, signed September 13, 1993, intentionally left the status of Jerusalem undecided until the two sides began negotiations over the "final status" issues, which also include borders, refugees, and settlements. The Declaration of Principles did specify that until an agreement was reached, the Palestinians would have no jurisdiction over Jerusalem. Meanwhile, Israel retained the right to build anywhere it chooses in Jerusalem and continues to exercise sovereignty over the undivided city. The PLO insisted that Jerusalem should be the capital of a Palestinian state, and, the day the Declaration of Principles was signed, Arafat declared that the Palestinian flag "will fly over the walls of Jerusalem, the churches of Jerusalem, and the mosques of Jerusalem."[19]

Muslim states have lived with the status quo since 1967; they may not like it, but there is no evidence they are prepared—despite their rhetoric—to go to war over Jewish control of the city. This may only be a pragmatic decision based on their estimation that they are too weak to challenge Israel at this time; whatever the explanation for Muslim inaction, the fear that Israel maintaining control of the city will provoke a holy war is exaggerated. Moreover, a compromise may yet be reached in the context of a peace agreement whereby Israel will cede some authority or territory in Jerusalem. Daniel Jonah Goldhagen has a much more pessimistic view of the outcome of the drumbeat of accusations that the Jews are threatening one of Islam's holiest places:

> This delegitimization, together with the obvious need and the concomitant right of the threatened people to defend themselves against such a demonic and dangerous foe, justifies, and not only justifies, but suggests, even propels forward the seemingly obvious conclusion that such an entity, and its people, need to be eliminated, in other words *destroyed* [author's emphasis].[20]

CHAPTER 9

SHATTERED DREAMS OF PEACE

FROM CAMP DAVID'S SUCCESS TO OBAMA'S FIASCO

One of the many myths about the conflict between Israel and the Palestinians is that the Palestinians have never had the opportunity to establish an independent state. In fact, they have had several opportunities dating back more than 70 years. The best hope for peace appeared to be following the mutual recognition of the PLO and Israel in 1993 and the beginning of what is referred to as the Oslo peace process. Those negotiations literally and figuratively exploded, however, and the wreckage remains while continuing aftershocks contribute to today's widespread skepticism that any peace agreement is possible.

Contrary to international opinion regarding Israeli settlements, the fundamental obstacle to peace has always been the Muslim Arabs' refusal to accept the existence of a Jewish state in the heart of the Islamic world. This fact has been highlighted during peace talks mediated by Secretary of State John Kerry, who has agreed with Israeli prime minister Benjamin Netanyahu that the Palestinians must recognize Israel as the state of the Jewish people as part of any agreement. PA president Mahmoud Abbas adamantly refuses to do so.

The conflict has often been simplified to a dispute between two peoples over one land, which led to the seemingly obvious conclusion early on that the solution would be to divide the territory between them. The Muslims, however, have never been willing to compromise and settle for anything less than the entire area, while the Jews accepted partition, even at the expense of most of the territory that constituted the Land of Israel, the promise made in the Balfour Declaration, and the loss of Jerusalem.

The Palestinians' first opportunity to achieve statehood was in 1937, when the commission led by Lord Peel suggested the partition of Palestine into Jewish and Arab states; the Arabs rejected the proposal.

The Arabs squandered the second chance for statehood in 1947 when the UN partition plan was rejected. Had they accepted it, a Palestinian state would be celebrating its sixty-eighth anniversary along with Israel in 2015.

From 1949 until Israel's victory in the 1967 War, the Gaza Strip was controlled by Egypt and the West Bank by Jordan. At any point during that time, a Palestinian state could have been established in one or both areas, but neither of the occupiers had any interest in doing so, and the Palestinians themselves made no demands for independence. To the contrary, they began to engage in terror attacks against Israel and Jews around the world in the continuing hope that Palestine could be liberated and the Jews driven into the sea. As a reminder to those who insist settlements are the obstacle to peace, it is worth noting that *not one* Israeli settlement existed in the West Bank or Gaza during this period, and yet the Muslims were still unwilling to contemplate peace.

Prior to 1967 no Muslim state was prepared to make peace with Israel even though no settlements existed and a majority of ancient Palestine was under the illegitimate control of Jordan. After the Six-Day War, Moshe Dayan said he was waiting for a phone call to negotiate a territorial compromise, but the call never came. Though Israel talked about the possibility of a confederation of the West Bank with Jordan, it never seriously considered annexing the West

Bank or Gaza Strip because of the large Palestinian populations in both and the prospect that a state incorporating all of those Arabs would have posed a security threat, as well as a democratic one, as they would be capable of changing Israel's character through the ballot box. A minority of Israelis suggested that Israel should either expel the Palestinians or allow them to stay but deny them the right to vote. Neither alternative was palatable to Israel's leaders or the general public. Eventually, some argued that Israel should unilaterally withdraw from the territories, but for nearly 40 years after the 1967 War, the public was unwilling to concede land without any guarantees of peace or security in return.

Israel essentially was stuck with two territories with rapidly growing Muslim populations that were irrevocably hostile toward their neighbor. Given that reality, Israel began to resettle parts of the West Bank and Gaza. The early settlers were primarily directed to strategically valuable areas. Other Jews sought to rebuild communities destroyed by Jordan in the 1948 War. The numbers remained small, however, until the political earthquake in Israel that resulted in the election of Israel's first prime minister from outside the Labor Party.

Menachem Begin, the former leader of the Irgun and longtime government opponent, was elected prime minister in 1977, and Israelis knew that he believed the Jews were entitled by history, by justice, and by law to the entire Land of Israel. To fulfill that dream, Begin's government began to support the expansion of settlements throughout the territories and to offer incentives to encourage Israelis to move to areas where they could buy houses much larger than most in the cities for a fraction of the cost and still live close to many of their jobs.

This was the backdrop for Israel's peace negotiations with Egypt that began openly in 1977 after Sadat's dramatic trip to Jerusalem and culminated in the signing of a treaty in 1979. Those talks presented the Palestinians with yet another opportunity for eventual statehood. Largely because Sadat was afraid of being accused of selling out the Palestinians and abandoning the Arab world's cause célèbre, he insisted on including a resolution to Palestinian demands as part of the talks.

At President Carter's insistence, Begin agreed to freeze settlement construction for three months, hoping the gesture would entice other Arabs to join the Camp David peace process. Though Carter would later claim Begin deceived him and had promised to keep the freeze in place longer, the documentary evidence indicates that Begin kept his word. It didn't matter because none of the other Arab states supported the negotiations and, after they were concluded, did everything they could to sabotage the peace treaty Israel and Egypt signed.

Carter had been assured by the Saudis, in particular, that they would support the peace talks, leading the president to believe the success of the Camp David negotiations treaty would create the momentum for the comprehensive peace he craved. Instead, the Saudis mobilized the other Arab states to isolate Sadat, cutting off aid to Egypt, moving the Arab League headquarters out of Cairo, and doing everything they could to sabotage the agreement.

Few recognized it at the time, but Begin's settlement freeze was, despite its brevity, a major concession for Israel. At that time most Israelis opposed the creation of a Palestinian state. The reasons included the fact that Jews had an equally strong claim to Judea and Samaria, lands where they had lived for millennia, while there had never been a Palestinian state there or anywhere else in recorded history. At that point, the Palestinians did not recognize Israel and engaged in an incessant campaign of terror against Jews and Israelis around the world (76 Israelis were killed in the years 1977–1979). Given that the 1967 frontier, which left Israel nine miles wide at its narrowest point, was referred to by Abba Eban as the "Auschwitz" borders, Israelis rejected the idea of returning to the pre-1967 lines. They believed that any Palestinian entity on its borders would pose an ongoing security threat given the Palestinians' violent irredentism. Also, Israel thought that a confederation with Jordan would be the best option for resolving the Palestinian issue.

Despite all the caveats, Begin offered the Palestinians "autonomy," a two-stage process whereby Israel would grant the Palestinians self-governing authority for an interim period to give them the opportunity to demonstrate they were prepared to live peacefully beside Israel. Once confidence was built, the plan was to negotiate an agreement on the final status of the territories and the permanent relationship between Israelis and Palestinians. Even though autonomy had limits, it would have been a step toward Palestinian statehood and, over time, Israel would have had a difficult time preventing limited self-rule from evolving into full independence. The plan fell far short of Palestinian demands; they rejected it and refused to participate in negotiations.

The Palestinian rejection of this opportunity to achieve eventual statehood had nothing to do with settlements. At that time fewer than 10,000 Jews lived in the disputed territories. Had they accepted autonomy, the Palestinians would inevitably have held onto more land for a future state with virtually no Jews to assimilate or expel.

Palestinian obstinacy left it to Sadat to negotiate on their behalf, though they did not acknowledge his right to do so. Ultimately, Sadat recognized the Palestinians would not agree to anything Israel was prepared to offer; moreover, he was far more interested in advancing Egypt's national interests, which included regaining the Sinai, improving ties with the United States, and removing a military threat from his border. Sadat gave up nothing beyond a promise to keep the peace. For that long-sought pledge, Israel gave up a huge strategic buffer (the Sinai Desert), relinquished oil fields that Israel had hoped to use to achieve energy independence, dismantled military bases, and uprooted more than 7,000 Jews who lived in the area. The painful scenes of Jews being dragged from their homes were difficult for most Israelis; nevertheless, they were carried out in the interest of peace, setting a precedent for what Israel might do to achieve an agreement with the Palestinians.

For his vision and courage Sadat was labeled a traitor by much of the Arab world, as well as by extremists within Egypt. Ultimately, he paid with his life when he was assassinated in 1981.

The failure to achieve any agreement only heightened Palestinian frustration. That tension was ultimately released in the violent uprising—the intifada—that began in 1987 and fizzled out following the U.S. invasion of Iraq in 1992. During the Gulf War the Palestinians won few friends with their support for Saddam Hussein; in fact, Kuwait expelled 300,000 Palestinians in anger over their support for the regime that attempted to overrun the country.

President Ronald Reagan was out of office by the time the fighting began, but before he left, he changed America's longstanding policy not to speak to the PLO. After Arafat met U.S. conditions to accept UN Resolution 242, to recognize Israel's right to exist and renounced terrorism, a U.S.-PLO dialogue subsequently began in Tunis. U.S. recognition put greater pressure on Israel to speak to "the sole legitimate representative" of the Palestinian people.

Reagan's successor, George H. W. Bush, soon demonstrated that he would not be the friend to Israel that Reagan had been, and his secretary of state, James Baker, lacked any emotional attachment to Israel. Their ambivalence toward Israel raised hopes in the Arab world that Israel would be compelled to give into their demands.

Prospects for an agreement improved when Israeli voters brought the Labor Party back to power. To ease tensions that had flared between his predecessor, Yitzhak Shamir, and Bush over the settlement issue, Prime Minister Yitzhak Rabin declared a settlement freeze (to win loan guarantees from the United States) and took a variety of confidence-building steps Israel hoped would advance negotiations with the Palestinians. Arafat, however, did not budge from his maximalist positions; in fact, with each gesture Rabin offered, the Palestinians raised the ante and made greater demands.

Negotiations continued, however, with the Palestinians now willing to discuss autonomy. Still, the talks made little headway, and the Bush administration became distracted by the president's reelection campaign, which Baker left the State Department to run. When Bush was defeated, and the very pro-Israel Bill Clinton became president, the Palestinians began to get a sense they would have to make the best deal possible while they still could.

Israel's government was still not prepared to negotiate with an organization they viewed as nothing but a bunch of terrorists who had murdered hundreds of Israelis. The ground began to shift and another opportunity for Palestinian independence emerged from secret talks between Israeli journalist Ron Pundak and Haifa University professor Ya'ir Hirshfeld and Abu Alaa, the number two man in the PLO. Contacts were set up by the Norwegians and were viewed as exploratory, but more than a dozen rounds of talks were held during which confidants of Arafat suggested a willingness to make concessions never offered before by the Palestinians.

When Rabin learned of the back-channel talks in Oslo, he was convinced enough progress toward an agreement had been made to grant permission to Foreign Minister Shimon Peres to continue the negotiations through Foreign Ministry Director-General Uri Savir. Arafat also sent his top lieutenants, including Mahmoud Abbas (today president of the Palestinian Authority).

The first major breakthrough occurred when the Palestinians in Oslo expressed a willingness to accept a phased plan whereby Israel would first agree to withdraw from most of Gaza and the city of Jericho in the West Bank. Israel had only wanted to concede Gaza, but the Palestinians wanted Jericho included to create a link between Gaza and the West Bank. The Palestinians would get territory, and the Israelis would have a chance to test their sincerity. By this time the government was fully informed of the talks, and surprised by how forthcoming the Palestinian negotiators were in Oslo. Savir and Alaa agreed on a draft declaration of principles that would form the basis of the first formal agreement between Israel and the Palestinians. The document, which they signed on August 20, 1993, came to be known as the Oslo agreement.

To convert the progress made in the back channel to a public agreement required one additional critical step: the mutual recognition of Israel and the PLO. The price of Israeli recognition amounted to Arafat's total capitulation to Israel's longstanding demands that the PLO recognize "the right of Israel to exist in peace and security"; accept UN Security Council resolutions; commit itself to the peace process; renounce terrorism; and agree to change provisions of the PLO covenant that called for the destruction of the Jewish state. Arafat agreed to these conditions in a letter to Prime Minister Rabin on September 9, 1993. The same day, Rabin wrote to Arafat that Israel "decided to recognize the PLO as the representative of the Palestinian people." Israel's concession was that it legitimized the PLO based on its words without first testing to see if they would be matched by deeds.

Paradoxically, the construction of settlements was a catalyst rather than an obstacle to negotiations. The number of settlers in the territories had ballooned from approximately 10,000 when the Palestinians turned down Begin's autonomy offer to more than 130,000 in 1993. "The Palestinians now realize," Bethlehem mayor Elias Freij said in 1991, "that time is now on the side of Israel, which can build settlements and create facts, and that the only way out of this dilemma is face-to-face negotiations."[1]

Not everyone in Israel or abroad was happy with the direction Israel was headed. Many could not countenance an agreement with the duplicitous Arafat, warned that it endangered Israel's security, and worried that the Palestinians were just carrying out their plan to liberate Palestine in stages. The dramatic change in relations between Israel and the PLO took place practically overnight, and many right-wing Israelis and their supporters believed that Israel rescued the PLO from the dustbin of history.

Even when the PLO later held a meeting to annul parts of its covenant that Israel found objectionable, and President Clinton certified that they had met their obligation, opponents of Oslo raised technicalities about the requirements for changing the covenant and argued it had not been altered. The hostility toward the negotiations grew to the point where large protests were held in which Rabin was portrayed in posters wearing an Arab headdress and accused of selling out the country. The vitriol directed against Rabin was especially ironic because he had fought in the War of Independence and spent most of his life in the military, reaching Israel's highest military rank, chief of staff, and could hardly be accused of being indifferent to Israel's security; nevertheless, opponents were convinced he was endangering the country.

Supporters of talks believed the PLO's weakness made it possible to get a deal favorable to Israel, that waiting for the PLO's complete collapse would have taken too long, and that it would have given Hamas the opportunity to gain greater influence. Most Israelis and their supporters were excited by the prospect of finally resolving the "Israeli problem" (that is, the dilemma of how to remain a Jewish state and stay a democracy if the country ruled more than 3 million Palestinians).

The PLO also faced criticism from its more militant factions that did not want to give up the armed struggle to liberate all of Palestine.

Some Palestinians, even among the supporters, also began to talk about the agreement as part of a phased plan where they would establish a state first in the West Bank and Gaza and then continue the struggle until they conquered the rest of "Palestine." Arafat's backers hoped the agreement would finally offer the Palestinians a measure of self-determination and believed this would lead in the not-too-distant future to the establishment of an independent Palestinian state.

Hamas was especially critical, viewing Arafat's recognition of Israel as unacceptable and any discussion of a compromise in which Jews continued to live on Islamic land and rule over Muslims as intolerable. Hamas remained irrevocably opposed to a two-state solution, which exacerbated the existing rift with the PLO and ensured the Islamists would do everything they could to sabotage the deal.

In an effort to prevent Hamas from out-maneuvering him and presenting themselves as the defenders of Muslim land and the group that could liberate Palestine from the Zionist usurpers, the supposedly secular PLO and Arafat used Islamic themes and rhetoric to inspire and incite the Palestinian population. Addressing Muslims at a mosque in South Africa, where he had attended the inauguration of President Nelson Mandela, Arafat said in English, "You have to come and to fight a jihad to liberate Jerusalem, your precious shrine."[2] After creating an uproar, Arafat claimed he was misquoted. Two years later (October 21, 1996), however, Arafat told a crowd in Bethlehem, "We know only one word: jihad! Jihad, jihad, jihad. When we stopped the intifada, we did not stop the jihad for the establishment of a Palestinian state whose capital is Jerusalem. And we are now entering the phase of the great jihad prior to the establishment of an independent Palestinian state whose capital is Jerusalem."[3] And again in 2002, Arafat declared: "Yes, brothers, with our souls and blood we redeem you, O Palestine. . . . This is a sacred bond. We are up to this duty. Allah is great! Glory to Allah and his prophet. Jihad, jihad, jihad, jihad, jihad!"[4] It was also no coincidence that the armed wing of Fatah is named the al-Aqsa Martyrs' Brigade and took directions from Arafat.

The Declaration of Principles was signed on the White House lawn on September 13, 1993. It specified that an elected Palestinian

Council with legislative powers would govern Palestinians in the West Bank and Gaza Strip for a transitional period of no more than five years, after which the final status of the territories would be determined. Ironically, the Palestinians were given far less territory than Begin offered as Israel insisted on the Gaza/Jericho first plan to test the Palestinian commitment to the agreement. Later, the two sides were to negotiate the details of autonomy for the rest of the territories. The Palestinians reluctantly agreed to delay for three years resolving the most sensitive issues—Jerusalem, refugees, settlements, security arrangements, and borders—which they preferred to tackle immediately. Israel also agreed to "early empowerment," giving the Palestinians responsibility for health, education, welfare, taxation, tourism, and other civil functions throughout the West Bank. The Israeli Defense Forces were to move out of heavily populated areas but not fully withdraw from the territories. Israel also retained responsibility for security throughout the territories and control over bridges to Jordan. All the Israeli residents were allowed to remain in the West Bank and Gaza under Israel's protection, and Israel made no commitments to alter its settlement policy.

During the signing ceremony, Rabin said, "Enough of blood and tears. Enough!" Sadly, both peoples would suffer many more years of both.

Over the course of the next decade, most Israelis concluded that Arafat was not a reliable negotiating partner. The most immediate problem was that Arafat would not or could not stop the terror attacks against Israel. In addition, the new Palestinian Authority kept up a steady drumbeat of incitement that took a variety of forms, including publishing maps showing Palestine replacing Israel, treating suicide bombers as martyrs, using textbooks in schools that contained anti-Semitic and anti-Israel material (they still do, but they've gotten better), broadcasting TV shows for children and adults that glorified martyrdom and promoted intolerance, allowing imams to give inflammatory and often anti-Semitic sermons, and even using something as mundane as crossword puzzles to delegitimize Israel by giving clues that erased Israeli cities and called them instead by Arabic names.

Israelis were particularly appalled by the indoctrination of children in schools, camps, and the media. For example, one Palestinian TV show featured a Mickey Mouse–like character named Farfour who encouraged children to fight against Israel and to work for "a world led by Islamists." After attracting criticism, the show was canceled, but not before a final episode aired in which Farfour was murdered by Israelis.

The Palestinians had their own complaints, in particular the slow process of the negotiations and the expansion of settlements, which they viewed as reflecting bad faith as well as creating facts on the ground that would impede the creation of a Palestinian state.

The Oslo agreement did not require Israel to stop settlement construction, and its continuation should have motivated Arafat to keep his commitments so a final agreement could be reached before the number of settlers made the establishment of a state impossible. By the time of Rabin's assassination in 1995, nearly 150,000 Jews lived in the territories.

Rabin used the military to respond to terror, but did not let any of the PLO's violations of the agreement derail the process. He was determined to get Israel out of the territories and relieve the country of the necessity of exercising control over more than 2 million Palestinians.

While the Oslo agreements sparked controversy, they dramatically changed the atmosphere in Israel. For the first time, at least since the treaty was signed with Egypt, Israelis felt hopeful about peace and the possibility of a better future for their children. Parents of very young children saw the possibility that by the time their kids reached the age of military conscription, peace with the neighbors would make compulsory service unnecessary.

Israeli optimism was not just based on the prospects for ending the conflict with the Palestinians; Israel was also enjoying an international honeymoon as countries that typically criticized Israel, particularly in Europe, cheered for Israel to succeed. The era of good feeling even extended to the Muslim world as Israel took steps toward openly normalizing ties with some of the Persian Gulf nations, such as Qatar and Oman.

Israelis were still realistic and believed it was more likely that these relations would be similar to Israel's ties with Egypt, that is, unidirectional, with virtually all of the interactions flowing from Israel to the Arab country.

The question arises why these Muslim states would engage in relations, even low-level ones, with Israel. The answer is that the Gulf countries, excluding Saudi Arabia, are more like trading posts than states. Like all countries in the region, Islam is the official religion, but like Jordan and Egypt, other interests, in this case commercial ones, trump their commitment to Islam. Also, despite the rhetoric, Muslims outside Israel have a very low opinion of the Palestinians and are not committed to their cause beyond rhetoric and token financial donations.

Perhaps the most important foreign policy development that arose out of Oslo was the decision by King Hussein of Jordan to enter negotiations with Israel. Unlike Sadat, Hussein had good reason not to make a separate peace with Israel. The majority of his subjects were Palestinians, Jordan also had its share of Islamists, and Hussein saw what happened to Sadat. Once the Palestinians reached an agreement with the Israelis, however, he felt that he had the cover to reach one as well. In 1995, a formal peace treaty was signed: Israel now had normalized relations with two Muslim Arab leaders and all but erased the threats on two of its borders.

The Jordan-Israel peace treaty, combined with the improvement in relations with other Arab countries, is probably the best point to recognize as the end of the Arab-Israel conflict. From this point on, it becomes much clearer that Israel and the Arab states can coexist; however, the reactions of Iran, Saudi Arabia, Hamas, and Hezbollah made it equally clear that radical Muslims were no closer to accepting a Jewish state in their midst and were no less committed to Israel's destruction.

The near euphoria that many Israelis felt as it appeared that peace was on the horizon disappeared overnight on November 4, 1995, when an Israeli Jew, Yigal Amir, assassinated Rabin following a peace rally in Tel Aviv. This was the first time an Israeli leader had ever been assassinated, and the impact on the whole country was shattering. On one level, the impact was similar to the way

Americans felt after the murder of John Kennedy, but for Israelis the pain went much deeper because it had been inconceivable that a Jew would ever resort to killing a Jewish political leader with whom he disagreed.

We can't know what he would have done had Rabin lived longer, but the end of the process ultimately led to the withdrawal of Israeli forces from approximately 80 percent of the Gaza Strip and 40 percent of the West Bank. The army withdrew from all the major Arab cities, and roughly 98 percent of the Palestinians were governed on virtually all domestic matters by the PA.

Though the Palestinians were successful in convincing gullible Westerners that they were interested in a "secular democratic state," this was an idea only expressed in English by propagandists. In Arabic, the Palestinians, including the supposedly secular Yasser Arafat, talked about liberating Jerusalem from the Jews. When Israel gave up parts of the West Bank and Gaza to allow the creation of the Palestinian Authority, it was immediately evident that the Palestinian leadership was not interested in democracy or civil rights. It wanted to impose a dictatorship much like the other Arab states, and, like those other nations, it was also to be an Islamic state, not a secular one. Once Arafat gained control over the lives of most Palestinians in the territories, he denied them most basic rights, including freedom of speech, freedom of the press, and freedom of assembly, and he did not recognize the rights of women or gays. Palestinians were free to agree with Arafat; public disagreement would usually result in arrest or worse.

Though Rabin's efforts won him the Nobel Peace Prize (along with Arafat and Peres in December 1994), and he was viewed as the great peacemaker, it is often forgotten that he vigorously opposed the creation of a Palestinian state, even if the Oslo agreements had been fulfilled to the letter. Rabin's position was consistent with that of the Israeli public at that time. Israelis wanted to rid themselves of responsibility for the lives of Palestinians in the territories, but they did not want to relinquish territory without ensuring their security. The distances between the Palestinian cities and Israeli cities had grown shorter as Palestinians in Gaza acquired rockets, and Israelis feared that if West Bank Palestinians had similar weapons they could threaten the demographic heart of Israel, Jerusalem and Ben-Gurion airport. Without IDF and intelligence forces on the ground, Israelis worried (and still worry) that the area could become another Lebanon, a base for terrorist operations, or that the Palestinian leaders might allow other Arab armies to use their territory as a staging ground.

While Rabin continued to move forward on the Palestinian track, he secretly was engaged in talks with Syrian president Hafez Assad in hopes of achieving a breakthrough that would lead to peace on the northern border. Some reports suggested they reached the outline of an agreement, but Rabin knew Assad would demand a complete Israeli withdrawal from the Golan Heights. The majority of the Israeli public trusted Rabin's judgment regarding Israel's ability to withdraw from the West Bank and Gaza without sacrificing its security, but Israelis would have a much harder time accepting evacuation of the Golan Heights after more than two decades of Israeli leaders emphasizing the area was essential to Israel's security.

Rabin died before finalizing a deal, and his successor, Shimon Peres, lacked Rabin's military credentials to sell a similar arrangement to the Israeli public. Ultimately, it didn't matter because Assad reverted to his longstanding position that he would not offer anything until Israel withdrew from the entire Golan Heights. Without any promise that Syria would offer at least the minimal normalization of ties that Israel received in the treaty with Egypt, the negotiations fizzled out.

Even with the death of Rabin, Palestinian terrorism, and the lack of progress toward resolving the conflict, Israelis did not completely give up hope. Peres believed in the possibility of peace with the Palestinians and liked to talk about a new Middle East in which Israel and its neighbors would cooperate in a variety of mutually beneficial activities.

Like other dreamers at the time, Peres had a difficult time accepting the reality on the ground, which was marked by an escalation in terror attacks. The idea that Peres would continue Rabin's legacy was popular with the Israeli left, but mobilized the opponents on the right who backed Benjamin Netanyahu, the Likud Party leader who virulently opposed the Oslo agreement.

Just six months after Rabin's murder, Israelis went to the polls to decide on his replacement. Peres appeared poised to win the election; however, a number of horrendous terror attacks occurred just before the election and reinforced Netanyahu's message that he was the candidate who would stop the terror and ensure that Israel's security would come first in talks with the Palestinians. These were the worst of a series of attacks:

- February 25, 1996: A suicide bombing of bus No. 18 near the Central Bus Station in Jerusalem kills 26 people (17 civilians and 9 soldiers).
- March 3, 1996: A suicide bombing of bus No. 18 on Jaffa Road in Jerusalem kills 19 people (16 civilians and 3 soldiers).
- March 4, 1996: Outside Dizengoff Center in Tel Aviv, a suicide bomber detonates a nail bomb, killing 13 people (12 civilians and 1 soldier).

Israel had been scheduled to remove troops from most of the city of Hebron, but was forced to postpone the withdrawal because of the upsurge in violence. The decision was ultimately taken out of Peres's hands. In an election decided by less than 1 percent of the total number of votes cast, Netanyahu was elected prime minister in May 1996.

It didn't take long for Netanyahu's ideology to come face-to-face with the pragmatic realities of continuing the process that Rabin started. In September 1996, Netanyahu met Arafat for the first time, and, after several months of shuttle diplomacy by U.S. envoy Dennis Ross, the two leaders concluded an agreement on January 15, 1997, in which the opponent of territorial compromise agreed to redeploy Israeli forces in Hebron and to carry out three additional redeployments from the West Bank. Netanyahu's decision to withdraw from Hebron—the town with the greatest religious significance to Jews in the West Bank, and the most zealous settler population—marked an irrevocable shift away from the Likud's ideology that maintained the West Bank was part of "Greater Israel" and must remain under Israeli control.

In each round of negotiations, Israel would make concessions while the Palestinians would simply promise to take the same steps they had agreed to in previous talks but never implemented. In October 1998, Clinton brought Netanyahu and Arafat together at the Wye River plantation in Maryland and convinced Israel to withdraw from an additional 13 percent of the West Bank and to release 750 Palestinian prisoners. The Palestinians said they would arrest Palestinian terrorists, formally revoke the PLO covenant's controversial articles, and take measures to prevent anti-Israel incitement.

Two months later, Clinton traveled to Gaza to witness the Palestine National Council revise the covenant. Many Israelis, to this day, insist the covenant was never changed because the proper procedures were not followed for amending the charter; nevertheless, Netanyahu accepted Clinton's recognition of the PNC's action, carried out the first of three planned withdrawals amounting to about 9 percent of the West Bank, and released the required number of prisoners.

The Palestinians never fulfilled their commitment to halt terror and incitement, and the Israelis were again taken. Listening to the mantra that they should trade land for peace, they gave up territory but only received more terrorism in return. It is a pattern that was repeated from the first Israeli withdrawals in 1993 until the last one in 2005.

Netanyahu's government collapsed and he was replaced as prime minister in May 1999 by Ehud Barak, a former chief of staff and Israel's most decorated soldier. After agreeing to repeated withdrawals, it became increasingly clear to most Israelis that the establishment of a Palestinian state was inevitable and that Israel could coexist with such an entity provided its security interests were protected. Rather than continue the incremental approach of the prior seven years, Barak decided to seek a final agreement that would resolve all outstanding issues and end the conflict with the Palestinians.

President Clinton saw an opportunity to rewrite his legacy, which had been tarnished by the Lewinsky affair, by facilitating a peace agreement. He invited Arafat and Barak to Camp David in July 2000. Discussions continued a few months later at the White House, during which Barak agreed to give the Palestinians nearly everything they had demanded—statehood, an Israeli withdrawal from approximately 97 percent of the West Bank, evacuation of all but a handful of settlements, compensation for refugees, and Palestinian sovereignty on the Temple Mount in Jerusalem.

Arafat, however, rejected the proposal out of hand without even trying to improve the terms. A variety of explanations can be given for Arafat's reaction, including his inability to give up on the dream of liberating all of Palestine, the fear of being viewed as a traitor, especially by the Muslim extremists, and his identification with resistance. The religious element was also an important factor. As irreligious as he was, Arafat still could not agree to recognize the right of a Jewish state to exist in the Islamic world and to rule over Muslims. In fact, he refused to acknowledge the Jewish connection to their homeland. At one point in the discussions, for example, Arafat said that there had never been a Jewish Temple on the Temple Mount in Jerusalem, a remark that Ambassador Dennis Ross said "denied the core of the Jewish faith."

At one point Clinton told Arafat, "If the Israelis can make compromises and you can't I should go home. You have been here 14 days and said no to everything. These things will have consequences. Failure will end the peace process."[5]

For Israelis, Arafat's true intentions could be found on the Palestinian Authority website, which showed a map that did not have a Palestinian state beside Israel, but one that replaced Israel. The Fatah logo also depicted "Palestine" in the shape of Israel. Arafat wore his kaffiyeh draped over his shoulder in the same shape.

Not only did the negotiations fail to achieve an agreement, but the level of violence significantly increased as Palestinians began to attack Israeli police and soldiers and a new round of suicide bombings began. Though this new uprising was blamed on a visit to the Temple Mount by Ariel Sharon, it was actually planned by Arafat.[6] A familiar battle cry was carried by the Voice of Palestine, the PA's official radio station, on September 29, 2000, calling "all Palestinians to come and defend the al-Aqsa mosque." The PA closed its schools and bused Palestinian students to the Temple Mount to participate in premeditated riots. The following day, thousands of Arabs began throwing bricks and rocks at Israeli police and Jewish worshippers at the Western Wall. Rioting then spread to towns and villages throughout Israel, the West Bank, and Gaza Strip. In October, Palestinian mobs destroyed Joseph's Tomb in Nablus, tearing up and burning Jewish prayer books, and attacked Rachel's Tomb in Bethlehem with firebombs and automatic weapons. The "al-Aqsa intifada," or Palestinian War, continued for five years, during which time more than 1,000 Israelis were killed.

Jerusalem also was a focal point in Israeli politics as Barak's offer to make concessions to the Palestinians on the city's unity became a major issue in the next Israeli election. Barak thought he would gain support by demonstrating to the Israeli people that he could reach a deal with the Palestinians, but his failure to do so even after making so many compromises, combined with his inability to curb the growing violence, made him look weak. His opponent, Ariel Sharon, had no problem with presenting an image as a strong leader based on his long career as one of Israel's most valiant and hardnosed commanders. Sharon promised to end the violence and to ensure that Jerusalem remained undivided, and the voters were convinced, electing him prime minister in February 2001 by a landslide.

Palestinian terrorists seemed determined to prove that Sharon could not stop them. The Islamization of the conflict with the Palestinians was now reflected by the willingness of more and more Palestinians to strap explosives to their bodies and blow themselves up, along with Israeli men, women, and children, in the belief that they were defending Islam, carrying out the will of Allah, and would be rewarded for their actions in the afterlife. These human bombs produced unprecedented carnage that horrified the Israeli public. For example, on June 1, 2001, a Hamas suicide bomber blew up a disco in Tel Aviv, killing 21 and injuring 120. On August 9, 2001, a man walked into a pizzeria in downtown Jerusalem and exploded, murdering 15 people and injuring 130.

Even as Israelis were being murdered, Sharon was under international pressure to resume negotiations. The advocates of talks insisted the Palestinians only turned to violence because they had no alternative and saw no hope of achieving independence. This reflected the failure to realize the change in the conflict from political to religious. The men and women blowing themselves up were not interested in Israeli concessions, coexistence, or even independence; they were devoted to the destruction of Israel.

Under U.S. pressure, Arafat periodically condemned the violence—in English. When he spoke to the public in Arabic, however, he would call for a jihad against Israel and a million martyrs to liberate Jerusalem. Arafat was also getting support from Iran, which had no interest in promoting a compromise with Israel. This came as a surprise to the United States and others, but was proven in January 2002 when Israeli forces intercepted a ship bound for the Palestinian Authority carrying 50 tons of Iranian weapons that were paid for by one of Arafat's top aides.

The failure to comprehend the religious motivation for the violence was reflected in President George W. Bush's declaration of support for the creation of a Palestinian state in November 2001. The rationale for making this official U.S. policy for the first time was the belief that the Palestinians would stop the violence and return to the bargaining table once they knew the United States supported their demand for statehood. The Palestinians did not waste any time, however, in demonstrating that Bush was mistaken. A series of suicide bombings and other attacks killed more than 30 Israelis and wounded hundreds more.

Some of the Palestinians may have thought that by inflicting enough pain on Israel they would force the government to capitulate to their demands; however, Sharon refused to negotiate "under fire" to show the Palestinians Israel would not be coerced by terror to make concessions. As the violence intensified, Israeli troops were sent into the West Bank to root out the terrorists there and confine Arafat to his office in Ramallah. Sharon declared Arafat "irrelevant," reflecting his belief that the PLO leader was unwilling to stop the attacks and would never agree to end the conflict.

From September 2000 through the end of February 2002, nearly 300 Israelis were murdered by Palestinian terrorists. The violence escalated in "Black March," when Palestinians carried out 15 suicide bombing attacks—nearly one every other day—as well as other shooting and grenade attacks that killed at least 130 people. The most heinous attack, which killed 28 people and injured more than

130, was perpetrated by a Hamas suicide bomber at a hotel in Netanya during a Passover Seder. The high casualty total, combined with the fact that the attack occurred on a religious holiday, convinced most Israelis that the time had come for a strong military response. Sharon responded by launching Operation Defensive Shield, sending troops and tanks into the major cities of the West Bank on March 28. Arafat expected the Arab states to come to the Palestinians' rescue, but they did nothing more than criticize the Israelis, demonstrating again that their support for the Palestinians was limited to rhetoric and financial aid.

As the Palestinian casualty total grew, Sharon came under pressure to withdraw the troops. He resisted the pressure at first before ending the operation on April 21, 2002. Although the Israeli operation did not completely stop the suicide bombings, it significantly reduced the number.

Israel adopted a different strategy for Gaza, especially for responding to Hamas operations. The IDF began to target Palestinians in Gaza who were responsible for carrying out terrorist attacks or ordering them. In July 2002, for example, an Israeli strike killed Hamas's military commander in Gaza. Two years later, Israel killed Hamas founder Sheikh Ahmed Yassin and his successor, Abdel Aziz al-Rantisi.

While the Palestinians were intent on bombing Israel into submission, a peace initiative was launched by an unlikely source. Saudi Arabia's crown prince Abdullah gave an interview to the *New York Times'* Tom Friedman in which he suggested that the Arab states would be prepared to normalize relations with Israel if the Israelis fulfilled a number of conditions. The Arab League subsequently adopted Abdullah's initiative with a number of additions that made it unpalatable to Israel. The plan called for Israel to withdraw to the 1967 frontier, recognize the right of Palestinian refugees to return to their homes (in Israel), and to accept the establishment of a Palestinian state with East Jerusalem as its capital.

The plan was met with enthusiasm in Washington and hailed as a bold new initiative. What made it newsworthy, however, was less the content than the fact that it had been proposed by the Saudis, who had previously shown little interest in recognizing Israel or participating in the peace process.

There was good reason to be skeptical of the Saudis' intentions as well as the true implications of the plan. Twelve of the 22 Arab leaders did not attend the summit where the proposal was debated, and rejectionists such as Iraq and Syria had no intention of agreeing to normalize relations with Israel. Western supporters of the plan also did not seem to notice the word *peace* was nowhere to be found in the proposal. Moreover, the beneficiaries of the initiative, the Palestinians, walked out of the Arab League meeting after Lebanon stopped Arafat from making a live televised speech from his West Bank headquarters.

The Arabs' sincerity seemed dubious given that the summit's final communique praised Palestinian martyrs. Subsequently, it became clear they had no interest in negotiating; Abdullah was unwilling to go to Jerusalem or invite the Israelis to Riyadh to discuss the proposal. The plan was also presented as a take-it-or-leave-it proposition; in fact, the Arabs warned that if Israel didn't accept the plan they might go to war.

Given the rabid anti-Semitism of the royal family, Israelis were justified in being skeptical. The only other time the Saudis had proposed a peace agreement was in 1981 when they were trying to win congressional approval of a major arms sale. King Fahd had floated a peace plan but reversed course as soon as the arms transfer was ratified. He then denounced the Camp David Accords, rejected Resolution 242, and called for a jihad against Israel.

The timing of Abdullah's initiative was also suspect because it came just months after 9/11. At the time the Saudis were on the defensive because most of the hijackers were Saudis, and the country was being vilified for its support of terrorism. Rather than a sincere offer, the peace initiative was more likely a public relations ploy designed to change the image of the Saudis from sponsors of terror to peacemakers. The Saudis did succeed in attracting positive publicity, but the initiative went nowhere after the Arabs refused to enter negotiations with Israel and the Israelis raised objections to major elements of the plan. In June 2003, President Bush asked the Saudis to sign a joint statement supporting normalization with Israel and Abdullah refused.

Bush had tried to avoid the pitfall of his predecessors who became enmeshed in the Israeli-Palestinian issue; however, he came under increasing pressure to become involved as the violence escalated. In June 2002, he proposed a peace plan, which subsequently formed the basis for an initiative, referred to as the "road map," formulated in April 2003 by the European Union, Russia, the United States, and the United Nations ("the Quartet").

Both sides had a variety of obligations under the road map, but the plan essentially came down to another chicken-and-egg fight with Israelis insisting the Palestinians end all violence before they fulfilled their responsibilities and the Palestinians refusing to act until Israel froze all settlement construction. The road map laid out a timetable for performing the required steps as the Quartet believed that deadlines would pressure the parties to act. Neither Israel nor the Palestinians, however, felt any need to stick to a timeline, and the same issues that bedeviled the Oslo negotiations turned the plan into a road map to nowhere.

It was clear to Sharon the Palestinian leaders were unable and unwilling to negotiate a peace agreement that recognized the right of Israel to exist even beside a Palestinian state. Moreover, he recognized the demographic dilemma that had prevented previous Likud governments from fulfilling their dream of "Greater Israel," namely that Israel could not annex the disputed territories and remain a democratic Jewish state because of the likelihood the Palestinians would be either a significant minority or majority of the population. These realizations led Sharon to announce in December 2003 his intention to withdraw all Israeli soldiers and civilians from the Gaza Strip. The disengagement plan ultimately called for the dismantling of the 21 settlements in the Gaza Strip, which were home to approximately 8,500 Israeli Jews, and the evacuation of four small communities in northern Samaria.

Before implementing the disengagement, a new and unexpected opportunity arose for a negotiated peace when Arafat died on November 11, 2004. A few weeks later, Mahmoud Abbas was elected president of the Palestinian Authority. Abbas, it was hoped, would adopt more moderate policies than his predecessor, reform the Palestinian Authority, and put an end to more than four years of senseless violence. Abbas had other ideas; he did not fundamentally alter the Palestinians' position toward peace with Israel and decided not to cooperate with the Israeli disengagement from Gaza.

Despite hysterical warnings of a civil war, the disengagement was carried out in September 2005 with little opposition from the Jews in Gaza. The evacuation was supposed to take two months to complete, but every civilian was out in less than a week.

The Palestinians now had yet another opportunity to lay the groundwork for statehood. After 38 years of military rule in Gaza, the Palestinians now governed themselves. After years of being urged to trade land for peace, Israelis hoped the Palestinians would demonstrate that the sacrifice they had made would pay off with an end to the five years of unremitting terror. Moreover, if the Palestinians proved they could live in peace now that the occupation of Gaza had ended, Israelis would have greater confidence that a withdrawal from the West Bank would terminate the conflict. That was the dream, but instead the disengagement resulted in a nightmare.

Almost immediately after leaving Gaza, terror attacks resumed. Instead of building the infrastructure for a state and proving to Israelis that they would get peace in return for territory, violence from the West Bank and Gaza escalated. The Palestinians smuggled weapons into Gaza from Egypt and launched barrages of mortars and rockets into southern Israel.

Just a few months after the disengagement, Israelis were shocked when Sharon suffered a massive brain hemorrhage and was incapacitated. His deputy, Ehud Olmert, became prime minister initially on an interim basis and then for a full term after winning a special election in March 2006. Olmert ran on the platform that he would continue Sharon's legacy and withdraw from most of the West Bank. His plans were derailed by Hezbollah's kidnapping of Israeli soldiers and his subsequent decision to go to war with the Lebanese terrorists, as well as a dramatic shift in power within the Palestinian Authority from Fatah to the Islamists of Hamas.

Bush had hoped the Palestinians would lay the groundwork for a democratic government by holding elections, despite Israeli warnings that the winners were likely to be fundamentalists who believed in theocracy rather than democracy. This is what happened when Hamas won the Palestinian election in January 2006 and took control of the Palestinian Authority's legislature. Abbas remained president, but he was politically handcuffed by Hamas. The Hamas victory also exacerbated the religious conflict because the Islamists refused to recognize Israel, honor past agreements signed with Israel, or negotiate with Israel. Shortly after the election Hamas leader Khaled Mashaal declared: "[Hamas will] never recognize the legitimacy of the Zionist state that was founded on our land."[7]

Abbas and the international community tried to marginalize Hamas; however, the organization grew more popular and influential in its base in Gaza. In June 2007, Hamas seized power in Gaza, leaving the government of President Abbas in control of only the West Bank. From 2007 to the present, Israel has considered Abbas too weak to implement a peace agreement, even if he were willing to sign one, and realized whatever he agreed to would only apply to the West Bank. Hamas, moreover, is committed to ensuring that Abbas does not make any compromises that leave a Jewish state on Islamic land.

To emphasize its commitment to Israel's destruction, Hamas and Islamic Jihad launched thousands of rockets at Israeli towns and cities. Thanks to weapons imported from Iran, Hamas obtained the capability to hit targets deep inside Israel, putting approximately 3.5 million Israelis in harm's way. At one point Hamas was firing an average of 80 rockets into Israel each day. Schools in Ashdod, Ashkelon, Beersheba, and other southern cities were closed as Hamas targeted civilian centers. The rocket attacks were largely ignored or, at times, excused by the international community, but when Israel used force to protect its citizens, it was roundly condemned. Israel, nevertheless, sent troops into Gaza in Operation Cast Lead at the end of December 2008. After nearly a month of fighting, Israeli forces significantly degraded the Hamas arsenal, and a cease-fire was arranged that ended the bombardment.

Terrorist attacks increased dramatically in 2011–2012 when more than 1,300 rockets were fired from Gaza. The escalation prompted the Israeli Air Force to kill Hamas military commander

Ahmad Jabari in hopes of convincing Hamas that continued terror would come at a price. The rocket fire continued, however, prompting Israel to launch another military operation—Pillar of Defense—on November 14, 2012. A week of fighting followed before a cease-fire was implemented. Since that operation, Hamas has been careful not to provoke Israel while simultaneously continuing to smuggle in weapons to replace those destroyed by Israel. The group remains as belligerent as ever, however, as reflected by this statement by Ismail Haniyeh:

> Resistance and jihad is the only strategic option for the Islamic ummah. . . . As the representative of the Palestinian nation, we have (already) announced to the children of the Arab um-mah, the Islamic ummah, and all free-thinkers in the world and (again) insist . . . that we will never recognize the Zionist regime and announce that the Palestinian nation will continue their resistance until the holy Palestinian land is liberated.[8]

The behavior of Hamas following Israel's disengagement had a profound impact on the Israeli public. Even Israelis on the left who favored a withdrawal from the West Bank became distrustful of the Palestinians. Israelis on the right never trusted the Palestinians to begin with, but virtually all Israelis now fear that a Palestinian state will become a haven for terrorists who could threaten their capital, their airport, and their population with the type of rocket barrages Hamas launched from Gaza. And these concerns assume Fatah re-mains in power; the prospect of a Hamas takeover of the West Bank makes any territorial concessions appear suicidal. It is in this context that Barack Obama launched his peace initiative.

George W. Bush was reviled in the Muslim world in part because he was viewed as an unabashed supporter of Israel. When Obama entered office, he was determined to demonstrate that he was differ-ent and immediately declared his support for a Palestinian state and confronted Israeli prime minister Netanyahu with a demand that Israel freeze all settlement construction in the West Bank and Jeru-salem. Combined with his outreach to Muslims, the Palestinians and their supporters were optimistic that an American president would, at last, force the Israelis to capitulate to their demands. They were quickly disappointed.

Netanyahu resisted Obama's call for a settlement freeze, but ultimately agreed to a ten-month suspension of building in the West Bank. He refused to extend the freeze to Jerusalem, however, because the city is Israel's capital and not part of the disputed territories. The conflict over settlements proved catastrophic to Obama's hope to restart peace talks.

From the Israeli point of view, Obama's policies were disturbing on multiple levels. First, Israelis were alarmed by the extent to which the president appeared to be solicitous of the Muslim world. Second, they believed he misunderstood the region, a view exemplified by Obama's apparent subscription to the Arabist belief that the Palestinian issue was the root of all problems in the Middle East. Third, Obama was publicly critical of Israel and publicly snubbed the prime minister. Fourth, Netanyahu was given no credit for accepting a two-state solution in which a Palestinian state would be created beside Israel. Not even Rabin was willing to do this; nevertheless, he was still pigeon-holed by the administration and media as hardline, right-wing, and anti-peace. Fifth, while most Israelis favored a withdrawal from the West Bank and opposed settlement construction, there was a consensus that Jerusalem should remain the undivided capital of Israel and that it was not part of the occupied territories. Sixth, Obama placed no demands on the Palestinians and was therefore seen as insensitive to Israeli concerns. Finally, after the disengagement experience, Israelis were unwilling to make new territorial compromises without assurances that the West Bank would not become "Hamastan." The upshot of all these concerns was that Israelis did not trust Obama, and they were not willing to take the risks necessary for reaching an agreement with the Palestinians if they did not believe the United States was behind them.

The Palestinians and others in the Middle East were disappointed in Obama's inability to force Netanyahu to freeze settlements in Jerusalem. This led them to believe the president was weak and unable or unwilling to exert the necessary pressure on Israel to cave in to Palestinian demands.

The focus on settlements also created a previously non-existent impediment to negotiations. Since the first Oslo talks, the Palestinians never made a settlement freeze a condition for negotiations. In fact, Abbas met with Olmert 36 times before Obama's election without Israel changing its settlement policy. Once Obama raised the issue, however, Abbas could not afford to demand less than the president. Hence, Abbas refused to enter negotiations. In addition, Hamas used terror to demonstrate it could not be ignored, that Abbas could not deliver peace, and that Gaza would not be part of any agreement.

By alienating both sides the president's peace initiative was essentially stillborn. This did not discourage him from trying again after his reelection.

By 2012, the Arab Spring had turned to an Islamic Winter, the Syrian civil war was escalating, the Palestinians had tried to circumvent negotiations by asking for UN recognition of a Palestinian state, and the Iranian nuclear threat loomed over the region. Nevertheless, Secretary of State John Kerry decided, in true Arabist spirit, that he should devote most of his attention to an Israeli-Palestinian peace agreement.

The timing also was dubious because of the public pronouncements of the Palestinians. On November 29, 2012, Abbas had given a vitriolic speech at the UN accusing Israel of "one of the most dreadful campaigns of ethnic cleansing and dispossession in modern history"; of unprovoked "aggression" in Gaza; and of "an apartheid system of colonial occupation, which institutionalizes the plague of racism." These were hardly the words of a leader interested in peace.

Similarly, in December 2012, Hamas leader Khaled Mashaal used his first visit to Gaza to declare: "From the sea to the river, from north to south, we will not give up any part of Palestine—it is our country, our right and our homeland." He added that Palestinians are "all united in the way of resistance."[9]

The Palestinian public also seemed in tune with Hamas, with 41 percent in a December 2012 poll saying that armed attacks on the army and settlers can force Israel to withdraw from the territories. Only 24 percent believed peaceful non-violent resistance would force Israel to withdraw, and only 30 percent agreed that negotiations with Israel would result in a withdrawal from the territories. When Palestinians were asked whose way is the best to end the Israeli occupation and build a Palestinian state, Hamas's way or Abbas's way, 60 percent said Hamas's way and 28 percent Abbas's way. By contrast, more than 60 percent of Israelis said they were willing to give up some or all of the West Bank.[10]

On the other hand, a 2014 poll shows that 76 percent of Israelis (and 83 percent of Israeli Jews) say that a withdrawal to the 1967 lines and a division of Jerusalem would not end the conflict, and 61 percent (up from 49 percent in 2005) think that defensible borders are more important than peace to ensure Israel's security. More than three-fourths of Israelis believe the Palestinians should recognize Israel's right to exist as a Jewish state, but only one-third believe it will happen. More than two-thirds don't believe the Palestinian leadership is capable of negotiating a binding peace agreement. Israelis (77 percent) also don't trust Palestinians to ensure freedom of worship for Jews if Israel withdraws from Jewish holy places.[11] Seventy percent of Israelis said they had little or no trust in the United States to support Israel's interests in a peace agreement.[12]

Meanwhile, Abbas resisted Kerry's repeated efforts to bring him to the negotiating table and stuck to the irredentist demands that Israel withdraw to the 1967 lines, accept the right of refugees to return to their homes, dismantle settlements, and recognize a Palestinian state in the West Bank and Gaza with East Jerusalem as its capital. The PA's religious affairs minister insisted that even the Western Wall would have to be inside a Palestinian state.[13] If Israel does not accept his terms, Abbas has threatened to circumvent negotiations and ask the UN to recognize a Palestinian state.

None of these positions was acceptable to Israel, but Netanyahu still called on Abbas to meet with him. The Israeli prime minister maintained that the root of the conflict with the Palestinians is their unwillingness to accept Israel as a Jewish state and set that recognition as a requirement for any deal. Here again, the transformation of the conflict from political to religious made it impossible for Abbas to agree. Hamas, of course, reiterated it would never accept a Jewish state under any conditions.

CHAPTER 10

CAN THE ISLAMIC-JEWISH/ISRAELI CONFLICT BE RESOLVED?

On one hand, the religious conflict seems irreconcilable. How can Muslims ever accept infidel Jews in their midst? On the other hand, Muslims have demonstrated remarkable pragmatism throughout their history. As historian Efraim Karsh noted, "The legendary Saladin himself spent far more time fighting Muslim rivals than the infidel crusaders; while he was busy eradicating the Latin Kingdom of Jerusalem he was closely aligned with the Byzantine Empire, the foremost representative of Christendom's claim to universalism."[1]

Even today, while Muslim nations rage against American policies, they also closely cooperate with the United States when it suits their interests. Though more infrequent, this is true for Israel as well. For example, though Jordan was technically at war with Israel, King Hussein was willing to accept Israeli help in 1970 to prevent the PLO from taking over his country. Similarly, the virulently anti-Semitic Saudis were willing to make a deal with Israel during "Charlie Wilson's War," in which they paid for Soviet arms captured by Israel for transfer to the anti-communist fighters in Afghanistan. The Saudis are now reportedly covertly cooperating with Israel to find a solution to the Iranian nuclear threats.

Muslim pragmatism also allowed both Anwar Sadat and King Hussein to sign peace agreements with Israel. This proved it is possible for Israel to have peace with Muslim states.

Meanwhile, radical Islamists are unlikely to ever accept a Jewish state in their midst. Groups such as Hezbollah and Hamas are committed to Israel's destruction. Could they change? It is highly unlikely, and, if they did, they would cease to be the same organizations. Hamas has been courted by the West to change its policy toward Israel in exchange for recognition, but the group has refused to bend. The good news is that both terrorist organizations have been weakened by developments arising from the Arab Spring.

Hezbollah chose to intervene in Syria to defend Bashar Assad, their patron (along with Iran) and source of arms. The group's involvement has been costly and unpopular. Hundreds of Hezbollah fighters have been killed, and their families and community have not reacted well to seeing body bags returning from the war. Shiites with the courage to challenge Hezbollah have questioned the justification for sending men to fight someone else's battle. Sunnis and others backing the rebels against Assad have new confidence that Hezbollah is vulnerable and have initiated a number of suicide bombings in Hezbollah strongholds in Lebanon. Sunni-led nations have been critical of Hezbollah since it provoked the war with Israel and have intensified their denunciations. Much of the Arab world dissociated itself from Nasrallah and rejected his call to join a holy war against Israel. The Arab media is also now openly critical of Hezbollah. For example, the Saudi paper *Al Watan* labeled their kidnapping of an Israeli soldier "irresponsible," and Kuwait's *Assi Assa* newspaper called Nasrallah an "adventurer" who was "unaware of his actions" and "does not understand what he has done to Lebanon."[2]

Hamas has suffered from the twists and turns in the revolution in Egypt. When the Muslim Brotherhood came to power, Hamas, which is an outgrowth of the Brotherhood, expected to receive financial, diplomatic, and military support. The hope was that smuggling tunnels would become superhighways for transferring goods and people, and that Egypt would no longer maintain a blockade. Before most of the benefits could be collected, however, the Egyptian military seized power and began to crack down on Hamas. The military accuses Hamas of aiding Sinai terrorists that have been attacking Egyptian soldiers and the gas pipeline serving Jordan and Israel. The government has used the state-run media to publicly attack Hamas, smuggling tunnels have been closed, militants arrested, and the group declared an enemy of the state.

The bad news for Israel is that both Hamas and Hezbollah remain dangerous threats to the Israeli civilian population. Hamas is still believed to possess thousands of rockets and, in early 2014, resumed sporadic attacks in the south. Despite the Syrian war, Hezbollah still is believed to have acquired tens of thousands of rockets. Israel fears that any military action against Iran would trigger a massive missile bombardment from Lebanon and that Hezbollah now has rockets with ranges sufficient to reach almost anywhere in Israel. Reportedly, Russia has provided Hezbollah with more sophisticated weapons systems, and, on at least two occasions, Israel is believed to have bombed supply trucks and depots holding these arms. Israeli intelligence also has learned the United Nations Interim Force in Lebanon has been useless and that Hezbollah has established arms caches and rocket launch sites in southern Lebanon. Unless the Lebanese government disarms Hezbollah, as called for by UN Security Council Resolution 1701, the group will remain a threat to Israel as well as to Lebanon. Fears that the Lebanese army would break up along Sunni and Shiite lines if it was ordered to move against Hezbollah have constrained the government from fulfilling its obligation. Consequently, Israel may have to launch a major offensive to degrade or, ideally, eliminate the missile threat.

When the Islamic Winter brought Egypt's Muslim Brotherhood to power, the region became a much more dangerous place. The prospect of Islamic extremists controlling one of the largest and most powerful armies (mostly supplied by the United States) raised the specter of radical forces from Egypt infiltrating and subverting Jordan and the Gulf states. The MB also repeatedly threatened to tear up the peace treaty with Israel, which would have dramatically intensified the strategic danger on Israel's southern border.

If Jordan were to fall to extremists, a plausible scenario given the presence of Hamas in the country and the momentum of the Islamic Winter, the peace treaty with Israel would be in peril, and Israel would have to concentrate more of its forces along its border with Jordan. This would also end any chance for an agreement with the Palestinians because Israel could not risk giving up territory and allowing a radical regime in Amman to join forces with the Palestinians to create a new, more dangerous eastern front.

In the north, Syria's future is uncertain with the civil war's outcome still in doubt. Regardless of the conclusion, the strategic picture in the region is likely to worsen. The situation is already perilous for Israel because of the possibility that the fighting might spill across the border. To date, only a few minor incidents have occurred, but any significant attack resulting in Israeli casualties could force Israel to become a combatant. An estimated 40,000 fighters from al-Qaeda and other radical Muslim groups have joined the fighting in Syria in hopes of establishing an Islamic state, and their presence poses both a short-term and long-term threat to Israel.

If Assad prevails, he will certainly be weaker, but he will continue to be a key ally for Iran and a conduit for bolstering Hezbollah. The West hopes Assad will be replaced by a "moderate" government; however, the rebels are divided between radical and more radical Muslims. Shiite extremists are backed by Iran while Sunni fighters are supported by Saudi Arabia and other Gulf states. If the Shiites prevail, Iran will be one step closer to creating an arc of allies in the region. If the Sunnis emerge victorious, it is less clear what policies they will adopt. Israel hopes that it has at least won some goodwill from the Syrian people by allowing many civilians injured in the fighting to cross the border for medical treatment. If any of the Islamists prevail, however, Western interests in the Middle East will be threatened and Israel could find itself eventually surrounded by fundamentalists bent on its destruction.

In the 1950s and 1960s, Israel survived despite being surrounded by nationalists trying to drive the Jews into the sea, but the nationalists had non-religious interests that were ultimately the basis of compromise. Radical Islamic states, however, are governed by religious law and faith and will not necessarily act pragmatically. The

Islamization of the Arab-Israeli conflict, therefore, is likely to make it far more difficult to resolve and herald a long period of instability and confrontation in the Middle East.

The Arab/Muslim street remains hostile toward Jews and Israel, and has grown tolerant of Muslim extremists. For example, at least 8 in 10 respondents in Lebanon (99 percent), Jordan (96 percent), the Palestinian territories (94 percent), Egypt (92 percent), Turkey (86 percent), and Tunisia (86 percent) have unfavorable views of Israel.[3] When asked specifically their opinions of Jews, it was not just the radicals who were anti-Jewish (if not anti-Semitic). A Pew poll found, for example, that only 2 percent of Egyptians, Jordanians, and Lebanese had favorable opinions of Jews.

Pew also found that anti-Israel Muslim terrorist organizations enjoy widespread support in the Middle East among Arab countries, but much less support from Muslim countries removed from the Islamic-Jewish conflict (e.g., Pakistan, Malaysia, Nigeria, and Senegal). For example, support for Hamas ranged from 43 percent in Jordan to 48 percent in the disputed territories and Egypt (just after the military coup and before the crackdown on Hamas). Hezbollah's standing is significantly lower, with support at 18 percent in Egypt, 26 percent in Jordan, 43 percent in the territories, and 46 percent in Lebanon. Support for al-Qaeda ranged from 1 percent to 35 percent in the territories. When asked if suicide bombing could be justified, 25 percent of Egyptians said sometimes or often; 33 percent of Lebanese (39 percent of Shiites) agreed, as did 62 percent of Palestinians. For Israel, the degree of Palestinian support for terrorists is a red flag.[4]

A poll a few months earlier reported that 51 percent of the Palestinians supported attacks on Israel. A huge 74 percent majority considered locally made rockets fired from the Gaza Strip toward Israeli regions helpful. The survey also showed a rise in supporters of armed resistance among the Palestinian public, from 25 percent in November 2012 to 33 percent in December 2012. A majority (63 percent), however, still said peaceful negotiations and non-violent resistance are the best methods to achieve an end to the occupation.[5]

About the same time, another survey found that 56 percent of Palestinians opposed a proposal to recognize Israel as the state of the Jewish people even after a Palestinian state was created and the refugee, settlement, and Jerusalem issues were resolved. Nearly half the respondents (45 percent) said reconciliation between Palestinians and Israelis will never be achieved, and 22 percent said it wouldn't happen for many generations to come. Fewer than 5 percent believed it would happen in the next few years.[6]

In contrast, more than 60 percent of Israelis said they were willing to give up some or all of the West Bank.[7] Yet another poll from December 2012 found that 77 percent of Israelis (79 percent of Jews) said it is important that the Palestinians recognize Israel's right to exist as a Jewish state, but only a third of Israelis believe it will happen. Nearly two-thirds do not believe the Palestinians will renounce the demand for the refugees to return. A whopping 77 percent of Jews (68 percent overall) do not believe the Palestinian leadership—Fatah and Hamas—is capable of making a binding decision. Three-fourths of all Israelis (83 percent of Jews) do not believe withdrawing to the 1967 borders and dividing Jerusalem will end the conflict. A small percentage of Israelis called for an intensification of efforts to make peace with the Palestinians (21 percent) or believe this had any connection to events in the Arab world (25 percent). A majority (51 percent—55 percent of Jews) said territories vital to Israel's security should not be returned. Similarly, a majority of Israelis preferred defensible borders over peace to ensure Israel's security.

When asked whether specific areas should be given up for peace, large majorities opposed withdrawing from the Jordan Valley, Gush Etzion, Ariel, the 67 borders with minor adjustments, territories overlooking Ben-Gurion Airport or Road 443 between Tel Aviv and Jerusalem, Rachel's Tomb (Bethlehem), the Machpelah Cave (Hebron), and the Western Wall. When asked if they were willing to give up all East Jerusalem neighborhoods except the Old City or putting the Temple Mount under Palestinian rule while keeping the Western Wall in Israel's hands, nearly two-thirds of respondents said no.

The poll was sponsored by an Israeli think tank that leans to the right, but most of the results are not surprising and illustrate the depth of feeling Israelis have toward certain areas and their concerns with giving them up. The only compromises that had any significant support were withdrawing from 50 percent of the West Bank—42 percent of all Israelis agreed, 34 percent of Jews—and placing the Temple Mount under international rule and the Western Wall in Israel's hands, which was favored by 51 percent (47 percent of Jews). The proposals by Barak and Olmert to withdraw from 95 percent of the West Bank were opposed by 52 percent of all Israelis and 62 percent of Jews.

The poll also demonstrated a strong belief in self-reliance and a skepticism toward depending on others for security or guaranteeing Jewish religious freedom. Only 26 percent of Israelis believed Israel could rely on foreign forces to preserve Israeli security if it gave up the Jordan Valley, and 68 percent (77 percent of Jews) did not believe the Palestinians would ensure freedom of worship if Israel gave them control of Jewish holy places. Israelis narrowly 53–43 agreed they could rely on an international force to guarantee their freedom to worship at Jewish shrines if they were evacuated.[8]

These and other polls consistently show a lack of faith on both sides, with Palestinians doubting Israeli sincerity and Israelis convinced that meeting all the Palestinians' demands would not bring about peace. They also display an alarming degree of Palestinian support for violence. Little encouragement can be found in any of these results.

Israelis are under almost constant pressure to ignore their fears, however. This pressure comes from the United States and European powers, which are determined to achieve a two-state solution at almost any cost—to Israel. This longstanding Arabist understanding of the Middle East, which pervades the U.S. State Department and foreign ministries around the world, will compel the West to appease the Muslims, just as they did during the 1974 oil embargo and in the years before and after the establishment of Israel.

To summarize the Arabist view: The root of all problems in the Middle East, including America's relations with the Arab/Muslim world, is the conflict between Israelis and Palestinians. And the reason for the clash between Israelis and Palestinians was, first, the creation of Israel, and is now Israel's "occupation" of the disputed territories. The logical conclusion for foreign policy makers is that Israel should be forced to withdraw all soldiers and settlers from the West Bank, East Jerusalem, and the Golan Heights.

Given how easy it is to empirically prove the absurdity of the Arabist conception, it is hard to believe it remains so prevalent among serious decision makers. Consider, for example, the Arabist fantasy of a world without Israel. Would any of the following problems in the Middle East disappear: the Shiite-Sunni rivalry, the Syrian civil war, the violence in Iraq, the upheaval in Egypt, Iran's nuclear program, or al-Qaeda's war on the United States? The answer is obvious: of course not. Israel has nothing to do with any of these issues; yet it is often blamed for them or their impact on the United States.

Moreover, the disappearance of Israel would not satisfy radical Muslims who believe the destruction of Israel and the eradication of the Jews is necessary to satisfy their interpretation of the will of Allah. For example, Egyptian cleric Muhammad Hussein Ya'qub said in a televised sermon in 2009, "If the Jews left Palestine to us, would we start loving them? Of course not," he explained. "The Jews are infidels not because I say so but because Allah does. . . . They aren't our enemies because they occupy Palestine; they would be our enemies even if they had not occupied anything."[9]

Thus, if Israel withdrew from 100 percent of the West Bank, 100 percent of the Golan Heights, and 100 percent of Jerusalem—in addition to the already total evacuation of the Gaza Strip—Hamas, Islamic Jihad, Hezbollah, and the other radical Islamists would not stop murdering Jews. Rather, they would intensify their terrorist campaign in the belief that if they could force Israel to withdraw that far, more violence would eventually force the Jews into the sea. This is one reason the Islamic-Jewish conflict will never end.

The radical Islamic focus on Israel is partly a matter of convenience; it serves as an easy rallying point for the masses. These Muslims have little doubt that Israel can be destroyed because time is on their side. Given the perspective of centuries, the current situation in which the United States is the global superpower and Israel is considered the region's dominant power is deemed a temporary phenomenon. Many Muslims believe that the Palestinians will outnumber the Jews in the area between the Mediterranean and Jordan River (not to mention the 300 million Muslims in surrounding countries) and will then overwhelm the Jews by the sheer force of their numbers. They also believe that it is just a matter of time before they acquire nuclear weapons, regardless of the outcome of the effort to halt Iran's nuclear program. At that point they will also have the military means to destroy Israel. As the Arab maxim says, "A man who gains his revenge after 40 years is acting in haste." Muslims recognize it took 200 years to expel the Crusaders, but they did it, and, though it may take 200 years to expel the Zionists, they are confident they will do so. The political adviser Ahmed Yousef to then-Palestinian prime minister Ismail Haniyeh of Hamas said it all in the title of his book, *The End of the Jewish State: Just a Matter of Time.*

Without waiting for centuries, Islamists believe they're already on the march. Hamas believes its terror campaign forced Israel's withdrawal from the Gaza Strip. Iran's support for terrorists throughout the region, defiance of the international community's efforts to curtail its nuclear program, and ability to suppress internal dissent demonstrates that it is a power to be reckoned with on the regional and world stage. Hezbollah's ability to survive a war with Israel showed how an insurgency can fight and "win" against infidel forces constrained by Western values. The United States did not have the wherewithal to sustain its operations in Iraq and Afghanistan, proving that the Judeo-Christian emphasis on self-preservation is no match for the self-sacrificing spirit of Islamists seeking martyrdom.

The hatred of Israel has intensified with the Arab Spring, according to Middle East scholar Ali Salim, who observed, "The unique prosperity and power of the Jews in Palestine compared with the slaughter, poverty and backwardness of their Arab neighbors, create antagonism, jealousy, rage and an increasingly murderous desire for 'revenge' among Muslims still under the heady influence of the Arab Spring and incited by the sheiks of the Muslim Brotherhood."[10]

The groundwork for genocide is also being laid throughout the Muslim world by the perpetuation of anti-Semitic stereotypes. Cartoonists, for example, portray Jews as Nazis, murderers of God, apes, pigs, spiders, vampires, and devils. "To the cartoonists, death seems the only worthy punishment that 'the Zionist enemy' merits."[11]

The destruction of Israel is only a small part of the Islamist agenda. As Osama bin Laden and others have emphasized, the grand plan is to reconstitute the glorious Islamic empire, so Israel is just an obstacle on the way to the reconquest of Spain, the rest of Europe, and, ultimately, the entire world. The war may initially be most intensely focused on Jews and Israel; however, the Islamic revival is also aimed at the Christian world.

A popular Muslim slogan is "First the Saturday people, then the Sunday people." Islamic sages believe that Christianity and Judaism have merit as monotheistic religions, but they are anachronistic and "while temporarily they can exist . . . eventually all Christians and Jews will convert to Islam." Jews are even seen as the source of evil behind Christianity, with imams suggesting that "the Crusaders" are "manipulated by the Jews who control them."[12]

The United States, in particular, believes the Muslim world can be reformed if nations adopt Western-style democracy. Every initiative (with the possible exception of Tunisia), however, has failed or, worse, brought Islamists to power with the legitimacy of an election. This was the case when President Bush thought he could push the Palestinians toward a representative government that would make peace with Israel. Instead, Hamas won the election and ultimately created its own theocratic government in the Gaza Strip. Fatah, meanwhile, is so frightened of losing power, Abbas has repeatedly canceled elections, which has allowed him to unilaterally extend the four-year term he won in 2005 and remain in power for ten years. By abusing his position, Abbas has given Hamas and other Palestinians justification to argue that he lacks the authority to sign a peace agreement with Israel while leading Israelis to question whether he can deliver and enforce any deal he makes.

The PA is not the only example of the calamitous results of elections in the region, with the other striking example being Egypt. Proponents of elections and democracy too often conflate the two. Elections are necessary but not sufficient to establish a free society. Countries such as Syria and Iraq (under Saddam Hussein) frequently held elections that typically featured one candidate, or the leader and a patsy, where the outcome was preordained. The dictators are always reelected with nearly 100 percent of the vote and no one in those nations seriously believes the elections are democratic.

Democracy means "rule of the people, by the people, for the people" and the granting of basic rights to citizens such as freedom of speech, religion, and assembly; press freedom; women's rights;

and gay rights. The only country in the Middle East where all those rights are protected is Israel. While President Obama has called on the countries destabilized by the Arab Spring to become more free and democratic, he has continued to apply the longstanding "democracy exception" to pro-American totalitarian nations such as Jordan and Saudi Arabia, which are not asked to adopt democratic principles out of fear the rulers would be ousted and the United States would lose its influence.

One element of Western appeasement is the reluctance—if not absolute refusal—to condemn Muslim anti-Semitism. As Kressel argues, "Otherwise reliable opponents of bigotry too often duck when confronted with massive evidence of Jew-hatred in Arab and Islamic countries; they offer either dismissive interpretations or complex justifications in lieu of plainspoken opposition."[13] Krausz adds, "Those who don't ignore the subject outright prefer to downplay it, dismiss it as a peripheral cultural phenomenon or justify it as a righteous response to Israel's maltreatment of the Palestinians."[14]

Just as Western leaders refused to take seriously Adolf Hitler's public declarations of his plan to exterminate the Jews, the threats against Jews made today by radical Muslims are typically brushed aside. Like Hitler, the Islamists make no secret of their genocidal intentions and willingness to use deceit, terrorism, and whatever else it takes to defeat the infidels. Still, the West has "incomprehensible trouble believing that radical Islam means exactly what it says," Middle East scholar Ali Salim says, adding, "For us Arabs it is not just wordplay; when someone tells you he means to kill you, he means to kill you."[15]

The West's confusion about how to respond to the Islamists is partly due to the reluctance to believe that religious wars are not just part of ancient history. It is inconceivable that adherents to a religion today would have the type of imperialist ambitions attributed to nation-states. Universalists also have difficulty processing the idea that some Muslims believe what their faith tells them and do seek the perfection of the world by recreating the caliphate and expanding it to encompass the planet.

The reluctance to believe in religious war is also a function of the ignorance and wishful thinking of Western analysts as well as the general public. This "we are the world" or "they love their children too" naiveté makes moving lyrics but assumes that extremists will not engage in actions that Westerners would eschew because they are rational. It does not occur to these universalists that it is possible for others to have a different view of rationality. It is inconceivable to most of us, for example, that Muslims would kill fellow Muslims, or that they would use women and children as suicide bombers or cannon fodder, and yet this is precisely what the extremists do.

Moreover, Westerners refuse to accept the goals and motivations of the terrorists and discount their guiding ideology and theology. "Our opinion-shapers will look into every possible angle of a terrorist's background and history to find some way to explain away, or on occasion sympathize with, the perpetrators' motives," observed Yair Shamir, a former Israeli Air Force commander. "In reality, our Islamist enemies' goals are aggressive by nature. Al-Qaeda's ideological underpinnings are found in the writings of Egyptian Islamist theorist Sayyid Qutb, which lauded offensive jihad, or a jihad of conquest. There is little that is reactive about his belief system—it is not aimed at defending its rights, but at conquering the world of disbelievers."

Some in the West believe *we* are the ones at fault; that our actions have provoked Muslims to become militant for any one of a number of sins: coveting Middle Eastern oil, supporting Israel, occupying "Palestine," displaying disrespect and intolerance for Islam, and keeping Muslim societies from developing. If we are indeed the cause of Muslim anger, then surely we can mitigate it by addressing their grievances.

Osama bin Laden's objectives, for example, were routinely said to be the removal of U.S. forces from the Middle East and the replacement of the Saudi monarchy with an Islamic republic. After 9/11, he tacked on the desire to liberate Palestine. However, even if the United States concludes that its interests in the region are secondary to the threat posed by al-Qaeda, abandons its support for both Saudi Arabia and Israel, and removes all American troops from the region, the jihad will not end until the Islamists remake the world as they believe Allah intended.

Israel is on the front line of World War III, though Muslims see it as a mere speed-bump on the way to world domination. Israel is forced to defend itself to survive; however, the rest of the world does not want to admit the threat exists or to contemplate what actions may be required to fight and win a religious war. Israel, the United States, and the rest of the Western world, however, have no desire to fight radical Muslims. President Bush emphasized the United States was fighting a war on terror, not Islam. President Obama went even further by ordering his administration to stop using terms such as Islamists or jihadists to describe Muslim extremists in response to protests from Muslims who objected to being tarred with such nomenclature, as well as from those who argue Islam is a religion of peace and terrorists are an aberration.

According to Salim, "The West's political correctness and refusal to listen to and believe what the political Islamist leadership openly says—and its refusal to defend itself—will lead to catastrophe."[16] By denying the problem, the war today is essentially being fought by only one side—the Islamists. No one, including the Israelis, expects the world to fight the extremists for Israel; it must be done to protect Western interests.

The Europeans are caught up in contradictory self-interests. On one hand, they are heavily dependent on trade and oil from the Muslim world and fear alienating their trading partners, but they are also afraid that Muslim extremists will target them, as they already have in terrorist attacks in London, Spain, and elsewhere. They are even more frightened of their own growing Muslim populations, who, in places such as France, are not assimilating their host nation's culture or political ethos. Some countries have subsequently approved measures aimed at stemming Muslim influence and forcing their acculturation, sometimes at the expense of the countries' democratic values, and at the risk of provoking a backlash. Examples include a French law banning face-covering headgear, such as veils and burqas (if it covers the face), and a Swiss law banning the construction of new minarets. These steps may exacerbate the problem by enraging what is becoming a significant voting bloc in many European countries.

Ironically, many Jews see European actions as reasonable responses to the threats they face, knowing that if they were to adopt similar policies the Europeans would be the first to condemn them as anti-Muslim and in violations of human rights. As in Israel, however, the Europeans are first and foremost concerned with their own self-interest.

One of the few clear-eyed Europeans is former British prime minister Tony Blair. After the murder of a British soldier in London by a Muslim extremist, Blair said that if the killing was simply the act of a crazy person, many people would say not to overact. However, Blair believes the ideology that inspired the attack "is profound and dangerous." He argues, "There is no problem with Islam . . . there is a problem within Islam." Blair cautions that "the seeds of future fanaticism and terror, possibly even major conflict, are being sown." The response, he insists, is to "help sow seeds of reconciliation and peace. But clearing the ground for peace is not always peaceful." He acknowledges that military force is not always the answer, "but disengaging from this struggle won't bring us peace." Contrary to the Muslim view, Blair argues "there has to be respect and equality between people of different faiths. Religion must have voice in the political system, but not govern it." While some Muslims are producing a new generation of radicals by teaching their children to hate and the superiority of Islam, Blair believes it is necessary "to educate children of different faiths across the world to learn about each other and live with each other."[17] Admirable as it is, Blair has taken on a Sisyphean task.

Education is often viewed as the key to a better future, which is why Israel has placed so much emphasis on Palestinian incitement and the educational curriculum. After reading a report on anti-Semitism and incitement in Palestinian textbooks in 2007, Hillary Clinton said, "We cannot build a peaceful, stable, safe future on such a hate-filled, violent and radical foundation."[18]

It's not just the Palestinians who are teaching their children hatred. On January 18, 2014, for example, Hezbollah's Al-Manar TV reported on a baby born in a Lebanese hospital who was then dressed in a Hezbollah uniform. "Military fatigues were the first garment to touch his tender body," the reporter said, adding that the child "is a potential resistance fighter from the first hour of his life."

Other than a violent clash sometime in the future between Islamists and the West, or the submission of non-Muslims to their "superiors," the only hope for an end to the conflict is a reformation of Islam led by Muslims. After centuries of accusing Jews of killing Christ, subjecting them to the inquisition and murder during the Crusades, Christians changed some of their beliefs toward Jews. Christianity still has its flaws, but it no longer threatens the lives of non-believers. The Church was prodded by outsiders to change, but ultimately the transformation had to take place according to its own rules and timetable. Similarly, non-Muslims cannot force change on the Islamic world; Muslim reformers will have to implement changes, a more difficult proposition given the belief that the Koran is the word of God.

Few Muslims have been willing to come forward to criticize extremists or to promote a "reformation" of Islam that might lead to the reinterpretation of traditions to suit modern times and expectations of tolerance. In a rare example of candor, a retired Saudi navy commodore, Abdulateef Al-Mulhim, wrote in the *Arab News* that the real enemy of Arab nations is not Israel; it is corruption, sectarian strife, oppression, and lack of education. "It is time to stop the hatred and wars," he added, "and start to create better living conditions for future Arab generations."[19]

Columnist Youssef Ibrahim, an Egyptian-born American who served as a senior Middle East regional correspondent for the *New York Times*, says reform will require the silent Arab majority to speak out. These are Muslims who believe

7th century Islam is not fit for the 21st century challenges. That women do not have to look like walking black tents. That men do not have to wear beards and robes, act like lunatics and run around blowing themselves up in order to enjoy 72 virgins in paradise. And that secular laws, not Islamic Shariah, should rule our day-to-day lives. And yes, we the silent Arab majority, do not believe that writers, secular or otherwise, should be killed or banned for expressing their views. Or that the rest of our creative elite—from moviemakers to playwrights, actors,

painters, sculptors and fashion models—should be vetted by
Neanderthal Muslim imams who have never read a book in
their dim, miserable lives. Nor do we believe that little men
with head wraps and disheveled beards can run amok in Lebanon, Saudi Arabia, Iran and Iraq, making decisions on our behalf, dragging us to war whenever they please, confiscating our
rights to be adults, and flogging us for not praying five times a
day or even for not believing in God.[20]

For now, Muslim radicals can only terrorize Jews, but can't
threaten Israel's existence. The long-term danger facing Jews and
Israel is the continued Islamization of Europe and the Middle East
combined with the acquisition by Muslim extremists of weapons of
mass destruction. By the time this book is published, the deadlines
will have long passed for a final agreement to be signed to ensure Iran
does not get a bomb. Huge questions remain, however, as to whether
the West will cave in to Iranian demands and permit them to continue
to enrich uranium, which would allow them to quickly weaponize if
they choose, or whether the West will allow Iran to build a bomb (or
wait too long to stop it) and rely on containment and deterrence to
discourage Iran from using the bomb. At this time, it appears very
unlikely that any military action will be taken, though force may be
the only way to slow, if not stop, Iran's nuclear program.

The issue is not just Iran. If Iran does get the bomb, the danger
will extend beyond Tehran to surrounding countries that are likely
to acquire or build their own bombs to deter Iran. The proliferation
of nuclear materials in the Middle East will increase the possibility
that a radical Islamic regime will use them directly against Israel or
another neighboring country. Alternatively, nuclear materials could
be given to, or fall into the hands of, terrorists who might use them
to create a dirty bomb or some other weapon that could target Israel
or Jews abroad.

Besides nuclear weapons, Israel faces potential threats from chemical or biological weapons. Syria was known to have large stockpiles
of non-conventional weapons, and Assad horrified the world when
he used chemical weapons against his own people. Under threat of

a military response by the United States, Syria agreed to allow inspectors to inventory their stocks and transfer them out of Syria for destruction. Assad was initially cooperative. However, not all of the weapons have been destroyed, and it is now believed that many of the chemical agents have been hidden in government strongholds and, possibly, smuggled into Lebanon. Though Assad used chemical weapons on his own people, he has never targeted Israel, presumably out of fear of massive retaliation from Israel. If Syria falls to a group of Islamists, however, the risk that Israel might face a chemical attack at some point will dramatically increase.

While Iran and some of the Islamist terror groups may envision the unification of the Muslim world to reestablish the caliphate, they face one serious impediment, namely, inter-Arab and intra-Muslim conflicts. For example, Turkish prime minister Tayyip Erdogan's efforts to establish Turkey as the dominant power in the Middle East ran afoul of the Saudis' claim to leadership of the Sunni world. Similarly, the Saudis see the Muslim Brotherhood as a competitor for influence among Sunnis. The civil war in Syria has revived radical jihadi groups, such as al-Qaeda, thanks largely to financial assistance from supporters in the Gulf who are now battling Shiites, including fighters sent from Lebanon by Hezbollah to defend the Assad regime. Meanwhile, the withdrawal of U.S. troops from Iraq has led to a breakdown in order and a possible plunge into civil war as Shiite-Sunni fighting escalates.

Turkish columnist Sinem Tezyapar observed that in the Islamic-Arab world today, "There is a continuous and unending stream of hate—hate of the Shia, hate of the Wahhabi, hate of the Sunni, hate of the Alawi, hate of the Christians, hate of the Jews and so on. . . . Hatred is deeply ingrained in their tradition, in their culture and in their own education. This fierce, venomous style is what is tearing the Islamic world apart; this is exactly what is happening in Egypt, Syria, Lebanon, Iraq, Libya, Yemen, Pakistan and others—Muslims killing Muslims."[21]

Unless and until the hatred ends, and these rivalries are overcome, it will be impossible for a pan-Islamist alliance to form that can challenge Israel and the infidel world beyond. Today's Muslim leaders show no more interest in pursuing pan-Islamism than pan-Arabism because they are unwilling to sacrifice their power and existing states for a unitary empire under someone else's rule.

In the absence of this alliance, the Islamic jihad is likely to be a gradual process whereby the radical Muslim population outside the Middle East, particularly in Europe, grows exponentially and gains greater and greater influence with the aim of ultimately overwhelming the non-believers. This will increase the level of peril for Jews, many of whom will conclude they will be safer in the United States or Israel. At some point, European Christians will wake up to their declining position and have to decide if they are prepared to take draconian steps to stem the tide.

Given all of the adverse conditions, is it conceivable for Israel to continue to exist and flourish and to achieve a peace agreement with the Palestinians?

It is unlikely in the immediate future because of several factors. One is that the Islamic Winter has created too much turmoil and uncertainty along Israel's borders. Israel is unlikely to agree to take the enormous risk of ceding territory to the Palestinians while all its borders have grown less secure. In addition, the disengagement was a harsh lesson for Israelis. The fact that the response to their peace gesture was an escalation of terrorism and the bombardment of the country with thousands of rockets made Israelis wary of any new concessions that could put most of their population, their capital, and their international airport within range of rockets that could be launched by terrorists from a Palestinian state.

The Palestinians squandered their opportunity to begin building their state. Meanwhile, Israelis were traumatized by the eviction of Jews from homes the government had encouraged them to live in, and by the poor treatment of many settlers who did not receive the government assistance they were promised. A withdrawal from the West Bank will be even more difficult because of the numbers involved, tens of thousands of Jews, compared to fewer than 10,000 who left Gaza. The Jews in Gaza offered minimal resistance; in fact, far less than expected. Many Jewish extremists live in the West Bank, however, and have vowed to fight any effort to remove them from their homes.

Gaza also had marginal religious significance to Jews, whereas Judea and Samaria are intertwined with Jewish history. In a peace agreement, Israel is expected to give up the holy city of Hebron, the resting place for Jewish patriarchs and matriarchs. Evacuating the city would also be an especially difficult sacrifice after the rebirth of a Jewish community that was driven out by an Arab massacre in 1929 and reconstituted after 1967.

Gaza is a small area bounded on one side by the sea, on two sides by Israel, and on its southern border by Egypt. It is relatively easy to contain. The West Bank is a much larger area, which can be partially contained by the security fence but, depending on the depth of the withdrawal, could leave the width of Israel little more than the nine miles of the pre-1967 lines. Israeli security officials also believe that their presence in the area has been critical to managing the ongoing terror threats.

Even though the PA security forces have received U.S. training, Israelis are skeptical they will be willing and able to control extremists. Israel also believes it must control the Jordan Valley, a possible smuggling and invasion route that the Palestinians maintain must be part of their state (though they have suggested compromises, such as stationing NATO troops in the valley for a limited period, an idea rejected by Israel, which does not trust others to look out for its security interests).

Israeli security concerns also have ramped up as a result of a sharp increase in terrorist incidents in 2013 and the beginning of 2014. Despite repeated promises in each negotiation and agreement that terror will cease, it has continued unabated since 1993. From 2012 to 2013, the number of attacks recorded in the West Bank more than doubled to 1,271. The Shin Bet reported that approximately 190 attacks were thwarted in 2013 (as opposed to 112 the year before), mostly from the West Bank. They included: 52 kidnapping plots, 52 shooting plans, the intention to use 67 improvised explosive devices, and 16 suicide bombing schemes.[22] In addition, more than 30 rockets were launched from Gaza at Israel in the first six weeks of 2014.

The PA is unable to meet its budget obligations, yet it manages to pay the families of "martyrs" and terrorists released from Israeli prisons. In 2014, the PA allocated an additional $46 million for former prisoners, Palestinian "heroes," many of whom were convicted of murdering Israelis. Since virtually the entire PA budget comes from foreign donors, Americans, Europeans, and other contributors are subsidizing rewards for terrorists.[23]

Given the level of continuing violence, and the PA's lack of control, Israelis fear the West Bank will be taken over by Hamas or other Muslim radicals who will ignore the terms of any agreement Fatah officials might sign with Israel. Moreover, an extremist group would be in a position to turn the West Bank into a terror base with most of Israel's industry and population in its crosshairs. Even if Fatah remains in control, many Israelis believe (and the PLO has given them good reason), the acceptance of a state in the West Bank and Gaza is just the first stage in their plan to gradually liberate all of Palestine. Unless Israelis are sure the conflict will end with the establishment of a Palestinian state in the territories, they have little incentive to change the status quo.

Hamas's tentacles have been spreading throughout the West Bank, but the combined efforts of Israeli and Palestinian security forces have kept the organization from developing a stronghold. While the focus has been on Hamas, however, other radical Islamists have been infiltrating the West Bank to challenge the Palestinian Authority. In June 2013, for example, hundreds of Muslim fundamentalists belonging to Hizb-ut-Tahrir marched through the streets of Ramallah, the site of the PA's government offices, to commemorate the ninety-second anniversary of the fall of the caliphate. They called for a "march toward Palestine to liberate the Aqsa Mosque and the rest of Palestine" from the "filthy Jews." Like other Muslim extremist groups, Hizb-ut-Tahrir seeks the unification of the Muslim world under a caliph who rules according to the Sharia. The organization considers the PA's leaders "traitors and collaborators with the enemies of Islam." So far the group has been kept in check by the PA, but it was allowed to march, some Palestinians believe, to show the Americans the PA needs greater support to prevent an Islamist takeover.[24]

An al-Qaeda–linked group also is reportedly operating in the West Bank. "By the will of God Almighty, the global jihadi doctrine has reached the bank of pride, the West Bank, planting its foothold after all attempts to thwart its presence," according to a website posting by a group calling itself Majles Shura al-Mujahideen (Holy Warriors Assembly). This statement appeared after Israeli security forces killed three Palestinians belonging to a radical Salafi cell, which was planning attacks and kidnappings of Israelis and PA officials they deem collaborators.

"Salafi jihadism is an idea, not an organization," a source told the *Jerusalem Post*. "According to this idea, everything that is a state but not ruled according to Islamic law is an infidel entity. For them, this holds true of the Palestinian Authority and Israel."[25] Recognizing the danger of these radical Salafists (not all Salafists, believers in a puritanical brand of Islam, are jihadis), the PA arrested 20 in West Bank cities.[26]

The danger is perhaps greater to the PA than to Israel at this point. While the Palestinians have warned of a third intifada if their demands are not met, it may be more likely that an uprising will be directed at the PA leadership if it is seen as making concessions to Israel on any significant issue. Abbas uses this potential threat as an excuse for intransigence.

"Palestine" may be radicalized even if Muslim radicals do not rule. Many Palestinians are Western-educated and have adopted Western habits, and a significant number, especially among the PLO leadership, are not known for being devout Muslims; nevertheless, the draft constitution prepared for a future Palestinian state, like all other Muslim states in the region, establishes Islam as the official religion, and an overwhelming 89 percent of Palestinians favor the imposition of Sharia law.[27]

Peace activists argue that an agreement with the Palestinians will improve Israel's security because Israelis will no longer have to worry about Palestinian terrorists, and the other countries in the region will no longer have any reason for antagonism toward Israel. This is the naiveté of those who refuse to acknowledge the conflict is rooted in Islam and not politics. Equally foolish is the notion that converting the conflict from one that matches a powerful state against "powerless, stateless victims" to one between sovereign states will lead to greater sympathy for Israel if Palestinian terror continues. This is pure fantasy; Israel will continue to be blamed and constrained even if it acts in self-defense against provocateurs from a Palestinian state. Besides, the last thing Israelis want is to be forced to reconquer the territories to pacify the border between Israel and Palestine.

On the positive side, Jews have craved peace with their neighbors since the first Jewish pioneers settled in the land in the nineteenth century. They have repeatedly demonstrated a willingness to make great sacrifices to achieve peace, as in the withdrawals from the Sinai and Gaza and offers to evacuate almost the entire West Bank. Most Israelis have supported territorial withdrawal in exchange for peace and security; they do not want to continue to be responsible for the lives of millions of Palestinians. Moreover, Israeli parents dream of the day when their children will no longer need to serve in the military.

Western officials are in a hurry to end the conflict because they want this annoyance to disappear so they can improve ties with the Muslims. They believe that once the Palestinian issue is resolved, the Middle East will become a utopian paradise. This, of course, is nonsense, but even if it were true, Israelis have to think beyond the immediate benefits that might derive from peace with the Palestinians. What will Palestine look like in 10 years? 20? 50? Israelis can see all around them how quickly regimes can change. What if the peacemakers of today are replaced by Hamas or other radical Muslims? Israel insists that a Palestinian state be demilitarized, but how will that be enforced? What will happen years from now when instead of homemade rockets, the Palestinians have access to sophisticated weaponry, especially considering they already have the means to threaten Israel's industrial, spiritual, and demographic heart? The signers of a peace agreement may bathe in the glow of international applause and Nobel Peace prizes, but will peace last? Israel's government has an obligation to protect the country against the worst-case scenarios not only of today, but of tomorrow, situations the rest of the world neither contemplates nor cares about.

The intractability of the Arab-Israeli, and now the Islamic-Jewish, conflict has never deterred American officials from seeking to cement their legacies by achieving what no one has done before. Every administration proffers its own formula because officials have never understood that the lack of peace has nothing to do with the failure of a diplomatic Einstein to invent the unified theory of negotiations to bring all the parties together. The United States can help nudge the parties to talk and offer suggestions for compromises or bridging proposals to try to bring the parties closer to an agreement. For example, the United States agreed to station troops in the Sinai to reassure Israelis returning the area to Egypt that the desert would not become a future invasion route. Similarly, Secretary Kerry is discussing various security arrangements for the Jordan Valley to try to meet Israel's security concerns while not compromising a Palestinian state's long-term sovereignty.

President Obama is the latest president to believe he knows how to break the logjam, and his desperation to have some foreign policy success has led him to aggressively pursue an agreement. However, no U.S. plan has ever been the basis of a peace agreement because, in the end, the parties themselves must decide that they want peace and are prepared to make concessions to bring it to fruition. Still, no deal can be achieved if the parties are not talking, and by keeping the pressure on both parties to continue negotiations, Obama can at least create the possibility of an agreement.

Two precedents for Middle East peace do exist. They are not ideal relationships, but Israel has nevertheless enjoyed peace with Egypt for more than three decades, and Jordan for nearly two. Though both have unique qualities that made peace more plausible, they are still Muslim countries.

The key to peace is not new permutations of the same old formulas for dividing the territory; the prerequisite, as it was in the Egyptian case, is a psychological breakthrough. One or both sides have to make a dramatic gesture that will convince the other that attitudes have changed and the time for conflict is over. The two sides may not become friends, but they must coexist. The question is whether such a breakthrough can occur so long as radical Islamic ideology dominates Palestinian thinking.

The end of the Arab-Israeli conflict has made it possible for Israel to improve relations, if only discreetly, with Muslim states beyond its immediate borders, such as Qatar and Oman. Ties would become more robust if not for the pressure placed on the Muslim states by the Arab League. These countries are far more interested in commerce than "Palestine," ideology, or religious fundamentalism. The same holds for North African countries such as Morocco. All of these countries broke off relations after the outbreak of Palestinian violence in 2000, but they still cooperate in a variety of areas outside the public eye.

Saudi Arabia is more problematic. The Saudis have at times demonstrated a willingness to work with Israel, if it can help them stay in power. Despite the massive arms buildup over the last three decades by the Saudis, Israel does not see them as a significant threat. Still, the Saudis create a variety of problems, some derived from their interests and others from their rabid anti-Semitism. The Saudis try to use their economic clout to drive a wedge between Israel and its Western allies. They also do everything in their power to obstruct any peace efforts in the region. They tried to sabotage the Egypt-Israel peace treaty and did succeed in preventing progress toward a comprehensive peace. Since then they have refused to cooperate with succeeding American administrations seeking their help to advance the peace process. They also actively interfere with peace efforts by indoctrinating Muslims with hatred for the Jews through Saudi-financed schools and materials, and they contribute millions of dollars to terrorist groups inside and outside the PA that target Jews, Israelis, and Americans. Saudi money has also gone to Hamas and undermined Fatah while the United States was trying to bolster Abbas. For now, Israel and the Saudis share an interest in preventing Iran from building a nuclear weapon; however, if they fail, and Saudi Arabia carries out its threat to acquire its own bombs, the Saudis could present Israel with an additional existential threat.

The prospect of any accommodation between Israel and other states in the region will depend on the outcome of the Islamic Winter. If the spread of radical Islam is stemmed, Israel may have potential partners for peace; however, if a series of dominoes fall to the Islamists, the danger to Israel will grow exponentially. For now, the situation is fraught with danger.

Imagine walking out the front door of your house one day to find that the house across the street is on fire. Sensing danger, you look around and see that the homes of the neighbors on both sides of you are ablaze. You look behind you and see smoke billowing out of the house behind you. Does this seem like the time to have a neighborhood block party?

This is essentially the situation Israel finds itself in since the Islamic Winter began. Israel is almost totally surrounded by countries that are antagonistic, unstable, heavily armed, and likely to become more dangerous as the upheaval continues and, possibly, escalates. It is a remarkable change from two decades ago, when the region was relatively stable and the prospect for a comprehensive peace became imaginable. Conditions today have reverted back to what they were prior to the 1973 War, when Israel faced enemies in all directions.

Most Israelis agree that expanding ties with their neighbors would significantly improve their lives. Israelis are realistic enough to know, however, that even in the best case, it is impossible to have the kind of peace they fantasize about, like America's relations with its neighbors. Once Israel reaches agreements with the Palestinians or others in the region, detractors who wish to see Israel disappear will simply refocus their attention on relations between Israel and the Palestinian state (e.g., water rights, air rights, and demilitarization) as well as the treatment of Arabs within Israel, which will be held up as the new case studies of Jewish treachery.

Moreover, the transformation of the dispute into an Islamic-Jewish conflict guarantees that radical Muslims will continue to do everything in their power to fulfill their conception of what Allah wants them to do, namely, kill Jews in the hope of destroying Israel. From their perspective the current clash is "nothing less than a continuation of Muhammad's battles with the Jews of Arabia" in the seventh century.[28]

It is often said that you make peace with your enemies, not your friends. The problem, Golda Meir explained more than 30 years ago, is that Israel's enemies do not want anything concrete, such as territory; the crux of the conflict is the unwillingness of Muslims to accept Israel's existence. "We intend to remain alive," Meir said. "Our neighbors want to see us dead. This is not a question that leaves much room for compromise."[29]

No one should confuse the Muslim states' unwillingness to engage in a war with Israel as a permanent acceptance of Israel's presence in the Middle East. If the balance of power in the region shifts, and a coalition of governments can form with the capability to destroy Israel, it is possible the conflict will intensify. In the short run, most Muslim states will do the minimum required to satisfy their populations' animosity toward Israel (which the leaders have indoctrinated and stoked); namely, spout pious slogans about the Palestinian cause, sponsor anti-Israel resolutions at the UN and other international forums, support terrorists, and engage in anti-Semitic rhetoric. It isn't pretty, and it isn't peace, but Israel can survive provided the radicals do not obtain weapons of mass destruction.

Israel and Jews around the world will remain in danger in the long run, however, unless the West recognizes it is in a fight to the death with radical Islam. No permanent accommodation can be reached between Islam and the Jews because Muslims believe that Allah is the one true God and that his teachings are the final word for all people. Muslims believe they will triumph over the Jews, even if it takes centuries to do it, and then they will proceed to restore the caliphate and impose their beliefs on the entire world.

As history has taught us, the Jews may be the first victims, but they will not be the last. Remember the words of Pastor Martin Niemoeller speaking about the Nazis:

> First they came for the Communists, but I was not a Communist so I did not speak out. Then they came for the Socialists and the Trade Unionists, but I was neither, so I did not speak out. Then they came for the Jews, but I was not a Jew so I did not speak out. And when they came for me, there was no one left to speak out for me.

NOTES

CHAPTER 1: ISLAM AND THE JEWS

1. Yossi Melman, "A Price Tag for Jewish Terror," *Jerusalem Report*, May 6, 2013, p. 18.
2. Efraim Karsh, *Islamic Imperialism* (New Haven, CT: Yale University Press, 2007), p. 15.
3. Aluma Solnick, "Based on Koranic Verses, Interpretations, and Traditions, Muslim Clerics State: The Jews Are the Descendants of Apes, Pigs, and Other Animals," MEMRI, November 1, 2002, http://www.memri.org/report/en/0/0/0/0/0/0/754 .htm#_edn56, accessed December 21, 2013.
4. Ibid.
5. Ibid.
6. Ibid.
7. Ibid.
8. Neil J. Kressel, *The Sons of Pigs and Apes: Muslim Antisemitism and the Conspiracy of Silence* (Dulles, VA: Potomac Books, 2012), p. 31.
9. Tibor Krausz, "Plumbing the Depths of Islamic Jew-hatred," *Jerusalem Report*, April 22, 2013, pp. 45-46.
10. Kressel, *The Sons of Pigs and Apes*, p. 33.
11. Carmen Matussek, "Fertile Ground for a Poisonous Weed: The Protocols of the Elders of Zion in the Arab World," *Israel Journal of Foreign Affairs* 7, no. 3 (2013): 71.
12. "Al-Shatat: The Syrian-Produced Ramadan 2003 TV Special," MEMRI, Special Dispatch No. 627, December 12, 2003, http://www.memri.org/report/en /0/0/0/0/0/0/1018.htm, accessed December 22, 2013.
13. *Al-Mussawar*, August 4, 1972, quoted in Bernard Lewis, *The Jews of Islam* (Princeton, NJ: Princeton University Press, 1984), p. 187.
14. Interview with Salman Al-Odeh on Rotana Khalijiya TV, August 13, 2012, translated by MEMRI, August 13, 2012.
15. *Assyasah* (Kuwait), translation from Saudi magazine '*Ain-Al-Yaqin*, November 29, 2002.
16. "Egyptian Cleric Abu Zayd: The Jews Use Internet Porn to Corrupt the Muslims," YouTube, translated by MEMRI, https://www.youtube.com/watch?v=Ah DhEIiMWgw, accessed May 29, 2014.
17. Middle East Media and Research Institute (MEMRI); *Al-Hayat Al-Jadeeda*, May 15, 1997; *Jerusalem Post*, May 23, 2001; Palestine News Agency WAFA, April 28, 2005.
18. Examples of cartoons from the Egyptian press can be found at http://www.jewish virtuallibrary.org/jsource/Peace/egtoons.html and a selection from multiple countries produced during the 2009 war in Gaza at http://www.jewishvirtuallibrary .org/jsource/anti-semitism/ascartoonsgaza.html.

19. Kressel, *The Sons of Pigs and Apes,* p. 47.
20. Iqraa Television, Saudi Arabia/Egypt, May 7, 2002, in Solnick, "Based on Koranic Verses, Interpretations, and Traditions, Muslim Clerics State."
21. Krausz, "Plumbing the Depths of Islamic Jew-hatred."
22. Martin Kramer, "Jihad 101," *Middle East Quarterly* vol. IX, no. 2 (Spring 2002): 87–95.
23. Karsh, *Islamic Imperialism,* p. 4.
24. Bernard Lewis, "Jihad vs. Crusade," *Wall Street Journal,* September 27, 2001.
25. Quoted in Karsh, *Islamic Imperialism,* p. 66.
26. Mitchell G. Bard, *Will Israel Survive?* (New York: Palgrave, 2007), p. 105.
27. Dore Gold, *Hatred's Kingdom* (Washington, DC: Regnery Publishing, 2003), pp. 7-8; Bernard Lewis, *The Middle East: A Brief History of the Last 2,000 Years* (New York: Scribner, 1995), p. 233; and Daniel Pipes, "Jihad and the Professors," *Commentary,* November 2002.
28. Karsh, *Islamic Imperialism,* pp. 66-67.
29. Ibid., p. 80.
30. Norman Stillman, *The Jews of Arab Lands* (Philadelphia: The Jewish Publication Society of America, 1979), pp. 247, 281–286; Maurice Roumani, *The Case of the Jews from Arab Countries: A Neglected Issue* (Tel Aviv: World Organization of Jews from Arab Countries, 1977), pp. 26-27; and Bat Ye'or, *The Dhimmi* (Rutherford, NJ: Fairleigh Dickinson University Press, 1985), pp. 60–61.
31. H. E. Wilkie Young, "Mosul in 1909," *Middle Eastern Studies* 7, no. 2 (1971): 232.
32. Daniel Jonah Goldhagen, *The Devil That Never Dies: The Rise and Threat of Global Antisemitism* (New York: Little, Brown, 2013), p. 96.

CHAPTER 2: JEWS INVADE THE HEART OF ISLAM

1. "PA Negotiator Saeb Erekat Claims Family was Canaanite, in Israel for 9,000 Years," *Algemeiner,* February 2, 2014.
2. Jacob Lassner and S. Ilan Troen, *Jews and Muslims in the Arab World* (Lanham, MD: Rowman & Littlefield, 2007), p. 73.
3. Robert D. Kaplan, *The Arabists: The Romance of an American Elite* (New York: Free Press, 1995), p. 7.
4. Hillel Cohen, *Army of Shadows: Palestinian Collaboration with Zionism, 1917–1948* (Berkeley: University of California Press, 2008), p. 15.
5. Ibid., pp. 49-50.
6. Ibid., p. 122.
7. Yehuda Bauer, "From Cooperation to Resistance: The Haganah 1938–46," *Middle Eastern Studies* (April 1966): 182-183.
8. Clemens Heni, *Antisemitism: A Specific Phenomenon* (Berlin: Edition Critic, 2013), pp. 487-488.
9. Joseph S. Spoerl, "Islamic Antisemitism in the Arab-Israeli Conflict," *Journal for the Study of Antisemitism* vol. 4, issue 2 (2012): 598.
10. Ibid., p. 599.
11. Ibid.
12. Mitchell Bard, *The Arab Lobby: The Invisible Alliance That Undermines America's Interests in the Middle East* (New York: HarperCollins, 2010).
13. Official British document, Foreign Office file no. 371/20822 E 7201/22/31; Elie Kedourie, *Islam in the Modern World* (London: Mansell, 1980), pp. 70–74.
14. Peter Grose, *Israel in the Mind of America* (New York: Knopf, 1983), p. 151. Michael Oren, *Power, Faith, and Fantasy: America in the Middle East, 1776 to the Present* (New York: W. W. Norton, 2007), p. 469.
15. Eliahu Elath, *Zionism at the U.N.* (Philadelphia: Jewish Publication Society, 1976), 316n.

16. Grose, *Israel in the Mind of America,* pp. 149-153; Oren, *Power, Faith, and Fantasy,* p. 471; Benny Morris, *1948* (New Haven, CT: Yale University Press, 2008), p. 393.

17. King Abdul Aziz ibn Saud to President Truman, October 30, 1947, in *FRUS: The Near East and Africa* v (1947): 1212.

18. Cohen, *Army of Shadows,* p. 211.

19. Efraim Karsh, *Islamic Imperialism* (New Haven, CT: Yale University Press, 2007), p. 140.

20. See Mitchell Bard, *The Water's Edge and Beyond: Defining the Limits to Domestic Influence on U.S. Middle East Policy* (New Brunswick, NJ: Transaction, 1991), pp. 159–188.

21. "Interview with Abd al-Rahman Azzam Pasha," *Akhbar al-Yom* (Egypt), October 11, 1947; translated by R. Green.

22. Security Council Official Records, S/Agenda/58 (April 16, 1948), p. 19.

23. Cohen, *Army of Shadows,* pp. 3 and 263.

24. Folke Bernadotte, *To Jerusalem* (London: Hodder and Stoughton, 1951), p. 113.

25. Quoted in Bernard Lewis, "The New Anti-Semitism," *American Scholar,* based on a lecture delivered at Brandeis University on March 24, 2004.

26. Lassner and Troen, *Jews and Muslims in the Arab World,* p. 102.

CHAPTER 3: ARAB UNITY AND DISUNITY

1. Clemens Heni, *Antisemitism: A Specific Phenomenon* (Berlin: Edition Critic, 2013), p. 473.

2. *Middle Eastern Affairs,* December 1956, p. 451.

3. Jacob Lassner and S. Ilan Troen, *Jews and Muslims in the Arab World* (Lanham, MD: Rowman & Littlefield, 2007), p. 22.

4. Mitchel Bard, *The Arab Lobby: The Invisible Alliance That Undermines America's Interests in the Middle East* (New York: HarperCollins, 2010), p. 41.

5. Eisenhower's message to Ben-Gurion, October 31, 1956.

6. Michael Oren, *Power, Faith, and Fantasy: America in the Middle East, 1776 to the Present* (New York: W. W. Norton, 2007), p. 514.

7. Efraim Karsh, *Islamic Imperialism* (New Haven, CT: Yale University Press, 2007), p. 162.

8. "The Campaigners," *Near East Report,* October 4, 1966, p. 79.

9. Karsh, *Islamic Imperialism,* p. 171.

10. Ibid., p. 113.

11. Raymond Close, "Intelligence and Policy Formulation, Implementation and Linkage: A Personal Perspective," Remarks at the 13th Annual Arab-US Policymakers Conference, Washington, DC, September 13, 2004.

12. Lassner and Troen, *Jews and Muslims in the Arab World,* p. 23.

CHAPTER 4: FROM TERRORISTS TO JIHADISTS

1. Jacob Lassner and S. Ilan Troen, *Jews and Muslims in the Arab World* (Lanham, MD: Rowman & Littlefield, 2007), p. 138.

2. Ahram Online, February, 19, 2012, http://english.ahram.org.eg/NewsContent /1/64/34912/Egypt/Politics-/Im-proud-my-son-Khaled-killed-Anwar-Sadat -Mother.aspx, accessed January 8, 2014.

3. Martin Kramer, "The Oracle of Hizbullah: Sayyid Muhammad Husayn Fadlallah," in *Spokesmen for the Despised: Fundamentalist Leaders in the Middle East,* R. Scott Appleby, ed. (Chicago: University of Chicago Press, 1997), pp. 83-181.

4. Col. Timothy J. Geraghty, *Peacekeepers at War: Beirut 1983—The Marine Commander Tells His Story* (Dulles, VA: Potomac Books, 2009), p. xv; "Gov. Cuomo Directs Flags to Half Staff," Albany, NY Governor's Press Office, October 22, 2013.

266   DEATH TO THE INFIDELS

5. Efraim Karsh, *Islamic Imperialism* (New Haven, CT: Yale University Press, 2007), p. 230.
6. Jonathan Masters, "Hezbollah," Council On Foreign Relations, July 22, 2013, http://www.cfr.org/lebanon/hezbollah-k-hizbollah-hizbullah/p9155#p1, accessed January 11, 2014.
7. Lassner and Troen, *Jews and Muslims in the Arab World*, pp. 143-144.
8. Ibid., p. 153.
9. Itamar Marcus and Barbara Cook, "How Fatah got religion and lost power," *Jerusalem Post*, September 12, 2008.
10. Palestinian Authority TV (Fatah), October 21, 1996.
11. Daniel Byman, *A High Price: The Triumphs and Failures of Israeli Counterterrorism* (Oxford: Oxford University Press, 2011), p. 212.
12. Quoted in Amal Saad-Ghorayeb, *Hizbullah: Politics and Religion* (London: Pluto Press, 2002), p. 170.
13. Daniel Jonah Goldhagen, *The Devil That Never Dies: The Rise and Threat of Global Antisemitism* (New York: Little, Brown, 2013), p. 347.
14. Mira Tzoreff, "The Palestinian Shahida: National Patriotism, Islamic Feminism, or Social Crisis," in *Female Suicide Bombers: Dying for Equality?*, Yoram Schweitzer, ed. (Tel Aviv: Jaffee Center for Strategic Studies, 2006), pp. 13-24.
15. Yoram Schweitzer, "Palestinian Female Suicide Bombers: Reality vs. Myth," in *Female Suicide Bombers: Dying for Equality?*, pp. 25-42; "For Palestinians, a New Low," *National Post*, November 25, 2006.
16. *Jerusalem Post*, January 15, 2003.
17. Interview with Jerusalem district police chief Aryeh Amit by Etta Prince Gibson, "The Back Page," *Jerusalem Report*, March 31, 2008.
18. Jitka Maleckova and Alan Kreuger, "Education, Poverty, Political Violence and Terrorism: Is There a Causal Connection?" July 2002, quoted in the *Daily Star* (Lebanon), August 6, 2002.
19. Jewish Telegraphic Agency, December 18, 2001.
20. Daniel Pipes, "Palestinian Responses to an Israeli Withdrawal from Gaza," Danielpipes.org, September 6, 2005.
21. *Washington Post*, January 30, 2001.
22. IDF Spokesperson, June 26, 2013.
23. Rory McCarthy, "Hizbullah Leader: We Regret the Two Kidnappings That Led to War with Israel," *The Guardian*, August 27, 2006.
24. Anne Barnard, "Pressed on Syria, Hezbollah Leader Urges Focus on Israel," *New York Times*, August 2, 2013.
25. "Intransigent Hamas," *Washington Post*, October 7, 2006; referenced in *Post*, October 11, 2006.
26. *Canadian Jewish News*, August 17, 2007.
27. Itamar Marcus and Nan Jacques Zilberdik, "Hamas: Martyrdom Death for Allah Is Ideal," Palestinian Media Watch, December 9, 2012, http://palwatch.org/main.aspx?fi=157&doc_id=8094, accessed January 15, 2014.
28. "Palestinian Rockets and the Children of Sderot," *FrontPage Magazine*, February 23, 2010.
29. Eli Ashkenazi and Mijal Grinberg, "Study: Most Sderot Kids Exhibit Post-Traumatic Stress Symptoms," *Haaretz*, January 17, 2008.
30. "The Invisible Victims of the Gaza Conflict," *New York Jewish Week*, November 16, 2012.

CHAPTER 5: THE ARAB SPRING'S TRANSFORMATION INTO THE ISLAMIC WINTER

1. Rafael Israeli, *From Arab Spring to Islamic Winter* (New Brunswick, NJ: Transaction Publishers, 2013), p. 297.
2. Con Coughlin, "The Arab Spring Is Becoming an Islamist Takeover," *Telegraph* Blogs, October 25, 2011.

3. Israeli, *From Arab Spring to Islamic Winter*, p. 298.

4. Ibid., pp. 1-2.

5. Herb Keinon, "Sharansky: PA Election Not 'Truly Free,'" *Jerusalem Post*, January 10, 2005.

6. Dina Khayat, "The Rapid Fall of the Muslim Brotherhood," *Wall Street Journal*, January 8, 2014.

7. Khaled Abu Toameh, "Palestine Was Never a Jewish Homeland," *Jerusalem Post*, May 9, 2013.

8. Josh Rogin, "Morsi Implies Jews Control the American Media," *Foreign Policy*, January 23, 2013; "Beyond 'Apes and Pigs': Ten Morsi Quotes That Tell All," *Algemeiner*, January 25, 2013, http://www.algemeiner.com/2013/01/25/beyond-apes-and-pigs-ten-morsi-quotes-that-tell-all/, accessed January 17, 2014; Daniel Jonah Goldhagen, *The Devil That Never Dies: The Rise and Threat of Global Antisemitism* (New York: Little, Brown, 2013), pp. 237-238.

9. "$2.5 Bn Lost Income for Egyptian Tourism since 2011," Ahram Online, February 21, 2013.

10. Leila Hatoum, "Gulf States Curtail Online Dissent," *Wall Street Journal*, April 2, 2013.

11. Jeffrey Goldberg, "The Modern King in the Arab Spring," *The Atlantic*, April 2013.

12. "Hezbollah Leader Nasrallah Vows Victory in Syria," BBC, May 25, 2013.

13. Jim Michaels, "Kerry: Syrian Rebels Have Not Been Hijacked by Extremists," *USA Today*, September 5, 2013; Neil Macfarquhar and Hwaida Saad, "As Syrian War Drags On, Jihadists Take Bigger Role," *New York Times*, July 29, 2012.

14. Jay Solomon, "France Accuses Syrian Regime of Multiple Chlorine Gas Attacks," *Wall Street Journal*, May 13, 2014.

15. Marwan Muasher, "Year Four of the Arab Awakening," Carnegie Middle East Program, December 12, 2013.

16. David Littman, "Universal Human Rights in Islam," *Midstream*, February/March 1999.

CHAPTER 6: IRAN AND LITTLE SATAN

1. "Iran," *Encyclopaedia Judaica* (Farmington Hills, MI: The Gale Group, 2008).

2. David Littman, "Universal Human Rights and Human Rights in Islam," *Midstream* (February/March 1999).

3. Efraim Karsh, *Islamic Imperialism* (New Haven, CT: Yale University Press, 2007), p. 221.

4. "Iran," *Encyclopaedia Judaica*.

5. E. Zigron and A. Savyon, "The Image of the Jew in the Eyes of Iran's Islamic Regime—Part I: Theological Roots," MEMRI, January 27, 2013.

6. Efraim Karsh, "Why the Middle East Is So Volatile," *Middle East Quarterly* (December 2000): 13–22.

7. Zigron and Savyon, "The Image of The Jew in the Eyes of Iran's Islamic Regime."

8. "Antisemitic Statements, Publications by Iranian Regime," MEMRI, January 25, 2012, http://www.memri.org/report/en/print6024.htm, accessed January 22, 2014.

9. Adam Entous, Charles Levinson, and Julian E. Barnes, "Hezbollah Upgrades Missile Threat to Israel," *Wall Street Journal*, January 3, 2014.

10. 32. Daniel Jonah Goldhagen, *The Devil That Never Dies: The Rise and Threat of Global Antisemitism* (New York: Little, Brown, 2013), p. 232.

11. Clemens Heni, *Antisemitism: A Specific Phenomenon* (Berlin: Edition Critic, 2013), p. 487.

12. Mahmoud Ahmadinejad, "Speech, United Nations General Assembly, Sixty Third Session, General Debate," September 23, 2008, http://www.un.org/en/ga/63/generaldebate/pdf/iran_en.pdf, accessed November 3, 2013.

13. Goldhagen, *The Devil That Never Dies,* p. 232.

14. Ibid., p. 450.

15. "Hold Iran Accountable for Incitement to Genocide, Irwin Cotler Urges," *The Times of Israel,* December 21, 2012, http://www.timesofisrael.com/hold-iran-accountable-for-incitement-to-genocide-irwin-cotler-urges/#ixzz2rEbiX0B0, accessed January 23, 2014.

16. Bernard Lewis, "August 22," *Wall Street Journal,* August 8, 2006.

17. Prince Turki Al Faisal speech to the 22nd Annual Arab-U.S. Policymakers Conference, Washington, DC, October 22, 2013.

18. Friedrich Steinhausler, "Infrastructure Security and Nuclear Power," *Strategic Insights* 8, no. 5 (December 2009).

19. Jason Burke, "Riyadh Will Build Nuclear Weapons if Iran Gets Them, Saudi Prince Warns," *Guardian,* June 29, 2011.

20. Mark Urban, "Saudi Nuclear Weapons 'On Order' from Pakistan," BBC News, November 6, 2013.

21. "Sunday Times: Israel, Saudi Arabia Cooperating to Plan Possible Iran Attack," *Haaretz,* November 17, 2013.

22. Jay Solomon, "Panetta Warns of Iran Threat," *Wall Street Journal,* June 27, 2010.

23. "Bolton: Obama's Policy on Iran Like Sleepwalking Past the Grave," *Arutz Sheva,* quoting interview with John Bolton on Fox News, July 3, 2012.

24. "Iran's Leader: War Would Be Detrimental to U.S.," CNN, February 3, 2012, http://edition.cnn.com/2012/02/03/world/meast/iran-warning/?hpt=wo_c2, accessed January 23, 2014.

25. Asher Zeiger, "Netanyahu at Shoah Ceremony: 'We Won't Leave Our Fate in the Hands of Others," *Times of Israel,* April 7, 2013.

26. Agence France Presse, April 16, 2013.

27. Mark Perry, "The Entebbe Option," *Foreign Policy,* September 27, 2012.

28. Netanyahu speech to the AIPAC Policy Conference in Washington, DC, March 5, 2012.

29. "Views of the Israeli Public on Israeli Security and Resolution of the Arab-Israeli Conflict," Jerusalem Center for Public Affairs/Dahaf Institute Survey, December 2012; Stephen Miller, "Only One in Five Israelis Trusts Obama on Iran," *Times of Israel,* January 20, 2014.

30. "Iran Heeds Israel's Warning of Uranium 'Red Line,'" *Washington Post,* April 8, 2013.

31. "Iran Agrees to Curb Nuclear Activity at Geneva Talks," BBC News, November 24, 2013, http://www.bbc.co.uk/news/world-middle-east-25074729, accessed January 23, 2014.

32. "Limited Support for Iran Nuclear Agreement," Pew Research Center and *USA Today,* conducted December 3–8, 2013, December 9, 2013, http://www.people-press.org/2013/12/09/limited-support-for-iran-nuclear-agreement/, accessed January 21, 2014.

33. David Simpson and Josh Levs, "Israeli PM Netanyahu: Iran Nuclear Deal 'Historic Mistake,'" CNN, November 25, 2013, http://edition.cnn.com/2013/11/24/world/meast/iran-israel/, accessed January 23, 2014.

34. Charles Krauthammer, "The Real Rouhani," *Washington Post,* September 27, 2013.

35. Transcript of the Third Presidential Debate, October 22, 2012, National Public Radio, http://www.npr.org/2012/10/22/163436694/transcript-3rd-obama-romney-presidential-debate, accessed April 2, 2014.

36. James Zogby, "What Iranians Think," Huffington Post, December 7, 2013, http://www.huffingtonpost.com/james-zogby/what-iranians-think_b_4403946.html, accessed April 2, 2014.

37. "Iran and World Powers Reach Agreement on Nuclear Deal Start," CBS News, January 12, 2014, http://www.cbsnews.com/news/iran-and-world-powers-reach-agreement-on-nuclear-deal-start/, accessed January 23, 2014.

38. "Iran Says It Won't Scrap Any Nuclear Facility," Associated Press, February 18, 2014.
39. "George Will: 'Iran is Claiming Victory And I think Probably Rightly So,'" Real Clear Politics, January 15, 2014, http://www.realclearpolitics.com/video/2014/01/15/george_will_iran_is_claiming_victory_and_i_think_probably_rightly_so.html, accessed April 2, 2014.
40. Goldhagen, *The Devil That Never Dies*, p. 348.

CHAPTER 7: THE GLOBAL JIHAD

1. "Number of Chechens Leaving Chechnya Grows: Jews Are to Replace Them," KavkazCenter.com, January 20, 2013, http://www.kavkazcenter.com/eng/content/2013/01/20/17280.shtml, accessed, January 31, 2014; Nadav Shragai, *The "Al-Aksa Is in Danger" Libel: The History of a Lie* (Jerusalem: Jerusalem Center for Public Affairs, 2012), pp. 74-75.
2. Neil J. Kressel, *The Sons of Pigs and Apes: Muslim Anti-Semitism and the Conspiracy of Silence* (Dulles, VA: Potomac Books, 2012), pp. 101-151.
3. Daniel Jonah Goldhagen, *The Devil That Never Dies: The Rise and Threat of Global Antisemitism* (New York: Little, Brown, 2013), p. 387.
4. Henry Rome, "Author Jacobson Unravels 'Logic' Behind Holocaust Denial, Anti-Semitism," *Jerusalem Post*, October 9, 2013.
5. Yossi Melman, "Jewish Intelligence," *Jerusalem Report*, April 22, 2013, p. 20.
6. Drew DeSilver, "The Future of the Global Muslim Population," Pew Research Center, January 27, 2011, http://www.pewforum.org/2011/01/27/future-of-the-global-muslim-population-regional-europe/, accessed January 31, 2014.
7. Tony Blair, "Why the Middle East Matters," Office of Tony Blair, April 23, 2014, http://www.tonyblairoffice.org/news/entry/why-the-middle-east-matters-keynote-speech-by-tony-blair/, accessed June 8, 2014.
8. Alan Cowell, "Britain Orders Inquiry into Muslim Brotherhood in London," *New York Times*, April 1, 2014.
9. Andrew Higgins, "Jews in Europe Report a Surge in Anti-Semitism," *New York Times*, November 8, 2013.
10. "Survey of American Jewish Opinion," American Jewish Committee, 2013, http://www.ajc.org/site/apps/nlnet/content3.aspx?c=7oJILSPwFfJSG&b=8479755&ct=13376311, accessed February 1, 2014.
11. Michel Gurfinkiel, "You Only Live Twice," *Mosaic*, August 2013, http://mosaicmagazine.com/essay/2013/08/you-only-live-twice/, accessed April 4, 2014.
12. "ADL Global 100: A Survey of Attitudes Toward Jews in Over 100 Countries Around the World," New York, Anti-Defamation League, 2014.
13. Manfred Gerstenfeld, "Muslim Anti-Semitism in Western Europe," *Jerusalem Post*, February 19, 2013.
14. Günther Jikeli, "Antisemitism among Young European Muslims," in *Resurgent Antisemitism*, Alvin H. Rosenfeld, ed. (Bloomington: Indiana University Press, 2013), pp. 272-273.
15. Günther Jikeli, "Myths and Truth about Muslim Anti-Semitism in Europe," in *Demonizing Israel and the Jews*, Manfred Gerstenfeld, ed. (New York: RVP Press, 2013), p. 151; Günther Jikeli, "Antisemitism among Young European Muslims," p. 281.
16. Kressel, *The Sons of Pigs and Apes*, p. 49.
17. Gerstenfeld, "Muslim Anti-Semitism in Western Europe."
18. "50% Belgian Muslim Teens Have Anti-Semitic Views," *Jewish Telegraphic Agency*, March 28, 2013.
19. Jikeli, "Antisemitism Among Young European Muslims," p. 292.
20. "The World's Muslims: Religion, Politics and Society," Pew Research Center, April 2013, p. 29.
21. Pew Research Center's Global Attitudes Project, September 10, 2013.

22. Robert Satloff, "Just Like Us! Really?" *Weekly Standard,* May 12, 2008; John L. Esposito and Dalia Mogahed, *Who Speaks for Islam? What A Billion Muslims Really Think* (New York: Gallup Press, 2007).

23. Robert S. Wistrich, "The Slow Death of European Jewry," *Jerusalem Report,* April 22, 2013, p. 5.

24. "Manifestations of Anti-Semitism in the European Union—Analysis," commissioned by the E.U. Monitoring Center on Racism and Xenophobia, March 2003, https://www.jugendpolitikineuropa.de/downloads/4-20-1949/eustudieantisem .pdf, accessed February 27, 2014.

25. "Report in France: The Majority of Perpetrators of Hate Incidents— Muslims," The Coordinating Forum for Antisemitism, 2013; "Report on Antisemitism in France," Jewish Community Security Service, 2012.

26. "French Jewish Leader: Concerns of Anti-Semitism Keeping Jews from Enrolling in Public Schools," Jewish Telegraphic Agency, November 27, 2013; "Discrimination and Hate Crimes Against Jews in EU Member States," European Union Agency for Fundamental Rights, November 2013; Liam Hoare, "Could Spreading European Anti-Semitism Drive Jews from Homelands?" *Forward,* November 29, 2013.

27. *Attitudes Toward Jews In Ten European Countries* (New York: Anti-Defamation League, March 2012), http://www.adl.org/assets/pdf/israel-international/adl_anti -semitism_presentation_february_2012.pdf, accessed February 1, 2014.

28. "Poll: Israel Viewed Negatively Around the World," *Jerusalem Post,* May 17, 2012.

29. Catherine Philip, "West Turns Blind Eye to Friend It Dare Not Offend," *Times Online,* March 26, 2009.

30. "Poll: Israel Viewed Negatively Around the World."

31. "Unfavorable Views of Jews and Muslims on the Increase in Europe," Pew Global Attitudes Report, September 17, 2008.

32. Bernard Edinger, "Is the Glass Half-Empty or Half-Full for France's Jews?" *The Jerusalem Report,* April 22, 2013, p. 9.

33. Manfred Gerstenfeld, "Muslim Anti-Semitism in Western Europe," *Jerusalem Post,* February 19, 2013.

34. "Murder Suspect Who Fought in Syria Fuels Concern in the West," *Time,* June 5, 2014, p. 12.

35. Seth G. Jones, "The Accelerating Spread of Terrorism," *Wall Street Journal,* June 4, 2014.

36. Edinger, "Is the Glass Half-Empty or Half-Full for France's Jews?" p. 8.

37. Rebecca Benhamou, "French Consider Jews 'Tolerant,' Distrust Islam," *Times of Israel,* January 30, 2013.

38. "French Jewish Leader: Concerns of Anti-Semitism Keeping Jews from Enrolling in Public Schools," Jewish Telegraphic Agency, November 27, 2013, http://www .jpost.com/Jewish-World/Jewish-News/French-Jewish-leader-Concerns-of-anti -Semitism-keeping-Jews-from-enrolling-in-public-schools-333189, accessed April 4, 2014.

39. Sam Sokol, "Israel Greets 16,884 New Immigrants," *Jerusalem Post,* April 29, 2014.

40. "French Jewish Leader: Concerns of Anti-Semitism Keeping Jews from Enrolling in Public Schools."

41. "Building a Political Firewall Against the Assault on Israel's Legitimacy—London as a Case Study," Reut Institute, November 2013, pp. 27-28.

42. Kressel, *The Sons of Pigs and Apes,* p. 49.

43. Nick Meo, "Jews Leave Swedish City After Sharp Rise in Anti-Semitic Hate Crimes," *Telegraph,* February 21, 2010.

44. "Anti-Israel Protest Staged at Sweden Tennis Match," Reuters, March 3, 2009; "Malmö Blacklisted Over Israel Tennis Shutout," *The Local* (Sweden), April 3, 2009, http://www.thelocal.se/20090403/18648, accessed February 2, 2014.

45. Gurfinkiel, "You Only Live Twice."

46. Frits Bolkestein, "Israel, the European Commission, Europe, and the Netherlands," in *Demonizing Israel and the Jews,* Manfred Gerstenfeld, ed. (New York: RVP Press, 2013), p. 27.

47. Stephen Schwartz, *The Two Faces of Islam* (New York: Anchor Books, 2002), p. 259; Blaine Harden, "Saudis Seek U.S. Muslims For Their Sect," *New York Times,* October 20, 2001; Laurent Murawiec, *Princes of Darkness: The Saudi Assault on the West* (Lanham, MD: Rowman and Littlefield, 2003), pp. 96–99.

48. Stewart Bell, "Updated: Board Suspends Toronto Islamic School's Operating Permit After Row over Anti-Jewish Curriculum," *National Post,* May 17, 2012.

49. Valerie Strauss and Emily Wax, "Where Two Worlds Collide: Muslim Schools Face Tension of Islamic, U.S. Views," *Washington Post,* February 25, 2002; "Islamic Groups Hit Curriculum at Saudi School," *Washington Times,* August 2, 2004; Jerry Markon and Ben Hubbard, "Review Finds Slurs in '06 Saudi Texts," *Washington Post,* July 15, 2008; Dore Gold, *Hatred's Kingdom* (Washington, DC: Regnery Publishing, 2003), 4.

50. Goldhagen, *The Devil That Never Dies,* p. 441.

51. Quoted from textbooks in Center for Religious Freedom of Hudson Institute, *2008 Update: Saudi Arabia's Curriculum of Intolerance* (Washington, D.C.: Hudson Institute, 2008).

52. Center for Religious Freedom of Hudson Institute, *2008 Update.*

53. "Saudi Arabia," International Religious Freedom Report 2009, U.S. Department of State, October 26, 2009. See also Neil MacFarquhar, "A Nation Challenged: Education; Anti-Western and Extremist Views Pervade Saudi Schools," *New York Times,* October 19, 2001.

54. Jack Fairweather, "Saudi-Backed Hate Propaganda Exposed," *Washington Post,* September 3, 2008.

55. Jikeli, "Antisemitism among Young European Muslims," p. 271.

56. Goldhagen, *The Devil That Never Dies,* p. 375.

57. Kressel, *The Sons of Pigs and Apes,* p. 56.

58. Ibid., p. 140.

59. Michael Whine, "Terrorism Targeting Jewish Communities and Israelis Abroad," in *Demonizing Israel and the Jews,* Manfred Gerstenfeld, ed. (New York: RVP Press, 2013), p. 40.

60. Council on Foreign Relations, *Terrorist Financing,* report of an Independent Task Force, October 2002, p. 1, http://www.cfr.org/pdf/Terrorist_Financing_TF.pdf; Jean-Charles Brisard, "Terrorism Financing," report prepared for the president of the Security Council, United Nations, December 19, 2002; Murawiec, *Princes of Darkness,* 100–101.

61. Kressel, *The Sons of Pigs and Apes,* p. 2.

62. Sebastian Rotella, "The Terror Threat and Iran's Inroads in Latin America," ProPublica, July 11, 2013, http://www.propublica.org/article/the-terror-threat-and -irans-inroads-in-latin-america, accessed April 4, 2014. The U.S. Drug Enforcement Agency has also discovered drug smuggling operations in the United States that are funneling money to Hezbollah.

63. Joby Warrick, "Mexican Depicts Iran's Wooing of Hispanic Youths," *Washington Post,* August 11, 2013.

64. Murawiec, *Princes of Darkness,* xiii–xv; Thomas E. Ricks, "Briefing Depicted Saudis as Enemies," *Washington Post,* August 6, 2002.

65. Prados and Blanchard, *Saudi Arabia;* Michael Abramowitz, "Oil Efforts Are Best Possible, Saudis Say," *Washington Post,* May 17, 2008; Michael Jacobson, "Saudi Efforts to Combat Terrorist Financing," *PolicyWatch* no. 1555, Washington Institute for Near East Policy, July 21, 2009; Andrew Quinn, "More Saudi Help Needed on Terror Finance, US Report," Reuters, September 29, 2009.

66. "About OIC," Organization of Islamic Cooperation, http://www.oic-oci.org /oicv2/page/?p_id=52&p_ref=26&lan=en, accessed February 4, 2014.

67. Abba Eban, "The Saudi Text," *New York Times*, November 18, 1981.

68. "The U.N. Expunges a Smear," editorial, *New York Times*, December 17, 1991.

69. Secretary-General's message to the Third Session of the Human Rights Council, United Nations, November 29, 2006, http://www.un.org/sg/statements/?nid=2333, accessed April 4, 2014.

70. Tim Franks, "UN Expert Stands by Nazi Comments," BBC, April 8, 2008, http://news.bbc.co.uk/2/hi/middle_east/7335875.stm, accessed April 4, 2014.

71. Tovah Lazaroff, "US Slams Richard Falk's 'Despicable and Deeply Offensive Comments,'" *Jerusalem Post*, December 21, 2013.

72. "IDF Releases Cast Lead Casualty Numbers," *Jerusalem Post*, March 28, 2009.

73. Richard Goldstone, "Reconsidering the Goldstone Report on Israel and War Crimes," *Washington Post*, April 1, 2011.

74. Ibid.

75. Colonel Richard Kemp, "UK Commander Challenges Goldstone Report," UN Watch, October 16, 2009.

76. "Goldstone: Claims of Israel's Gaza War Crimes Should Be Reconsidered," *Haaretz*, April 2, 2011.

77. Kofi A. Annan, "10 Years After—A Farewell Statement to the General Assembly," United Nations, September 19, 2006, http://www.un.org/News/ossg/sg/stories/statments_full.asp?statID=4.

78. Speech to UN seminar on religious tolerance and freedom, delivered December 5, 1984, quoted in Anti-Defamation League News, February 7, 1985.

79. Morris Abram, "Israel Under Attack: Anti-Semitism in the United Nations," *Earth Times*, December 16–31, 1997.

80. Ibid.

81. "Rapporteur Watch: Jean Ziegler's Abuse of Mandate," UN Watch, July 7, 2005, http://www.unwatch.org/site/apps/nlnet/content3.aspx?c=bdKKISNqEmG&b=1746395&ct=1747987, accessed February 27, 2014.

82. Goldhagen, *The Devil That Never Dies*, p. 432.

83. Kressel, *The Sons of Pigs and Apes*, p. 131.

84. NGO Forum, "World Conference Against Racism—Durban, South Africa," *NGO Monitor*, August 27–September 1, 2001.

85. Omar Barghouti, "Relative Humanity: The Essential Obstacle to a Just Peace in Palestine," Counterpunch.org, December 13-14, 2003.

86. Simone Rodan-Benzaquen and Daniel Schwammenthal, "Do Jews Have a Future in Europe?" *Wall Street Journal*, June 16, 2014.

87. Goldhagen, *The Devil That Never Dies*, p. 198.

CHAPTER 8: JERUSALEM

1. John Oesterreicher and Anne Sinai, eds., *Jerusalem* (New York: John Day, 1974), p. 1; Israel Central Bureau of Statistics; Jerusalem Foundation; Municipality of Jerusalem. The figures for 2000 include 9,000 with no religion classified. Total includes those classified as "other."

2. Jacob Lassner and S. Ilan Troen, *Jews and Muslims in the Arab World* (Lanham, MD: Rowman & Littlefield, 2007), p. 93.

3. Michael Brecher, "Jerusalem: Israel's Political Decisions, 1947–1977," *Middle East Journal* 32, no. 1 (Winter 1978): 14.

4. Ibid., p. 19.

5. Nadav Shragai, *The "Al-Aksa Is in Danger" Libel: The History of a Lie* (Jerusalem: Jerusalem Center for Public Affairs, 2012), p. 24.

6. "Arab Spring and Frozen Peace: Palestinian Opinion, Summer 2011: Key Findings From a National Survey of 1,101 Palestinian Adults in the West Bank and Gaza," The Israel Project, June 20–July 8, 2011.

7. Itamar Marcus and Nan Jacques Zilberdik, "The PA's Jerusalem Libel Continues: Organizations and Officials Claim Israel Plans to Destroy Al-Aqsa Mosque," Palestinian Media Watch, October 2, 2012.

8. Shragai, *The "Al-Aksa is in Danger" Libel.*

9. Ibid., p. 54.

10. Ibid., p. 61.

11. Ibid., p. 100.

12. Itamar Marcus and Nan Jacques Zilberdik, "PA: Israel Planning to Destroy the Al-Aqsa Mosque," Palestinian Media Watch, March 30, 2014, http://palwatch.org /main.aspx?fi=157&doc_id=11122, accessed April 4, 2014.

13. "Gov't Condemns Israeli Building on Al Haram Al Sharif," *The Jordan Times,* September 2, 2013.

14. Rafael Israeli, *From Arab Spring to Islamic Winter* (New Brunswick, NJ: Transaction Publishers, 2013), p. 291.

15. Mohammed Mar'i, "Israel Planning to Raze Al-Aqsa to Build 'Second Temple,'" *Saudi Gazette,* June 25, 2013.

16. Yasser Okbi, "Islamic Movement Leaders Warn of 'Israeli Plan to Destroy al-Aqsa Mosque,'" *Jerusalem Post,* September 20, 2013.

17. "Jerusalem Court Convicts Sheikh of Incitement," *Times of Israel,* November 7, 2013.

18. Mudar Zahran, "Who Is Destroying Al-Aqsa Mosque?" Gate Stone Institute, December 9, 2013, http://www.gatestoneinstitute.org/4074/destroying-al-aqsa -mosque, accessed January 16, 2013.

19. Jordanian television, September 13, 1993, quoted by Mona Charen, "What Happened to the Peace Process?" *Baltimore Sun,* June 9, 1994, http://articles.balti moresun.com/1994-06-09/news/1994160113_1_arabs-land-for-peace-palestine, accessed April 4, 2014.

20. Daniel Jonah Goldhagen, *The Devil That Never Dies: The Rise and Threat of Global Antisemitism* (New York: Little, Brown, 2013), p. 338.

CHAPTER 9: SHATTERED DREAMS OF PEACE

1. Charles Krauthammer, "The Settlements Are a Spur to Peace," *Washington Post,* November 1, 1991.

2. Clyde Haberman, "Rabin Says Arafat's 'Jihad' Remark Set Back Peace Effort," *New York Times,* May 20, 1994. A video of Arafat calling for a jihad is also available on YouTube at http://palwatch.org/main.aspx?fi=711&fld_id=723&doc_id =5253&sort=d, accessed April 5, 2014.

3. "In the Words of Arafat," *New York Times,* August 4, 1997.

4. Gaza TV, "Arafat Addresses Hebron Delegation, Notes People Opt for 'Jihad,'" January 2, 2002, Gaza Palestinian Satellite Television in Arabic—translated to English, 1700 GMT, cited at Understanding the Times, http://www.understand thetimes.org/commentary/c9.shtml#_ftn1, accessed April 5, 2014.

5. Alan Sipress, "Adviser: Clinton Exasperated With Barak During Talks," *Washington Post,* July 18, 2001, citing an article by Robert Malley and Hussein Agha in the *New York Review of Books* in which they quote the President at the Camp David summit in July 2000.

6. Jerusalem Center for Public Affairs, "One Year of Yasser Arafat's Intifada: How It Started and How It Might End," *Jerusalem Issue Brief* 1, no. 4 (October 1, 2001), http://www.jcpa.org/art/brief1-4.htm, accessed April 5, 2014.

7. *Al-Hayyat al-Jedida,* February 3, 2006, http://www.adl.org/anti-semitism /muslim-arab-world/c/hamas-in-their-own-words.html, accessed on January 29, 2014.

8. "Ismail Haniya Says Jihad Is Only Strategic Option for Islamic Ummah," *Tehran Times,* February 11, 2012, http://www.tehrantimes.com/politics/95345-ismail -haniya-says-jihad-is-only-strategic-option-for-islamic-ummah, accessed April 5, 2014.

9. "Mashaal Vows to Continue Fighting Israel Rather Than Give Up 'Any Inch' of Palestine," *Times of Israel,* December 8, 2012.

10. Joint Israeli Palestinian Poll, PSR–Survey Research Unit, December 2012.

11. "Views of the Israeli Public on Israeli Security and Resolution of the Arab-Israeli Conflict," Jerusalem Center for Public Affairs/Dahaf Institute Survey, December 2012.

12. Gil Hoffman, "70% of Israelis Don't Trust US on Security, Says Poll," *Jerusalem Post,* February 7, 2014.

13. Itamar Sharon, "PA Minister: Western Wall Must Be Under Our Rule," *Times of Israel,* February 10, 2014.

CHAPTER 10: CAN THE ISLAMIC-JEWISH/ISRAELI CONFLICT BE RESOLVED?

1. Efraim Karsh, *Islamic Imperialism* (New Haven, CT: Yale University Press, 2007), p. 239.

2. "Arab Papers Slam Nasrallah, Dub Him Irresponsible," *Jerusalem Post,* August 29, 2006.

3. "Despite Their Wide Differences, Many Israelis and Palestinians Want Bigger Role for Obama in Resolving Conflict," Pew Research Global Attitudes Project, May 9, 2013. The poll also found that majorities in France, Germany, and China had negative views of Israel. Only the United States had a majority that expressed positive opinions of Israel.

4. "Muslim Publics Share Concerns about Extremist Groups," Pew Research Global Attitudes Project, September 10, 2013.

5. "Gaza, Resistance and the UN Bid," Poll No. 78, Jerusalem Media & Communications Center, December 2012.

6. "Palestinian Public Opinion Poll No. 50," Palestinian Center for Policy and Survey Research, December 2013.

7. Joint Israeli Palestinian Poll, PSR–Survey Research Unit, December 2012. It is worth noting that Palestinians do not have freedom of speech and the reliability of polls in the territories is questionable. Moreover, opinion on many of these questions often changes significantly.

8. "Views of the Israeli Public on Israeli Security and Resolution of the Arab-Israeli Conflict," Jerusalem Center for Public Affairs/Dahaf Institute Survey, December 19, 2012.

9. Evelyn Gordon, "Ignoring Jew-Hatred in the Islamic World," *Commentary,* April 26, 2013, http://www.commentarymagazine.com/2013/04/26/ignoring-jew -hatred-in-the-islamic-world/, accessed February 28, 2014. The sermon is also available on YouTube at http://www.youtube.com/watch?v=kzlzDXWWRdM.

10. Ali Salim, "Begin on Saturday, Finish on Sunday," Gatestone Institute, August 21, 2013, http://www.gatestoneinstitute.org/3943/begin-saturday-finish-Sunday, accessed on August 21, 3013.

11. Joel Kotek, "Major Anti-Israeli and Anti-Semitic Motifs in Arab Cartoons," in *Demonizing Israel and the Jews,* Manfred Gerstenfeld (New York: RVP Press, 2013), pp. 32–34.

12. Salim, "Begin on Saturday, Finish on Sunday."

13. Neil J. Kressel, *The Sons of Pigs and Apes: Muslim Anti-Semitism and the Conspiracy of Silence* (Dulles, VA: Potomac Books, 2012), p. 56.

14. Tibor Krausz, "Plumbing the depths of Islamic Jew-hatred," *Jerusalem Report,* April 22, 2013, p. 44.

15. Salim, "Begin on Saturday, Finish on Sunday."

16. Ibid.

17. Tony Blair, "The Ideology Behind Lee Rigby's Murder Is Profound and Dangerous. Why Don't We Admit It?" *Daily Mail,* June 1, 2013.

18. "Senator Hillary Clinton and PMW in joint press conference introducing report on Palestinian schoolbooks," Palestinian Media Watch, February 8, 2007.

19. Abdulateef Al-Mulhim, "Arab Spring and the Israeli Enemy," *Arab News,* October 6, 2012.

20. Youssef M. Ibrahim, "The Arab Majority May Not Stay Silent," *Chicago Tribune,* July 19, 2006.

21. Sinem Tezyapar, "Muslims, Stop Blaming Israel," JewishJournal.com, September 11, 2013, http://www.jewishjournal.com/opinion/article/muslims_stop_blaming _israel, accessed April 5, 2014.

22. "Kerry Says No Deaths from West Bank Terror in 2013, Just Days After Shin Bet Lists Fatalities," *Algemeiner,* February 3, 2014.

23. Itamar Marcus and Nan Jacques Zilberdik, "PA Allocates $46 Million More for Terrorists in 2014," Palestinian Media Watch, February 12, 2014.

24. Khaled Abu Toameh, "Radical Islam Arrives in Ramallah," Gatestone Institute, June 5, 2013, http://www.gatestoneinstitute.org/3751/radical-islam-ramallah, accessed June 7, 2013.

25. Yaakov Lappin, "New Breed of Radical Islamists in West Bank Worries Israel, PA," *Jerusalem Post,* December 5, 2013.

26. Robert Tait, "Al-Qaeda Linked Group Claims to Be Operating in the West Bank," *Telegraph,* December 1, 2013.

27. "The World's Muslims: Religion, Politics and Society," Pew Research Center, April 30, 2013, http://www.pewforum.org/2013/04/30/the-worlds-muslims-religion-po litics-society-beliefs-about-sharia/, accessed April 5, 2014.

28. Jacob Lassner and S. Ilan Troen, *Jews and Muslims in the Arab World* (Lanham, MD: Rowman & Littlefield, 2007), p. 149.

29. Israel Shenker, "Golda Meir: Peace and Arab Acceptance Were Goals of Her 5 Years as Premier," *New York Times,* December 9, 1978.

INDEX

Abbas, Mahmoud, 92, 106, 116, 209–10, 215, 230–2, 235–6, 246, 257, 260
Abbasids, 43
Abdullah I of Jordan, 21, 46, 49–50, 192
Abdullah II of Jordan, 118–20
Abraham, 3, 5
Abu Zahir, Sami, 105
Acre, 24, 30
Afghanistan, 97, 183
Ahmadinejad, Mahmoud, 136–7, 140
Ahmadiyya, 171
Al-Aqsa Mosque, 15, 26, 30, 50, 70, 92–4, 98, 100, 103, 151–2, 178, 200–1, 203–5
al-Aqsa Intifada, 94, 98, 100, 103, 201
"al-Aqsa libel," 30
al-Aqsa Brigades, 92–3, 201, 217
al-Aqsa TV station, 105
Al-Azhar Mosque, 5
Al-Azhar University in Cairo, 38, 47
al-Banna, Hassan, 71–2
Al-Buraq, 190
al-Dawalibi, Marouf, 8, 183
Al-Faisal, Turki, 139
Al-Habbash, Mahmoud, 204
Al-Hulhim, Abdulateef, 251
Al-Manar TV, 250
al-Masjid al-Haram Mosque, 5–6
Al-Mukhalalati, Mufid, 105
al Musawi, Abbas, 93
Al-Odeh, Salman, 8
al-Qaeda, 114, 122–3, 154, 160, 171, 173–4, 177, 240–1, 244, 248, 253, 256–7
al-Qaradawi, Sheikh Yusuf, 32, 113, 173, 201
Al-Qassam Brigades, 105

Al-Shatat, 7
al-Sisi, Abdul Fatah, 114–15
Al-Sudais, Abdul Rahman, 5
al-Tunisi, Muhammad Khalifa, 7
Al Watan, 238
al-Zawahiri, Ayman, 173
Alaa, Abu, 214
Alawites, 1–2, 85, 121, 125, 132–3, 253
Albania, 155
Algeria, 58, 63, 108
Ali, Ayaan Hirsi, 187
aliyah, 18
Allah, 4–6, 9–10, 24, 32–3, 40, 59, 87, 90–3, 109, 113 135, 151–2, 166, 170, 174, 217, 226, 244, 248, 261–2
Allies (WWII), 33, 47
AMIA Jewish community center building bombing, 133, 175–6
Amit, Aryeh, 96
Amman, 46, 50, 59, 76, 240
Anglo-Egyptian Treaty, 47
Annan, Kofi, 181–4
Anti-Defamation League (ADL), 162
anti-Semitism, 2, 4, 7–9, 14, 17, 22, 33, 49, 61–2, 90–1, 132, 136, 140, 142, 152–72, 179–86, 201, 218–19, 229, 237, 240, 245–50, 260–2
"apes and pigs," Jews as descendants of, 5–9, 40, 48, 113, 152, 170–1, 245
Arab Higher Committee, 29–31, 38
Arab-Israeli War (War of Independence) (1948), 38–41, 49–57, 60–1, 64, 70, 72, 143–4, 211, 216
Arab League, 34, 36, 38, 44–5, 71, 152, 203, 212, 228–9, 259–60

Arab Nation, 55–6
Arab News, 251
"Arab Revolt," 29
Arab Spring, 107–26, 203, 235, 238, 245, 247
Arabic language, 7, 22, 32, 73–4, 80–1, 88, 105, 172, 218, 221, 227
Arabists, 1, 22–3, 51, 64, 110, 117–18, 121, 196–7
Arafat, Yasser, 71, 75–6, 79–80, 83–4, 92–4, 96, 105–6, 200, 203, 206–7, 214–30
Araghchi, Abbas, 148
Argentina, 100, 179
Argov, Shlomo, 84
Ariel, 242
Asociación Mutual Israelita Argentina (AMIA), 133, 175–6
Assad, Bashar, 73, 85, 109, 120–4, 132–4, 238–40, 252–3
Assad, Hafez, 57, 64, 73, 108, 120, 222
Assi Assa, 238
Aswan Dam, 52
Aufhauser, David, 177
Auschwitz, 168, 212
Austria, 17, 31, 162–3
Axis, 47
Azerbaijan, 176
Azzam Pasha, Abdyk Rahman Hassan, 36–8

Baha'i, 171
Bahrain, 108, 117, 139
Baker, James, 214
Balfour, Arthur, 20
Balfour Declaration, 20–3, 25, 35, 69, 90, 192, 210
Balkans, 13
Bar Giora, 69
Barak, Ehud, 93–4, 142, 200, 224–6, 243

Barghouti, Omar, 186
Battle of Al Alamein (October 23–November 11, 1942), 47
Battle of Iwo Jima, 87
Battle of Khaybar, 132
Bedouin, 19, 118–19
Begin, Menachem, 84, 87, 211–12, 215–16, 218
Beirut, 19, 22, 45, 84, 86, 102, 133
Belgium, 78, 155–6, 159, 169
Ben Ali, Zine al-Abidine, 108
Ben-Gurion, David, 31, 49, 53, 192, 194–5, 221–2
Ben-Gurion Airport, 73, 242
Bernadotte, Folke, 39–40
Berro, Ibrahim Hussein, 175
the "Big Lie," 8
"Big Satan," 130
Bin Laden, Osama, 82, 96, 154, 246
"Black March," 227–8
"Black September," 76, 78, 82–3
Blair, Tony, 250
Bolkestein, Frits, 169
Bosnia-Herzegovina, 155
Boycott, Divestment and Sanctions (BDS) campaign, 185
Brazil, 100, 164, 175
Bulgaria, 155, 176
Bush, George H. W., 214, 233
Bush, George W., 111, 135–6, 141–2, 227, 229–32, 249

Cairo, 19, 34, 38, 44–5, 47, 55, 59, 65, 71–2, 75, 113, 115–16, 212
Caliph, 12, 46, 90
caliphate, 12, 46, 81, 85, 90, 149, 171, 247, 253, 256, 262
Cameron, David, 156
Camp David, 82, 212, 224, 229
Canaanites, 16
Canadian Parliament, 137
Carter, Jimmy, 64, 212
Caucasus, 13
Center for Religious Freedom, 171
Central Intelligence Agency (CIA), 22, 141
"Charlie Wilson's War," 237–8
Chavez, Hugo, 177
Chechnya, 151–2
chemical weapons, 123–4, 253
China, 52, 141–3, 164, 179, 181

Churchill, Winston, 24–5
Clapper, James, 141
"clash of civilizations," 11
Clinton, Bill, 214, 216, 224–5
Clinton, Hillary, 250
Cohen, Hillel, 39
Columbia, 100
Committee on the Exercise of the Inalienable Rights of the Palestinian People, 179
"Committee of Free Officers," 48
Communism, 90, 141, 237, 262
Conseil Représentatif des Institutions juives de France (Representative Council of French Jewish Institutions) (CRIF), 166
Constantinople, 13
Copts, 47–8, 112
Cotler, Irwin, 137
Coughlin, Con, 109
Crusaders/Crusades, 11–12, 36–8, 154, 201–2, 245–6, 251
Cuba, 179–81
Cukierman, Roger, 166
Cyprus, 35, 46, 176
Cyrus the Great, 127

Dacey, Austin, 184
The Daily Telegraph, 168
Damascus, 19, 59, 64, 73, 119–20
Davis Cup, 168
Dayan, Moshe, 197–8, 210–11
"Death to America," 6, 143
Declaration of Human Rights in Islam, 125
Denmark, 154
dhimmis (non-Muslims under Muslim rule), 12, 127–8
Diaspora, 3, 127, 156
Division for Palestinian Rights, 179
Djibouti, 108
Dome of the Rock, 190, 204, 206
drug trafficking, 91, 100, 175, 177
Druze, 1–2, 45, 125
Dulles, John Foster, 51–2
"Durban Strategy," 185

Eban, Abba, 179, 212
Edinger, Bernard, 164
Egypt, 3, 7–9, 15–16, 28–9, 40–1, 44–66, 70–2, 75, 79, 81–2, 88–9, 103, 104,

108, 110–21, 124–5, 160, 164, 179, 203, 210–13, 219–20, 222, 231, 238–9, 241, 244, 246, 248, 250–1, 253, 255, 259–60
Eilat, 40, 57
Eisenhower, Dwight D., 51–2
El Al, 77, 129, 174
el-Husseini, Haj Amin, 22–5, 32, 201
el-Husseini, Kamal, 23
el-Kaukji, Fawzi, 29
el-Kourdieh, Haj Issa, 27
electromagnetic pulses (EMPs), 144
Encyclopaedia of Islam (Tyan), 10
Encyclopedia Judaica, 26–7
The End of the Jewish State: Just a Matter of Time (Haniyeh), 245
Erdogan, Tayyip, 124, 253
Erekat, Saeb, 16
Eshkol, Levi, 58
Esposito, John, 161
Ethiopia, 47, 129
European Council of Fatwa, 173
European Organization for Nuclear Research (CERN), 169
European Union (EU), 154, 156, 161–2, 166–7, 169, 176, 230
EU Fundamental Rights Agency (FRA), 162
EU Monitoring Center on Racism and Xenophobia, 9, 161
Evans, Jonathan, 163

Facebook, 93, 171
Fadlallah, Sheikh Mohammed Hussein, 85–6
Faisal of Saudi Arabia, 8, 62
Falk, Richard, 181
Fallahijan, Ali, 175
Farfour (character), 219
Farouk I of Egypt, 48
Farthest Mosque, 190
Fatah, 71–5, 88–9, 92, 102–3, 114–15, 177, 201, 217–18, 225, 231, 233, 242, 246, 256, 260
Fath, 73–4
fatwa, 24, 187
fedayeen, 22, 26, 50–1, 70–1
Federal Bureau of Investigation (FBI), 170
female martyrs, 83, 94–5
Fez, 13
Fifth Aliyah (1932–1938), 19

First Aliyah (1882–1903), 18
First Temple, 127
Fordow, 148
Fourth Aliyah (1924–1931), 19
France, 19–21, 43–7, 52–3, 83, 129, 140, 143, 154–7, 162–7, 169, 173, 249
Free Syrian Army (FSA), 121
Freij, Elias, 216
French, Lewis, 29
French Empire, 40
French Jewry, 162–7
French Revolution, 49, 90
Friedman, Tom, 228
Fuad I of Egypt, 47
Fundamental Rights Agency, 156

Gabriel (angel), 4, 190
Galicia, 18
Gallup, 161
Gantz, Benny, 143
Gaza Strip, 6, 8, 41, 55–6, 59–61, 73, 75, 81, 88–9, 92–4, 97–8, 102–5, 110, 113–14, 167–8, 180–4, 210–11, 215, 217–18, 221–2, 224, 226, 228, 230–3, 235–6, 244, 255
Geneva agreement, 145, 147
genocide, 4, 137, 143, 182, 185, 245, 247
Georgia, 155
Germany, 12, 19, 27, 31–3, 47, 49, 77–8, 83, 100, 140, 143, 154–7, 162–3, 168, 169, 179, 187
Germany Hungary, 156
Giora, Simeon Bar, 69
Golan Heights, 56–7, 59, 63, 120, 124, 180, 222, 243–4
"Golden Age" of Jewry, 13
Golden (Mercy) Gate, 190
Goldhagen, Daniel, 13–14, 149, 152, 187, 207
Goldstone, Richard, 182–3
Goldstone Commission, 182
Goldstone Report, 182
Goldwasser, Ehud, 100–2
Great Britain, 14, 17, 19–40, 43–9, 52–3, 128, 153, 156, 159, 162–5, 167, 170–3, 183, 192, 250. See Palestine Mandate
"Greater Syria," 18
Gush Etzion, 242

Habash, George, 73
Hadiths, 4–5
Haifa, 24, 77, 100, 138, 214

Hamas, 11, 32, 89–92, 96–8, 102–6, 111, 113–14, 119–20, 134, 160, 177, 182–3, 205, 216–17, 220, 226, 228, 231–6, 238–46, 256, 258, 260
Hammad, Fathi, 182
Haniyeh, Ismail, 103, 113, 233, 245
"Harakat al-Tahrir al-Watani al Filastini," 73
Hariri, Saad, 102
Harvard University, 11
Hashemi, Ali Akbar, 175
Hashemite dynasty in Arabia, 21, 46, 60–1
Hashomer (Guild of Watchman), 69
Hebrew Scriptures, 5
Hebrew University, 39, 109
Hebron, 26, 223, 242, 255
Herzl, Theodor, 17
Hezbollah, 6, 64, 66, 85–7, 89, 93, 98–102, 104, 120, 122, 124, 133–4, 138, 160, 173, 175–7, 181–3, 220, 231, 238–41, 244–5, 250, 253
hijackings, 73, 75–8, 83–4, 133, 151, 173, 176, 229
Hirshfeld, Ya'ir, 214
Hitler, Adolf, 7–8, 27, 31–3, 135, 247
HIV virus, 8, 184
Hizb-ut-Tahrir, 256
Holocaust, 28, 32, 35, 65, 136, 157, 168, 182
homosexuality, 171
House of Islam (Dar al-Islam), 10–11, 130
House of War (Dar al-harb), 10, 130
Human Rights Council (HRC), 181–5
Hungary, 162
Huntington, Samuel, 11
Hurva Synagogue, 203
Hussein, Saddam, 88, 109, 135–6, 213, 246
Hussein, Sharif, 46
Hussein of Jordan (King Hussein), 58–9, 63, 75–6, 79–80, 220, 237–8
Husseini, Jamal, 38

ibn Husseini, Faisal, 21
Ibn Saud, 46
Ibrahim, Youssef, 251
Idris, Wafa, 95
India, 2, 21, 97, 128, 164, 174, 176
Indonesia, 2

Inter-Muslim feuds, 37
International Atomic Energy Agency (IAEA), 140, 148
International Tennis Federation, 169
"International Year of Solidarity with the Palestinian People" (2014), 179
Internet, 171
intifada, 88–90, 92, 201, 206, 213, 217, 226, 257
Iqraa (television station), 9
Iran, 2, 44, 64, 73, 81–6, 89, 91–4, 100, 108–9, 114, 117, 119–20, 122, 124–49, 163, 170, 173, 174–6, 205, 220, 227, 232, 235, 237–40, 244–5, 252–3, 260; and "little Satan," 127–49
Iranian revolution, 81–4, 89, 129, 132
Iraq, 10–11, 19–21, 28, 40, 44–6, 58, 60, 66, 108–9, 124, 129, 135–6, 139–40, 143–4, 213, 229, 244–6, 252–3
Ireland, 97–8, 184
Irgun, 31–2, 211
Isa (Jesus), 33
Ishmael, 5
"Islamaphobia," 2
Islambouli, Khalid, 82
Islamic Association (Al-Mujamma Al Islami), 89
Islamic Jihad (Palestinian terrorist organization), 11, 98, 106, 134, 138, 176, 232, 244, 254
Islamic Movement, 205
Islamic Resistance Movement, 89
Islamic Revolution (1979), 129
Islamic Saudi Academy in Fairfax, Virginia, 170
Islamic theocracy, 109
Islamic Winter, 107–26, 235, 239
Islamists, 5–6, 72, 91–2, 96, 102, 105–6, 111–12, 115, 118–19, 122–3, 125–6, 133, 152, 154, 156–7, 161, 171, 217, 219–20, 231–2, 238, 240, 244–9, 251, 253, 256, 260
Islamization, 84, 151, 226, 241, 252
"Islamophobia," 157, 171–2, 184

Israel Defense Forces (IDF), 63, 65, 83–4, 99–101, 104–5, 143, 183, 222, 228
Israel's Independence Day, 56–7
Israel-Egypt peace treaty, 110
Israeli, Rafael, 107
Israeli-Palestinian conflict, 1, 206, 230, 235
Israeli Air Force, 101, 134, 232–3, 248
Israeli embassy in Buenos Aires, attack on (1992), 174–5
Israeli independence (1948), 38–9, 211. See State of Israel
Israeli Islamic Movement, 201–2
Israeli-Palestinian Declaration of Principles, 206–7, 215, 217–18
Israeli Supreme Court, 204
Israelis killed in terror attacks following the Oslo Agreement (table), 99
Istanbul, 13–14, 83
Italy, 20, 47, 156
Izz al-Din al-Qassam Brigades, 89

Jabari, Ahmad, 232–3
Jacobson, Howard, 153
Jaffa, 24, 223
Jerusalem, 3, 5–6, 12, 15–16, 22–4, 26–7, 30, 36–7, 40–1, 46, 50, 58–9, 62, 70, 75–7, 80, 83, 88, 94–6, 103, 113, 116, 138, 167, 180, 189–207, 210–11, 217–18, 221–9, 233–7, 242–4, 257; international zone of, 37; population of, 189–93
Jerusalem Embassy Act (1995), 196
Jerusalem Post, 257
Jewish Federation in Seattle, 174
Jewish immigration, 20–35, 128, 166–7
Jewish National Fund, 19
Jewish Quarter, 27, 192, 199, 203
Jewish state, 10, 17, 30–41, 45, 49, 51, 57–8, 66, 69, 72, 82, 86, 105–6, 125, 137, 140, 179, 181–2, 192, 200, 209, 215–16, 220, 225, 230, 232, 236–8, 242, 245

Jewish Temple, 16, 200, 225
Jibril, Ahmed, 73, 90
jihad ("holy war"), 2, 7, 9–12, 38, 69–106, 113–14, 123, 134, 138, 149, 151–85, 217, 227, 229, 232–3, 244, 248–9, 253–7
Jikeli, Günther, 158
Johnson, Lyndon B., 57
Jonas, George, 78
Jordan, 3, 20–1, 23–4, 36, 38–41, 45–6, 49, 51–63, 66, 75–7, 79, 82–3, 97–8, 108–10, 115, 118–20, 125–6, 160, 180, 192–5, 198–9, 203, 205, 210–12, 218, 220, 237–44, 247, 255, 259
Jordan Valley, 242–3, 255, 259
Jordanian Legion, 58–9
Joseph's Tomb, 226
Judaism, 3, 5, 16–17, 70, 128, 190, 199, 246

Karine-A, 94
Karsh, Ephraim, 3–4, 11, 237
Kashmir, 167
Kemp, Richard, 183
Kennedy, John F., 220–1
Kerry, John, 106, 115, 146, 209, 235–6, 259
Khaldun, Ibn, 10
Khamenei, Ali, 85, 132, 137, 141, 175
Khan, Abdul Qadeer, 136
Khan, Reza, 128
Khatami, Ayatollah Ahmad, 132, 141
Khomeini, Ayatollah, 81, 84–5, 108, 129–32, 134, 136–8, 187
kibbutzim, 18
King Fahd, 229
Kissinger, Henry, 62–4
Knesset, 91, 180, 194, 197
Knight without a Horse (TV series), 7
Koran/Qur'an, 2, 4–7, 9–10, 12–13, 32, 70–2, 85, 109, 131, 152, 169–70, 190, 251
Kosovo, 154–5
Kramer, Martin, 9–10
Krausz, Tibor, 6
Kressel, Neil J., 7, 247
Kristallnacht (the "Night of Broken Glass"), 31
Kuntar, Samir, 101
Kuwait, 8, 58, 66, 71, 88, 108, 117, 135, 139–40, 197, 213, 238

Labor party, 87
Labor Zionism, 17
Land of Israel, 2–3, 15–17, 19, 30, 127–8, 189, 201, 210–11
Land of Palestine, 92
Lashkar-e-Taiba, 173
Lassner, Jacob, 51, 61, 66
Latin America, 177
Latvia, 156
Lawrence, T. E., 22
Le Figaro, 166
League of Arab States, 44–5. See Arab League
League of Nations, 21, 90
Lebanon, 18, 20, 22, 28, 40–1, 44–6, 60, 66, 83–7, 93, 98–100–2, 120, 134, 139, 160, 175–6, 181, 231, 239, 241, 250, 253
Levant, 13
Levey, Stuart, 177
Lewinsky, Monica, 224
Lewis, Bernard, 4, 10
Lewis Commission, 29
Libya, 13, 63, 66, 108, 115, 253
Likud party, 87, 93, 222–3, 230
"limited-liability war," 17
"Little Satan," 130, 139
London Central Mosque, 170–1

Machpelah Cave, 242
Madhi, Sheikh Ibrahim, 6
Mahdi, 138
Majd, 89
Majles Shura al-Mujahideen, 257
Malaysia, 160, 241
Malmö, 168
Mandela, Nelson, 217
Marrakesh, 13
Marshall, George, 143–4
martyrdom, 9, 62, 87, 92, 94–7, 103, 113, 138, 151, 170, 177, 217–18, 227–9, 245, 255–6
"martyrs," 92
Mashaal, Khaled, 232, 235
Mauritania, 108
Mecca, 3, 5, 15, 33, 46
Medina, 3, 15, 33
Mein Kampf (Hitler), 7–8
Meir, Golda, 49, 62–3, 261
Melman, Yossi, 1, 154
Menem, Carlos, 175
Middle East Media Research Institute (MEMRI), 81
Mikati, Najib, 102

Military Administration in Palestine, 23
Mogahed, Dalia, 161
MI5, 163
Montenegro, 155
Morocco, 13, 63, 108, 124–5, 139, 260
Morsi, Mohamad, 111–15
Mossad, 78
Mount Mina, 5
Mount Moriah, 5
Mount of Olives, 194, 199
Moussa, Mohammed Ahmed, 98
Movement for the (National) Liberation of Palestine, 73–4
Muasher, Mawan, 125
Mubarak, Hosni, 82, 108, 110–12, 115, 117, 121
mufti, 23–32, 34, 70, 200, 206
Mughrabi Gate, 203
Muhammad, 2–7, 10–12, 15, 48, 71–2, 138, 184, 190, 261
Munich massacre (1972), 78
Murawiec, Laurent, 177
Muslim Association of Britain, 167
Muslim Brotherhood (MB), 32, 71–2, 81–2, 85, 89, 110–15, 118, 120, 133, 156, 167, 173, 201, 238–9, 245, 253
Muslim National Associations, 24

Nablus, 24, 226
Nakba (catastrophe), 41
Nashashibis, 22
Nasrallah, Hassan, 6, 93, 101–2, 122, 238
Nasser, Gamal Abdel, 48–59, 62, 70–5, 91, 108, 110, 125
Natanz, 148
National Bureau of Economic Research, 96
National Covenant, 55
National Socialism, 32
National Water Carrier, 56
Nayef of Saudi Arabia, 8
Nazareth, 24
Nazism, 8, 12, 19, 27, 32, 47, 49, 74, 91, 153–6, 162, 170, 181–2, 184, 187, 245, 262
Nebi Musa riots (1920), 23
Negev desert, 36–7, 40
Netanyahu, Benjamin, 83, 106, 116, 141, 143–6,

202, 209–10, 222–4, 233–6
Netherlands, 162, 169
New York Times, 180, 228, 251–2
Niemoeller, Martin, 262
Nigeria, 2, 160, 241
Nobel Peace Prize, 221
Non-Aligned Movement, 53
nongovernmental organization (NGOs), 182
North Africa, 13, 32, 108, 154–5, 173–4, 260
North Atlantic Treaty Organization (NATO), 169, 255
North Korea, 136, 163
Norway, 162, 168–9

Obama, Barack, 108–11, 115–18, 123, 139–42, 145–8, 233–6, 247, 249, 259
oil, 21–2, 31, 44, 46, 63–4, 107, 110, 129, 139–40, 143–4, 148, 154, 178, 195, 199, 213, 243, 248–9
Old City of Jerusalem, 40, 58, 70, 180, 192, 197, 199, 205, 242
Old Testament, 3
Olmert, Ehud, 100, 231, 243
Oman, 108, 118, 219, 259–60
Operation Cast Lead, 104–5, 167, 182
"Operation Defensive Shield," 228
Operation Entebbe (1976), 144, 151
"Operation Peace for Galilee," 84
Operation Pillar of Defense in Gaza, 104
Organization of Islamic Cooperation (OIC), 125, 178–81, 184–5
Organization of the Petroleum Exporting Countries (OPEC), 64
Orthodox Jews, 17–18, 204
Oslo Accords, 74, 92, 94, 99, 118, 206, 209, 215–16, 219–22, 230, 235
Ottoman, 3, 13–14, 19–21, 26, 43
Otunnu, Olara, 95
Otzar Hatorah School (Toulouse), 165

Pahlavi, Mohammad Reza, 128

Pakistan, 97, 136, 139, 160, 163, 174, 184, 241, 253
Palaestina, 3
Palestine British Administration, 23
Palestine Liberation Army, 71
Palestine Liberation Organization (PLO), 55–6, 61, 66, 71–84, 89–92, 98, 103, 201, 206–7, 209, 214–19, 224, 227, 237, 256–7
Palestine Mandate, 19–25, 186
Palestine Media Watch (PMW), 81
Palestine National Charter, 74
Palestinian Authority (PA), 6, 81, 94, 98, 102–4, 108, 184, 200, 204, 210, 215, 218, 221, 225, 227, 230–2, 236, 246, 255–7, 260
Palestinian Covenant, 74
Palestinian Diaspora, 61
Palestinian Islamic Jihad (PIJ), 88–9, 96
Palestinian Red Crescent, 95
pan-Arabism, 44–5, 48–9, 51–2, 54–6, 57–9, 61–3, 66, 70–2, 75, 91, 125, 129, 254
Panama, 177
Panetta, Leon, 141–2
Paraguay, 100
Passover Seder, 16
patriarchs and matriarchs, 26
Pearl, Daniel, 174
Peel, Earl, 29
Peel Commission, 31
Pentagon, 142
"People of the Book," 12, 127
Peres, Shimon, 215, 222
Persia, 37, 127
Persian Empire, 127
Persian Gulf, 140
Pew surveys, 154, 160
P5+1, 145, 147–8
Picot, François-Georges, 19–20
"Pillar of Defense," 233
Pipes, Daniel, 11
Poland, 18–19, 25, 33, 163, 168, 179
Popinski, Judith, 168
Popular Democratic Front for the Liberation of Palestine (PDFLP), 72–3
Popular Front for the Liberation of Palestine (PFLP), 72–3, 77–8, 83

Popular Front for the Liberation of Palestine-General Command (PFLP-GC), 72–3, 90
post-traumatic stress disorder (PTSD), 105
Protection of Holy Places Law, 197–8
Protocols of the Elders of Zion, 7–8, 86, 90–1, 132, 137
Psaki, Jen, 182
Pundak, Ron, 214
Putin, Vladimir, 123

Qatar, 118, 122, 219, 259–60
Qods Day, 132
"the Quartet," 230
Qutb, Sayyid, 71, 248

Rabin, Yitzhak, 214–23, 234
Rachel's Tomb (Bethlehem), 226, 242
racism, 74, 153, 161, 173, 179, 185–6, 235
Rafsanjani, Akbar Hashemi, 138, 175
Rajaie-Khorassami, Said, 125–6, 130
Ramallah, 227, 256
Rand Corporation, 177
Rantisi, Abdel Aziz, 96, 228
Reagan, Ronald, 87, 92, 214
Red Sea, 40
refugees, 31, 41, 55, 62, 76, 101, 118–19, 121–2, 168, 179, 206, 218, 225, 228, 236, 242
Regev, Eldad, 100–2
Rejectionist Front, 64
Religious Zionism, 17
Republic of Macedonia, 155
Right to Food, 184
rioting, 23, 25–7, 38, 88, 96, 126, 167–9, 202–3, 206, 225
rockets, 73, 91–3, 98, 100–2, 104–5, 119–20, 134, 183, 221, 231–3, 239–41, 254–5, 258
Romania, 18
Roosevelt, Franklin D., 33
Ross, Dennis, 223, 225
Rothschild, Edmond de, 19–20
Rouhani, Hassan, 145–7, 175
Rushdie, Salman, 187
Russia, 7, 18–19, 69, 122–3, 128, 133–4, 141, 143, 155, 164, 179, 181, 194, 230, 239

Sabri, Sheikh Akrama, 201
Sadat, Anwar (Anwar Al-Sadat), 62, 65, 72, 79–82, 108, 110, 120, 204, 211–13, 220, 238
Saladin, 12, 237
Salafists, 111, 166, 257
Salah, Sheikh Raed, 205
Salim, Ali, 245, 247, 249
Satanic Verses (Khomeini), 187
Saud of Saudi Arabia, 33, 54
Saudi Arabia, 3, 8, 33, 44–6, 54–5, 62–6, 92, 97, 108, 115, 117–18, 122, 133, 135, 139–42, 169–70, 173, 177–81, 183, 197, 220, 228, 240, 247–8, 252, 260
SAVAK, 129–30
Savir, Uri, 215
Sayyid Tantawi, Al-Azhar Sheikh Muhammad, 5
Second Aliyah (1904–1914), 18
Senegal, 160, 241
Sephardic Jews, 13
September 11, 2001 (9/11), 8, 10, 161, 171–6, 182, 229, 248
Shalah, Ramadan Abadallah, 89
Shalit, Gilad, 103–4
Shamir, Yair, 248
Shamir, Yitzhak, 214
Shaqaqi, Fathi, 88–9
Sharansky, Natan, 109–10
Sharia law, 72, 81–2, 109, 112, 125, 129, 161, 184, 251, 256–7
Sharif, Abu, 78
Sharon, Ariel, 84, 93–4, 98, 100, 201, 225–31
Shaw, William, 27
Shaw Commission, 27
Shazli, Sa'ad, 65
Shebaa Farms, 98–9
Sheikh Ijlin Mosque (Gaza City), 6
Shia/Shiites, 43–4, 84, 87, 100, 122, 125, 130, 135–6, 138–9, 238–41, 253
Shragai, Nadav, 198, 200
Shukeiri, Ahmed, 71, 74
Shukri, Hasan, 24
Sinai, 53, 56, 59, 63–4, 110, 114, 119, 213, 239, 258–9
Six-Day War (1967), 16–17, 57–66, 71, 74–5, 77, 79, 144, 178, 194–8, 201,

204, 207, 210–12, 228, 236, 242, 255
Solomon's Stables, 201–2
South Africa, 135, 185–6, 217
Soviet Union, 45, 50, 52–3, 59, 65–6, 76, 85, 133, 138, 237
Spain, 13, 36–7, 155, 163, 245, 249
Special Committee to Investigate Israeli Practices Affecting the Human Rights of the Palestinian People and Other Arabs of the Occupied Territories, 179
State of Israel, 9, 35, 36–41, 196
Stern Gang, 31–2
Straits of Tiran, 52–3, 57, 70
Sudan, 58, 63, 108
Suez Canal, 21, 47–8, 52–7, 61, 63, 70–1
Suez Crisis (1956) War, 52–7, 61, 70
Sufis, 2
Summer Olympics (1972), 78
Sunna, 10, 109
Sunnis, 5, 43–4, 85, 91–2, 102, 112, 121–2, 125, 133–6, 173, 238–40, 244, 253
Supreme Moslem Council, 23
Sweden, 156, 162, 168
Sykes, Mark, 19–20
Sykes-Picot agreement, 20
Syria, 3, 7, 18–21, 23–4, 28–9, 40–1, 44–6, 52, 54, 56–64, 66, 73–6, 85, 92–3, 97–100, 102, 108–9, 118–24, 132–4, 138, 144, 179, 183, 222, 229, 235, 238–40, 244, 246, 251–3
Syrian civil war, 73, 134, 235, 244

Talmud, 8, 104, 183
Taylor, Waters, 23
Tel Aviv, 18, 30, 77, 83, 104, 129, 134, 138, 167, 186, 195–6, 220, 223, 226, 242
Tel Aviv University, 186
Telegraph, 109
Temple Mount, 26, 30, 93–4, 180, 190–1, 197–206, 225, 242–3
Temple of Solomon (Solomon's Temple), 200, 202
Tenenbaum, Elchanan, 99

282   DEATH TO THE INFIDELS

terrorism, 11, 56, 29, 50, 53,
    56, 64, 66, 69–106, 110,
    114, 119–20, 133–4, 151,
    160, 165, 171–2, 174,
    176–8, 182, 189, 197,
    200–1, 214, 222, 224,
    226–8, 231–3, 238–9,
    241, 244–5, 248–9, 252,
    254–7, 260, 262. See
    fedayeen
Tet Offensive, 87
Tezyapar, Sinem, 253
Thailand, 176
theology, 5, 139, 248
Third Aliyah (1919–1923),
    18
Tiberias, 24
Timerman, Héctor, 176
Tisha B'av, 16
Tomb of the Patriarchs, 180
Torah, 5, 26–7, 191–2
Toronto District School
    Board, 170
Trade Unionists, 262
Transjordan, 21, 24, 36,
    38–40, 45–6, 192. See
    Jordan
"tribute" (jizya) to the ruler,
    12
Troen, Ilan, 51, 61, 66
Truman, Harry S., 51–2
Tunisia, 84, 92, 108, 110,
    115, 174, 241, 246
Turkey, 2, 83, 97, 124, 129,
    160, 176, 240, 253
Turks, 13, 16, 20–1, 31, 43,
    46, 160
Twelfth Imam, 138
Twitter, 117, 171
Tyan, Emile, 10
Tzoreff, Mira, 95

Ummayads, 43
United Arab Emirates, 66,
    118
United Arab Republic (UAR),
    54
United Kingdom (UK), 20,
    140, 154–5, 157, 162–5,
    167, 195
UN Educational,
    Scientific and Cultural
    Organization (UNESCO),
    180, 195, 203
UN General Assembly, 79,
    194–5

UN Emergency Force
    (UNEF), 57
UN Human Rights
    Commission, 8, 183
UN Interim Force in Lebanon
    (UNIFIL), 239
UN Relief and Works Agency,
    62
UN Security Council, 38, 50,
    60, 90, 123, 140–1, 143,
    175, 178, 195, 215, 239
UN Security Council
    resolutions, 60, 179–80,
    198–9, 214, 229, 239;
    Res. 242, 60, 198–9, 214,
    229; Res. 1701, 239; Res.
    3379, 179
UN Special Committee on
    Palestine (UNSCOP),
    35–6
UN Universal Declaration of
    Human Rights, 125
UN World Conference, 185
U.S. Congress, 146, 196
U.S. Defense Department, 22
U.S. embassy bombing (April
    18, 1983), 86–7
U.S. Foreign Affairs
    Committee, 137
U.S. State Department, 22,
    171, 182, 243
U.S. Treasury Department,
    177
Universal Declaration of
    Human Rights (Iran), 130
umma, 48–9, 233
uranium, 136, 140, 144–9,
    252

Vahidi, Ahmad, 175
Valls, Manuel, 166
van Gogh, Theo, 187
Vatican, 192, 194–5
Velayati, Ali Akbar, 175
Venezuela, 177
Vengeance: The True Story
    of an Israeli Counter-
    Terrorist Team (Jonas),
    78–9
Vietnam, 55, 59, 76, 87, 122,
    179
Voice of the Arabs, 57

Wahhabi, 33, 118, 170–1, 253
Wakf/Waqf, 201–2
Washington Post, 145, 170

weapon smuggling, 35, 83,
    92–3, 100–2, 119, 122,
    134, 231, 233, 253
weapons of mass destruction
    (WMDs), 136
Weinstein, Warren, 174
Weizmann, Chaim, 19–20
West Bank, 3, 41, 56, 59,
    75, 79–81, 88, 92–3, 97,
    100, 103, 116, 119, 134,
    180, 192, 195, 200, 205,
    210–11, 215, 217–18,
    221–9, 231–4, 236,
    242–4, 254–8
Western Wall, 180, 190–1,
    199–200, 202, 205, 225,
    236, 242–3
White Paper (1939), 31
Will, George, 148–9
Wilson, Woodrow, 19, 44
Wistrich, Robert, 32, 161,
    169
World War I, 13, 17–19, 27–8,
    31, 45–7, 90, 128
World War II, 19, 27–8, 33,
    44–7, 87, 90, 128, 168
World War III, 248–9
World Zionist Organization
    (WZO), 18–19
"Wrath of God," 78

Ya'qub, Muhammad Hussein,
    244
Yassin, Sheikh Ahmed,
    89–90, 94–5, 96, 228
Yathrib, 3
Yemen, 13, 45, 54–5, 97, 108,
    115, 139–40, 253
Yom Kippur War ("Ramadan
    War") (1973), 61–6, 70,
    79, 82–3, 112–13, 120,
    140, 261
Young, H. E. W., 14
YouTube, 172

Zahar, Mahmoud, 119–20
Ze'evi, Rehavam, 73, 94
Ziegler, Jean, 184
Zionism, 5–6, 17–19,
    22–5, 27, 31, 33–7, 39,
    41, 44–6, 50–1, 55–7,
    60–1, 74, 88, 90–1, 113,
    128, 131–2, 135–6, 141,
    151–3, 169, 179–80, 183,
    205, 217, 232–3, 245
Zionist Congress, 18